Helmut Digel

Sport in a Changing Society

Sociological Essays

VERLAG KARL HOFMANN SCHORNDORF

**This volume is financially supported by the
Federal Institute for Sport Science, Cologne**

Die Deutsche Bibliothek — CIP-Einheitsaufnahme

Digel, Helmut:
Sport in a changing society : sociological essays /
Helmut Digel. — 1. ed. — Schorndorf : Hofmann, 1995
  (Sport science studies ; 7)
  ISBN 3-7780-6471-1
NE: GT

Order Number 6471

Total production: Druckerei und Verlag Karl Hofmann GmbH & Co., D-73614 Schorndorf
Printed in Germany · ISBN 3-7780-6471-1

Contents

Acknowledgements

Behind every author there are numerous colleagues and friends who provide direct and indirect support and assistance. In my case there have been many.

I should like to express my gratitude to those of my friends and colleagues with whom I discussed various parts of the essays. I have benefitted considerably from their comments. I would particularly like to thank *Heidi Zimmer* who performed a variety of administrative and typing tasks as the manuscript was being prepared. Thanks are also due to *Peter Becker*, *Gunnar Drexel* and *Manfred Muckenhaupt* for many lively and enjoyable sessions which we had working on some essays. Last but not least I should like to thank *Peter Knapp* for his help in translating the whole book from German. The many hours of patient labor he put in went far beyond what could normally be asked of a friend.

Helmut Digel

The ICSSPE Editorial Board wishes to thank Mr. Bob Chappell of the School of Sport and Physical Education at West London Institute of Higher Education for proof-reading and checking of the text.

John F. Coghlan
Chairman Editorial Board ICSSPE

Introduction

At present sport is in a state of flux. Social change in sport is touching everybody, we all are witnesses of a process of differentiation. The interrelation between sport and society shows more and more interesting and critical patterns: Sport reflects culture and society; sport integrates groups and individuals; sport reinforces social inequalities; sport is a vehicle for resistance. Involvement in sport is more than making use of the body, using endurance and strength to achieve the objective of a game. More and more we are aware of the positive and negative consequences of the way sport is organized in society. We are concerned about some changes in sport, especially in most industrial societies we can observe the transition from performance and athlete-oriented activities towards the impersonality of what is called "corporate sport". Sport is reaching nearly everybody and sport is the most influential part of an everyday mass culture. Our knowledge about this process of transition is rather poor, and scientists at present are not particularly advanced to describe this process. Concept formation and theory construction in sport sciences are not sufficient to deal with this subject on a well founded basis. The following collection of essays is related to this failure. Therefore it is only possible to present essays of a largely preliminary kind. Firstly, they illustrate the type of questions which sport sociologists should ask in relation to sport and suggest a series of concepts and theses. They attempt to identify and explain observable trends in the development of sport and some of the consequences resulting from these trends. They propose opinions concerning the functions of sport, that is, concerning their intended and unintended effects on individual and social life. Some of the essays point out the respects in which sport science can help in the solution of problems.

I wrote this book with a variety of purposes in mind. Firstly I want to actively involve my readers in thinking about some sociological aspects of sport and to acquaint them with some interpretations which may be useful in the discussion of a variety of questions about the relationship between sport and society; secondly, I wish to develop our awareness and appreciation of the social significance of sport not only in modern societies and to promote an understanding of the social structure, social relations and social problems of sport and finally indicate how some selected theories and methods of the sport sciences we can use provide us with a better understanding of sport and thus supply a basis for developing policies to address the social problems of sport in general and in developing countries in particular.

This book is divided into four parts. Chapter I presents a brief introduction, a cursory survey of the significance of sport in industrial societies. It is also oriented to a problem, which is the most severe one today. Modern risks in modern societies, sport-related and social problems within these societies, sport and the environment are contents of this essay.

Chapter II presents an analysis of the process of mass communication and its relation to sport. Particular emphasis is given to the question about the standards and state of research, which meanwhile have been reached in this area. The social functions of the mass media and their relation to sport are reviewed as well as the influence of the mass media on sport (vice versa), and the role of sport journalists. A second essay deals with expectations towards sport journalism.

Chapter III constitutes the core chapter of the book. It is concerned with the role of sport in developing countries in relation to processes of social change. Sport as a means of modernization is recommended as well as sport as a means of intercultural learning.

In Chapter IV essays are oriented towards the future of sport in general and at the prospects of top-level sport in particular. The basic theme in this chapter is that since sport reflects society, as the society changes, sport will also undoubtedly undergo some transformation. Several current trends are discussed and it is shown how each trend is likely to be manifested in sport changes.

This book is based on the premise that sport is an integral aspect of society and culture all over the world. But it should be noted that the degree to which sport affects people can vary considerably from one country to another, and from one region to another. The focus of this book is on sport in Germany. There are many parallels with sport and society in neighboring industrial nations as well as important differences. This must be noted seriously.

Chapter I:

Sport and Society

The Relation between Sport and Society

1. Introduction

Today sport sociologists are not the only people frequently maintaining that sport is a social phenomenon. Politicians, sport officials and even some athletes also refer to society when talking about sport.

We assume that there are connections and correlations between a certain society and what we understand as sport. These assumptions are very plausible. But trying to describe the relations between these two fields confronts us with difficulties which are primarily based on the fact that today sport appears in a confusingly large variety of forms, which again are embedded in society in a no less multifarious way.

Finding an answer to the question concerning the relations between sport and society requires, above all, knowledge of the meaning of the terms 'sport' and 'society'. The title 'sport **and** society' indicates that we have to talk about the interdependence between two phenomena. Even if it seems obvious that both, society and sport are subject to constant change, a description of the relationship between sport and society has to take into consideration the present condition of a given political system. This is necessarily a generalization which is intensified by the fact that the relationship between sport and society can only be explained in an exemplary manner.

2. What is sport? What is society?

2.1 Sport

Obviously everyone who is asked this question resorts to experiences from everyday life, thinking about the many areas where sport takes place. The first differentiation can be made between organized and informal sport. We all know examples of organized sport in the form of high performance, competitive, and professional sport, etc. within the different sport associations.

The whole range of organized sport becomes visible when considering all other institutions of organized sport, like in schools or universities, sport in the military, in factories and in church organizations, just to name a few examples. However, sport does not necessarily have to be organized by institutions, as you can see from recreational and leisure sport, keep-fit programs and the 'sport for all' campaign.

Sport is obviously practiced by different people in different situations with varying intentions; but what is the common denominator, the internal structure of this activity?

The board of directors of the German Sport Association (DSB) commissioned its advisory board to produce a catalogue of characteritics which could help to describe or define sport. This description was meant to alleviate future decision-making processes in the DSB concerning the admission of sport associations. Another objective was a linguistic consensus regarding the definition of sport in the clubs and associations of the DSB. According to this description the internal structure of sport features seven characteristics:

1.   Motor activity
The main characteristic of sport is motor activity, it is constitutive for each sport discipline and requires coordination and fitness. The improvement of motor skills requires the athlete to develop them in a planned manner. Thus activities like dog racing, model building, etc. are excluded due to the fact that motor activity is not directly applied.

2.   Content of meaning
Contrary to motor skills as required in everyday activities and at the workplace, sporting activities are - as a matter of principle - unproductive; they can even be called artificial. They are not subject to existential pressure and mostly need their own organization. Ritualization and symbolization of real actions as well as self-promotion for the sake of sport gives sport an independent significance, thus distinguishing it from labour and production. This structural characteristic excludes from the range of sport such activities as fishing and driving if they do not possess the quality of a 'means to their own end'.

3.   Performance
Performance is an essential feature of sport. Practicing sports requires the setting, achieving and surpassing of standards. Efforts, pressure and strains are willingly and voluntarily accepted by the athlete in order to achieve a certain standard. Due to their lack of this feature cult dances, musical games, parades and acrobatics are to be excluded.

4.   Sport organizations
In order to perform sport with other people we need social structures such as teams, crews, etc. Hence, a sports association is characterized by comprehensive organization, a supra-regional competition system and a set of rules, which leads to the exclusion of social structures formed instantaneously, which are not subject to any general social rules, like those frequently to be observed in children's play.

5.   Sport rules
Actions in sport are subject to more or less defined rules (cf. I.3).

6.   Ethical values
The well-being of all participants, equality of opportunity, team spirit and fair-play are norms every athlete has to acknowledge. That these values are indeed existential for sport can easily be recognized whenever they are ignored, neglected or violated in games and sport. All-in Wrestling or sensational performance threatening the lives of participants have to be excluded from the range of sport as they do not meet these ethical standards.

7.   Forms of experience
Experiences such as fitness, vitality, self-control, creation of movement, aesthetic grace, adventure, risk and excitement are all possible and typical features in the world of sport.

The discussion of the question "what is sport?" makes apparent that those sports that are examined are already recognized as such, recognized and rendered legitimate by their admission as an association by the DSB. It is obvious, however, that these guidelines are often not clear at all and that they fail to comprehend the reality of sport in society. (Is, for instance, professional soccer a means to its own end? - Isn't downhill skiing sensationalism at 125 km/h? Whose motor skills are decisive in show jumping or horse racing, the riders' or the horses'? Is boxing to be considered life-threatening sensationalism?).

Considering the abundance of situations in which people think they are practicing sport we have to question the DSB guidelines. They are, however, certainly helpful in trying to describe the relations between sport and society. In particular the characteristic 'content of meaning' refers to the connections between sport and work, clearly distinguished sport as a partial system form other social systems. Before going into greater detail in this respect we have to explain what is to be understood by the term 'society'.

2.2 Society

'Society' is a very ambiguous term used in the social sciences as well as in the sector of everyday life. Terms like 'industrial society', 'bourgeois and class society' are just as commonly used as 'high society' or the notion of a 'good' society.

Table 1: Sport and selected systems of society

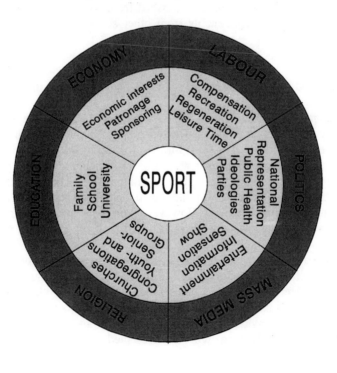

 SOCIAL SYSTEMS

 ASPECTS OF INFLUENCE

When the term 'society' is used here in the following it means the area between the state and the individual. It refers to a construct of interaction by individual and unrelated human actors. This interaction produces a relatively autonomous and complete system of society. The interactions themselves are based on a framework of mutually accepted and binding action patterns made available in single 'prefabricated' cultural values and social structures in order to free the individuals from the task of trying to solve all the social interaction problems on their own. The internal social structure of this system is determined by the division into economic, political, social and cultural sectors.

Working power and means of production are the most important elements in a social system, the interplay of these elements being constitutive for the social structure or the social conditions of production.

This definition indicates that there can be many forms of society because we can distinguish different societies by examining the significance of the different sub-systems. Thus, in the following, the term 'society' does not stand for human society as a whole but as a specific social unit, a framework consisting of a variety of sub-systems, which can be structured according to table 1.

This shows sport as one social system among many others. If we describe sports as a social system we assume that it is made up of a whole group of social values, norms and roles, which together form a social structure. This provides sport with an unmistakable identity and autonomy. Sport is also distinguished from its social surrounding to which it has specific relations, receiving benefits from other social systems as well as returning benefits to them.

3.   The correlation between sport and society - Two models of interpretation

It is by no means self-evident to ask in what respects there are relations between sport and society. Sport as a private matter and sport as aimless play are common labels having determined the evaluation of sport for decades. Sport was placed in a free space by relevant groups in society, a space that was to be protected and sheltered against all evil and particularly against politics. This idea is still prevalent today, and especially top-athletes understand their successes as individual achievements, and negate the social dependence of their sporting activities. However, even more than 20 years ago the idea of sport as an activity taking place in an isolated space free of values was found to be erroneous.

Sport as a part of our society has always had diverse relations to other partial systems, especially to those sectors that determine our society, such as economy and labour. Today this interdependence is undisputed. However, the kind and quality of this interdependence can still not be clearly defined. Philosophers, sociologists, educators and politicians have tried to provide answers to this question and have come up with a large variety, which in the following will be presented as two contrasting models of interpretation.

3.1 Sport as a desirable partner of society

Movement is a universal phenomenon that can be found in almost all cultures in the forms of dances, games and contests. The first patterns of typical sport movement, however, developed relatively late. They are the results of changing structures closely related to changes in the economy, in society and state. In this respect the alteration of development of norms related to performance, excitement and speed is decisive (cf. *Eichberg* 1973). This development already started before the Industrial Revolution in England. The typical features of modern sport, however, developed within capitalist industrial society, first in England at the end of the 18th century. Subsequently sport spreads to all other industrial societies as a parallel development to industrialization, that is, parallel to the deterioration of artisan production, to urbanization and the disintegration of class barriers but, above all, in relation to the particular emphasis on the principle of performance. Hence, the development of sport took place mostly parallel to the development of feudal society to a bourgeois meritocracy. It is not accidental that sport is governed by three principles: equality, achievement and rules. These principles can to a certain extent be more easily realized in sport than in other sectors of society.

For this reason sport is not only a phenomenon developing parallel to society but is considered an ideal model of an achievement-oriented society, a model providing the experience of a performance-oriented society. From society's point of view it is therefore desirable to introduce children and adolescents to this model by means of physical education in schools. Achievement motivation, fair competition and rules are just as essential for the maintenance of our culture as it is in the interest of culture that top-level performance takes place.

Therefore we have to promote commitment in sport, which becomes even more essential the more industrial society is alienated from its natural relationship to the human body (as *Plessner* 1967 expresses it).

Sport allows authentic experiences, and man needs a certain amount of movement, which sport provides, giving meaning to life, animating and stimulating, enabling man to experience tension, excitement and strain. In sport personal contacts are open which help to break down social barriers through communication. Everybody can achieve something in sport, in contrast to industrial production and even ideals, voluntary work and activity for its own sake are features of sport.

Sport provides for discussion and experience, they structure daily life and the activities of millions of people. In this respect it seems obvious that sport is a field of compensation for the pressure of work but also an ideal model which promotes the learning of the most important behaviour pattern of a performance-oriented society.

3.2 Sport - a guarantee of social injustice?

Whereas the first point of view suggests that sport is integrated adequately into society and that they are, so to say, 'correctly socialized', there is another group of experts holding the opposite view, maintaining that sport is not concerned with socialisation, and even though it is subsidized with tax revenues it is orientated towards capitalist interests. Thus, in their structure sport is a subject to the interests and conditions of capitalist utilization as well as its problems. These conditions, however, lead to an unjust social structure. Society is inhuman, the principle of achievement merely supports those who are successful, less successful people like those with disabilities or senior citizens are dumped. Sport is therefore not a model for a performance-oriented society but merely represents the ideology of a success-oriented one. Critics of sport try to demonstrate this on different patterns of sport.

The function of *school sport* or physical education, for example, is mainly physical maturing and compensation; it is a part of the qualifying process of the future labour force. It supports an understanding of sport as a recreational pastime by separating sport from production and placing it in the area of human self-realization.

Spectator and high-performance sport are subject to the principles of capitalist utilization. Clubs become business companies, athletes are treated as merchandise. The consumer-oriented attitude of the population towards recreation is intensified by spectator sport, also developing mass loyalty and a national consciousness that upholds the dominant social order.

Popular leisure sport serves the regeneration of working power; it takes place inside as well as outside of clubs, the club itself being an exercise ground for behaviour patterns essential for parliamentary and democratic forms. Furthermore it is an instrument of compensation for the strains at the workplace.

Factory sport serves the compensation for specific strains at work and the improvement of performance. It also helps to promote the public image of companies.

Military sport assists in the training of soldiers, thus making use of sport in a directly political manner.

In the last consequence institutionalized sport helps to maintain the existing conditions of power, having affirmative effects on the dominant norms concerning the prevalent sets of values and reinforcing bourgeois society. Sport is therefore an expression of the existing political and economic conditions, which provides insight into the social character of sport and discloses the ideology of its socio-political neutrality. In the face of this criticism it is consistent for the representatives of this view to demand alternative forms of sport culture, above all such forms that are characterized by their lack of achievement-orientation, competition and aggression.

Both views are based on plausible arguments, and it seems difficult to judge whether one is right and the other one wrong. However, it seems just as impossible to attribute a general positive socialization function to sport as it is to accept its general compensational function, as critics of sport claim to observe.

There rather seems to be a whole variety of factors determining whether someone practices sport or not. This view corresponds with the experiences we ourselves make when practicing sport. While, on the one hand, someone seeks diversion from his or her problems at work, someone else might, on the other hand, look for compensation for family problems. Someone might join a club because his/her friends are members, whilst somebody else might consider it an obstacle that one club only offers a limited range of sport that is inadequate for his/her needs.

Someone may join a club because he/she senses it as a rise in social terms, another person chooses a certain club because of his/her political beliefs. These examples indicate quite clearly that there is obviously no uniform way of describing the reasons why people practice sport, and that generalizations concerning the relations between sport and society can only correspond to reality to a limited extent. Moreover, it is apparent that the judgement concerning sport depends largely on the judgement about society. Apart from that, both points of view have in common that they attribute certain functions to sport, however, without providing any scientific proof that these functions are really fulfilled. The reason for this being that 'sport' is described in very general terms without taking into consideration the large variety of forms sport can take on.

However, a precise analysis of the connection between sport and society requires not only a differentiated examination of the aspects influencing the system of sport as environmental factors but also the internal structure of sport in its whole diversity. This process can be described in a triple-step: society-sport-society. The first step demonstrates the multivarious interdependences and features of sport within the social structure and its cultural sets of values. Hence, sport is not a natural phenomenon, it is rather influenced by specific social factors, which also mean that sport is possible in other forms too, as we can see in other societies or when looking back into the past. Looking at typical male or female sport also makes clear that the differences between them are not of a natural kind, it is, however an understandable difference if we comprehend sport within their specific social structure, because this is precisely what determines the specific forms sport can take.

The structures and processes of sport themselves must be considered in the second step which indicates that athletes (within their clubs and associations) have their own values and ideologies. Sport has its own norms, sets of rules and sanctions. The different types of sport have their own social structure, and individual groups of people practicing sport have specific communication structures (cf. *Digel* 1976).

The third step takes us back to society, showing how sport influences specific sociological areas such as family, work, politics, church, education and social classes as well as our system of society as a whole. To some extent sport helps to solve some social problems but on the other hand possibly obscure others (cf. *Klein* 1989). The question is, what meaning can, for instance, sport ethics have in other social sectors? Does the power of sport associations have anything to do with political power? Does sport have a stabilizing effect on certain economic and social systems?

4.   The influence of the environment on sport

So far we have talked about the environment of sport primarily in terms of work. Sport is, however, surrounded by a large number of social systems, which themselves are also influenced by other social systems. Therefore the question is, how a certain environment influences people's participation in sport in different situations. Wishing to participate actively in a sport club today requires playing a variety of roles: being a participant in an exercise group, a friend of some of the members, a member of a department, a club member, etc. But what factors determine that an individual plays the role(s) expected of him in everyday sport situations?

The answer to the question whether sport is practiced in a society, is who practices sport, and what kind of sport depends on a variety of social factors? Sport sociologists have shown that the following factors are particularly important:

- ·   conditions of production
- gross national product (GNP)
- forms of the division of labour
- family structure
- forms of education

- public health
- religion
- culture
- climate
- ecology

These factors can explain, above all, why, for example, one kind of sport is more popular in Egypt than in Finland, or why the majority of Olympic Champions tend to be citizens of a few industrialized nations only, why in some countries women are still excluded from sport, and why Protestants won proportionally more Olympic medals than Catholics.

With regard to industrial society these examples show that sport constitutes **one** aspect of movement culture typical of this society, which means it is tied to the conditions of a highly industrialized and differentiated society, and that this form is subject to social change, which, in turn, depends on transitions of society.

Table 2: The pyramid of sport (cf. *Renson/Careel* 1986)

Considering the problems and tasks which organizers of sport are confronted with, the question regarding the influence of environmental factors on people's involvement in sport is important in so far as it points out the limiting factors influencing the sport facilities and opportunities that are offered to as many people in a community as possible. On the other hand these factors can also highlight how alternative sport opportunities can be created or established if a sport organization wants to offer sport and games for groups with widely differing interests. The following factors are generally accepted as being of particular significance for people's participation in sport.

4.1 The family

The most decisive instance concerning our commitment to sport is the family. Parents are mostly responsible for their children joining a sport club or turning to other activities. Positive parental attitudes towards sport, like their membership in a club, usually result in their children's interest in sport, whereas negative or indifferent attitudes tend to prevent children from entering the world of sport. This is especially true for young girls. The parents' role model function does not merely affect active participation in sport but also their children's attitudes towards school sport, visiting sports events and using the media.

4.2 Social class

In order to determine the influence of the family more precisely we also have to consider the range of social positions of a family outside the sport club. Today we know that relationships within the family are determined by socio-structural features of inequality, which means that families can be distinguished by social class. This is important for the participation in sport in so far as professional position, income, financial possibilities and the standard of education are significant aspects determining if, and which, sport is practiced. Many investigations have shown that involvement in sport is more likely among the upper than the lower classes; the reason for this seems to be that the requirements to be met by sportsmen and women are congruent to behavioural expectations and values prevalent among the upper and middle classes in areas other than sport.

The typical middle and upper class values obviously encourage participation in sport, as the supreme principle of success guarantees that the participants' expectations won't be disappointed. Class differences already developed among teenagers are reflected in the unbalanced class membership of top-athletes. In terms of quality class differences are most apparent in the choice of certain sport disciplines.

The attractiveness of the various kinds of sport is not at all constant, it can, however, be assumed that the newer a sport is, the higher is the participants' social position. And the higher the expectations concerning the individual performance are, the more attractive is a sport for the upper classes (cf. Table 2). This means, on the other hand, that team sport is practiced more by the lower classes. Sport with frequent physical contact seems to be particularly attractive for the lower classes. The reasons, why class plays such an important role in choosing which type of sport to practice are basically self-evident. Limited financial possibilities do not allow the lower classes to practice exclusive sport. Above all, the specific set of values and the varying attitudes towards the human body in the different social classes, matters of health, success-orientation and family socialization encourage a differentiated approach to sport in our society. Transferring this description to the situation in our sport clubs enables us to explain, for instance, why today sport clubs are not very attractive for members of the lower classes.

4.3 Friends - peer group

In contrast to work where people can only decide to a limited extent, if at all, with whom they share their workplace, recreation situations are characterized by the fact that we enter them voluntarily. If we meet partners we like we are more likely to stick to a certain situation than if we are confronted those we dislike. In this respect sport is not just an occasion to form a group of friends, but the group of people in our direct surrounding is also important for our lasting involvement in sport. This is not only valid for the peer group, even though it is obvious that the peer group in the phase of puberty often is so effective that it has more power to decide in matters of participation in sport than any other instance of socialization (e.g. school and family).

Today we can maintain that the same peer group may support and protect commitment in sport, but it can also lead to its disintegration. During the age of adolescence the peer group is often opposed to organized instances and can suppress their influence in situations of conflict.

4.4 The media

Sport reporting can, in many respects, generate an interest in sport. The media can animate people to practice sport but it may have the opposite effect or no recognizable influence on socialization in sport at all. The fact that the media, above all, provide information about top-level competitive sport and basically neglect other information leads to the conclusion that they only to a limited extent show ways to active participation in sport, and that they even reflect an illusory image that is in sharp contrast to the usual situation in sport clubs. This applies primarily to those people who get their information about sport exclusively from the media. As far as the socialization of young people is concerned the media seem to have a decisive function. We have every reason to believe that particularly the media generate idols, which only contributes to a positive attitude of adolescents towards sport who already have obtained sufficient information about sport.

Finally it is worthwhile mentioning in this context that the contents of sport reporting are often also part of communication contents of club sociability.

4.5 Gender

If certain types of family interaction influence commitment in sport it is hardly surprising that the gender is important, when it comes to joining a sport club or practicing specific sport. In the same way as certain characteristics of sport corresponds to the demands of the upper classes, so the socialization process typical of males favours participation in sport more than that of females. However, class-specific features have to be taken into consideration too. Even today, in particular lower class females hardly practice any sport at all, consequently class membership is more important than gender with regard to active participation in sport. Nevertheless, there are still certain types of

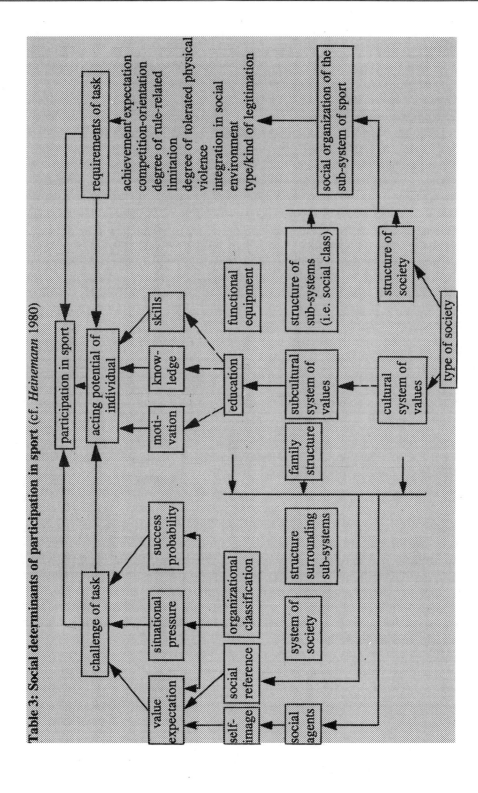

Table 3: Social determinants of participation in sport (cf. *Heinemann* 1980)

sport which are to be characterized as predominantly favoured by males or females, respectively.

Aggressive physical contact corresponds more to the image of male sport, whereas grace and elegance are characteristics of the typical female athlete.

Over the last few years these stereotypes have certainly been undergoing a process of change; women are taking over or demanding access to more and more male domains in sport. Today in Germany more than 400.000 women play soccer every weekend, previously purely a 'men's game'.

This tendency is also apparent concerning positions and functions in club management, which used to be dominated by men for decades. In fact, there are radical changes under way in this field today, and evidently many arguments and explanations prevalent in the debates about the disadvantages of women in sport in the past no longer hold true.

The reference, for example, to biological differences between men and women are only helpful to a limited extent, since daily women prove that they are capable of great achievements in nearly all types of sport.

Furthermore it ought to be seen as a positive development that the female identity meets the demands of modern sport only to a limited extent because this enables women to represent a corrective element against negative developments in modern sport.

4.6 Town - country - region

It has already been outlined in this essay that sport developed mainly in industrial societies. Sport was first organized wherever industry with all its advantages and disadvantages spread. Around the turn of the century, for example, in Germany a large number of sport clubs were founded in Berlin, Hamburg and other big cities. Thus sport became largely an urban phenomenon, a trend still apparent today, even though sport clubs are not only to be found in towns.

A differentiated variety of sport is not as common in rural as in urban areas, and consequently the place of residence as well as regional conditions seem to strongly influence which sport is or can be chosen. Clubs in rural areas usually differ from urban clubs only in terms of the range of sport they offer. The needs and demands of their members differ widely from those in the big cities. This is especially true in respect of club sociability, but there are also significant differences at the organizational level. Voluntary work is still, and always has been, a dominant feature in rural clubs, whereas in city clubs we observe a tendency towards professional management.

Regional differences regarding club life can only be presumed, however, regional idiosyncracies also seem to influence club life, and evidently sport clubs in Bavaria, for instance, differ from those in Berlin.

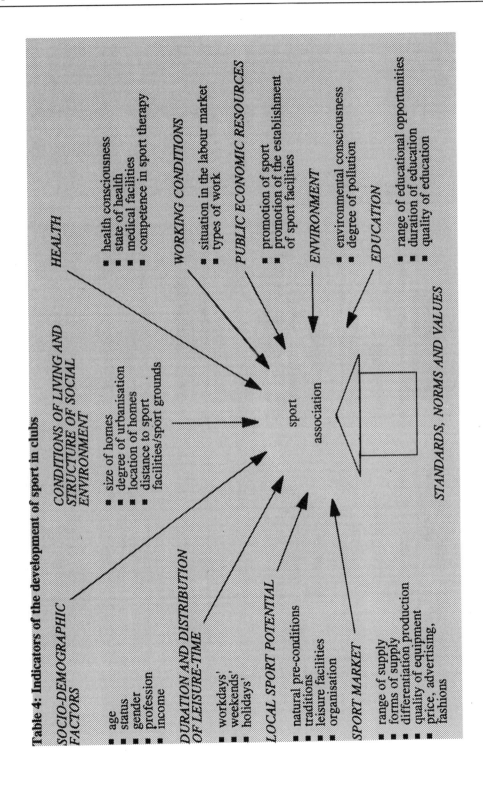

Table 4: Indicators of the development of sport in clubs

4.7 Age

Not only has sport been a male domain for many years, it is, above all, characterized by youth to the present day. Recalling the arguments of the critics of sport shows that particularly the weaker members of society are at a disadvantage in sport. This also applies to the elderly, and so it is not surprising that in a system that is geared towards high performance, those who only achieve less can only participate to a limited extent. For this reason the vast majority of sport club members in Germany have for decades been juveniles, whereas especially elderly women are only a small minority. This decisive mis-representation of the older generation begins already at the age of 35 and affects particularly the lower classes.

However, in recent years this feature has also been undergoing change. Before, the active phase of a club member was usually followed by passive membership after his or her competitive career, whereas today many people are able to continue practicing sport for fun after their time as competitive athletes, and elderly people are also given opportunities providing for their specific needs in terms of physical exercise. Clubs are becoming increasingly aware of how important physical activity is for their elderly members. Therefore sport has accepted the need to develop and offers a wide selection of sports that are not related to the principles of competition in order to satisfy the needs of older people. This will provide an important organizational challenge for clubs in the future.

4.8 Nationality

Ethnical problems do not only exist in developing countries, they can also be found, for example, in the German Sport Association (DSB). It is apparently an advantage to be German if you want to participate in sport in Germany. Far less favourable are the conditions for Italians, Yugoslavs or Greeks, and Turks have to face the most difficulties in Germany concerning their desire to practice sport. This applies to sport clubs as well as to communal sport facilities, and thus organized sport opportunities seem to be attractive only for a limited number of people in our society. In fact, there is sufficient evidence to believe that sport clubs tend to offer sport more or less exclusively for a specific type of person: he or she should be of good health, German, between 14 und 35 years of age, performance-oriented, sociable and fairly affluent. This somewhat exaggerated characterization of a typical sport club member merely serves the purpose of pointing out that people with other ethnic backgrounds have difficulties gaining access to sport clubs. Neither the communities nor the clubs have so far succeeded in solving the problem of ethnicity whose most pressing aspect is the integration of children of foreign workers. This is indeed a problem demanding our immediate attention. Its solution should also consider aspects of organization, and if we rightly expect from sport clubs - like from school sport - that they contribute to the integration of minorities, then we have outlined an important future task of sport clubs.

5.   The internal structure of sport

It has been pointed out that we can only talk about **the** sport and the relationship between sport and society in a relative way. In recent years sport has apparently developed into a very diverse phenomenon with a wide range of different facets which are quite difficult to bring into some kind of order. Following my research work, there can be already observed and distinguished five different models of sport (cf. Table 5):

1.   The *professional and commercial model of sport* comprehends sport as show business and commercial enterprise.

2.   The *model of organized competitive sport* emphasizes competition, performance, victory and defeat, thus being closely related to social reality.

3.   The *model of sport renouncing organized competition* is based on fun, pleasure, togetherness and self-expression; elements of performance and competition are not essential and sometimes obscured. Thus sport represents an alternative world in opposition to the social reality of our lives, especially with regard to industrial labour.

4.   The *alternative model of sport* emphasizes sub-cultural activities and opposes traditional sport, recruiting mainly from (ethnic) minorities at universities and regarding itself as part of the political opposition against capitalism.

5.   The *institutional model* of sport comprehends sport as an instrument determined by certain functions like socio-emotional, socio-integrative, political or biological and socialization functions. This model is in the focus of many debates about sport in education.

These descriptions only feature certain characteristics of the internal structure of sport. What are the special features of sport, and what distinguishes sport in particular? It is actually not difficult to find out what characterizes the internal structures of sport.

Looking at a city from the viewing platform of a TV-tower, we can easily detect it: rectangular sport fields and gymnasia or oval tracks represent typical features of sport, indicating its rule-structure which can be clearly distinguished from the absence of such rules in the surrounding area. Thus there are obvious differences between the world of sport and the world around it. In sport, different rules apply than in everyday life. In order to investigate the internal structure of sport more thoroughly it may be convenient to look firstly at its ethical values. Apart from specific rules in the different types of sport there are moral maxims (patterns of values) whose functions are the regulation of behaviour in sport. Typical patterns of this kind are, for example, fair-play, companionship, the absence of material objectives (which means sport has no material value in terms of results, yet, it is valuable in terms of experience), equal opportunity and open endings. These patterns could also be defined as typical motives determining individual behaviour in sport. The moral maxims of sport - this must be emphasized - do not have to be in accordance with other generally recognized maxims.

It is particularly typical of sport that tolerance, consideration and care, which are widely appreciated principles in everyday life, are often largely unsuitable in competitive sport and would make many competitions, like rugby or boxing, impossible because sport frequently has to be ruled by such principles like rivalry, domination and victory.

However, the strongest evidence concerning the internal structure of sport is provided by its rules. They are conventions to which athletes and players submit themselves voluntarily, which are defined by sport themselves, and which are subject to constant change. The internal structure is not solely based on constitutive rules as they can be found in the rule books of sport associations. It also comprises the informal strategic sector of acting in sport (- hence, strategic rules -) that determines, for instance, a team's tactical concept or the choice of figures as in gymnastics or figure-skating.

Norms and rules are, in fact, not the only determinants of the specific internal structure of sport; we also have to recognize the social character of sport, that is, the personality profile of an athlete as opposed to other social characters like a student, worker or businessman. The supposition of a sport-specific social character must not lead to the assumption that there is a typical biography for all in sport. As different athletes practicing different sport has different social backgrounds, as their interests are based on different experiences, as their active participation might end at different times, and as the professional prospects of former athletes may vary significantly, it would be wrong to speak of an autonomous social character of sport, even more so, since the athlete's role is not the only one in the social system of sport. In terms of their role structure sport is characterized by a large variety of roles, which also are a significant feature of its internal structure.

Finally, the specific norm, rule and role types of sport as a whole indicate another feature of their internal structure. Sport is organized according to its own needs and thus obtains a tendency towards autonomy, which is especially true for Germany. This institutional autonomy forms a framework for sport enabling it to present itself - at the level of the participants - as a specific field of experience. We have seen that it is obviously possible for sport, to a limited extent only, to distinguish themselves autonomously from their environment. It would indeed be desirable if sport could react to social change and influence society respectively. Therefore the final section will deal with the ways in which sport does or can affect society.

Table 5: Different models of sport

(1) Professional sport

- Commerce
- Mass media
- Competition
- Professionals
- Employment contracts

(2) Organized competitive sport

- Competition
- Excitement thrill
- "Amateurs"
- Membership in a sport association
- Sport clubs

(3) Sport without organized competitions

- Pleasure, amusement, recreation
- Fun
- Participation
- Individualism
- Open forms of organization

(4) Alternative sport

- Body (physical) culture (not sport culture)
- Subcultural phenomenon
- Relaxation, not excitement
- Open forms of organization
- Postmodernity

(5) Instrumental sport

- Instrument of social policies
- Instrument of educational policies
- Instrument of health policies
- Instrument of entertainment
- Instrument of research and further education

6.   The influence of sport on its social environment

For people practicing sport in clubs it is undisputed that sport provide them with something special: experiences before and after the game, companionship or friendship and solidarity which are to be found in the various departments of clubs, feeling well after strenuous running, all this indicates experiences people do not want to miss once they have made them. These examples demonstrate that sport certainly exercises an influence on their social environment. This influence is not restricted to the personal domain as described above, it can also be observed in partial systems like 'family' or 'work'. Top-level competitive sport undeniably influences the political system of a society, but nevertheless do we know much about the actual functions of sport regarding the different social systems and their environment? Considering the general functions assigned to sport, which are largely to be characterized as speculative, we now have to ask what precisely the influence of sport really is. Is a player who plays fair in a match also fair in his professional life? Does active participation in sport help people to cope in their professional lives at all? Is the social status acquired in sport reflected outside of sport? Does it possibly even assist in social climbing? These questions - we have to admit - cannot yet be accurately answered by sport sociologists. "Sportsmanship" has certainly gained access into many social areas. The use of typical sport terms in the field of politics demonstrates this influence quite clearly. Sport has become a model of behaviour orientation that is recognized far beyond the world of sport, and it is also a model for industrial work as far as achievement and performance are concerned. However, this model character of sport ethics is still disputed, and there are diametrically contradicting results the research on the influence of sport over family, economy, church and state, as well as, concerning the question to what extent personality qualities can be transferred from sport to other areas. As far as sport organizers are concerned it seems adequate in the face of this open situation to limit the question about the influence of sport on the sport clubs. At the higher level the following functions can be described: A club, that is not only a sport club, can successfully cope with problems caused by the polarization between the private domain and the formally organized sectors of business, politics and administration. This mediating function leads to many others that can be taken up by a sport club:
-    it can encourage emotional behaviour that is restricted to the formally organized world of work.
-    in a club the individual can feel responsible for his or her own actions in contrast to the situation at the workplace, where he or she is often deprived of responsibility.
-    success can be experienced directly and immediately in a club in contrast to daily life, where situations are becoming more and more obscure.
-    reality can become imaginable and experienced in contrast to daily life, where reality is often distorted.
-    the club is a place of local publicity permitting intensive and personal participation in contrast to the isolation of the individual in terms of social decisions.
-    clubs provide opportunities for relaxation and compensation for the strains at the workplace and in the family.
-    a club fosters the mentally and educationally valuable experience of "sportsmanship"; competition and solidarity can be experienced playfully in contrast to the tenser relationships at the workplace.

-     the social integration of different population groups (ethnic minorities, upper and lower classes) can be achieved in clubs.
-     a club can also have an integrating effect on the local community; community members can identify with the local sport club, especially if the club has a monopoly concerning the social life in the community or is successful in competitive sport.
-     a club can be an exercise ground and a selection potential for socially active personalities, which in particular requires learning democratic forms of leadership and administration.

These functions seem to make a sport club an ideal socially integrative system in our society. But it would be a grave error to assume that these positive functions come to the clubs overnight. On the contrary, the fulfillment of these functions depends decisively on the conditions established by the people responsible in the clubs. In this respect organizational conditions are of great significance, and that is why sport organizers have to be asked if their club is a centre of social life in the community, whether club members enjoy extensive social contacts with each other, whether new members are integrated into the club community and whether the members are given the opportunity to take on responsibility and show personal commitment.

Sport in a Risk Society

1. Life in a risk society

Since the Chernobyl disaster our knowledge about systems of society, their limitations, internal structures and dependencies has fundamentally changed. Until then, all the misery and sorrow, all the violence man had inflicted on man had been based on the category of the 'other person': Jews, blacks, women, foreigners, dissenters, communists.

On the one hand we used to have fences, camps, ghettos, military blocks and alliances, and on the other hand we had our homes as our 'castles' - real or symbolic boundaries used by non-affected people in which to withdraw and hide. They still exist, and yet they do not since the Chernobyl disaster, which defined the disappearence of 'the other guys', the end of our highly developed strategies of keeping distance. This experience has been imposed on us as a consequence of nuclear contamination (cf. *Beck* 1986). Nature, so it seems, has finally caught up with man.

The utopian vision of a better world for a long time has been accompanied by a negative anti-utopia of future catastrophies. Speaking reasonably about the future today is only possible if we also consider the scenario that this very future might not exist for man (cf. *Böhme* 1986, 929).

Despite all boundaries and enclosing strategies we are suddenly living in a 'risk society' and are part of a 'world-wide industrial system'. With regard to man's attempts to master or control this system, all that is visible is man's utter helplessness. Nature, for decades exclusively recognized in terms of its technical and industrial transformation, has become a fundamental and unchangeable condition for future ways of life in our modern industrial system.

The market and subsequent mass consumption have to be seen from a new perspective, as dependent on nature. Chernobyl, so it seems, might some day be regarded as a date marking man's realization of the end of our classical industrial society. This society's conceptions of national sovereignty, its idea of progress as an automatic process, of the class structures of society, the principles of performance, the availability of nature, the usefulness of the scientific results, the taking over of responsibility, of consumption and market seem to be in danger of disintegration. This is becoming apparent in many sectors of public and private life, at the workplace as well as in our free time, and not least in the field of sport.

Our present situation can best be characterized by the risks industrial modernization has consciously or unconsciously left us as subsequent problems. These risks have acquired a new quality, whose worst aspect is that they have to be managed and eventually mastered by generations that did not create them. These risks, however, also retaliate against those who have caused them - for example, as a radiation cloud encircling the earth depending on wind conditions. Therefore, in some ways, the dangers are spread equally.

The comprehensive process of individualization predominantly characteri-zing the social change in our society over the last few decades is by no means less risky. The subsequent dangers concerning the "we-I-balance" (*Elias*) have led to the disintegration of an increasing number of people's traditional lifestyles and relations.

Striking examples in this respect are the patterns of personal relationships in families and at the workplace. Whereas in the past family and work used to be supportive in the process of modernization and, above all, provided security, today many people can no longer rely on this security. Both sectors have lost their former reliability and protective function. The bourgeois family seems to be becoming a "negotiation family" staying together for a short time only, of which divorce statistics are a clear indicator.

At the workplace the boundaries between work and non-work are obscured. Working time, work place and, above all, labour legislation are factors becoming increasingly weaker, a fact supporting the growth of a risky and flexible market of "underemployment" beside official unemployment.

Jobs are placed next to vocations, professions and trades, and particularly education as an institution for vocational training has been in jeopardy for quite some time.

Women are no less affected by this change. In the process of modernization of our society women have certainly achieved emancipation to some extent. Women, however, also have to pay for their new liberties with new burdens. Today, women are more and more confronted with the fragility of marriage and are increasingly responsible for the financial support of the family; they are the most frequent clients of social welfare. Hence, women today are still dependent on men for their social security. Women are torn in the conflict between liberation from traditional arrangements, ties to their traditional roles as mothers and their gender-related inferior position in the labor market.

Often, as politicians search for strategies of risk management, they make use of science, which has acquired a more powerful position in this process. Today, it has, more than ever, the power of defining what is to be considered as hazard and what is not; it determines what is to be regarded as a relevant problem and what may be neglected as irrelevant. Science, however, can only use its new position of power to a limited extent, due to its shortage of solutions. Its position being beyond truth and enlightenment, science, has rather to be seen as a risk factor itself.

2. Risks related to practising sport - sport as a social problem

The Chernobyl disaster had very immediate effects on sport. In the same way as children were suddenly not allowed to play in their sandboxes any more, the play of adults was also in jeopardy. Tennis courts were closed, sporting activities in community sport facilities cancelled, and outdoor physical education disallowed. Sport, usually justified on the grounds of its supposed or real health-supporting functions, is being questioned in this very respect. According to health experts, everybody practising sport in those days seriously endangered his or her health and well-being.

What had been widely accepted standards for high performance sport, suddenly concerned a variety of sporting activities. Indicators for this danger, however, have existed for a long time. During severe smog conditions in cities, joggers and long-distance runners have been warned of the hazards of intensive endurance training. But probably only a few city joggers are aware of their paradoxical situation: running on city streets through the exhaust fumes of industry and traffic, an activity generated by the desire for well-being and good health, becomes an undertaking with backfiring effects; the advantages may well be diminished or even reversed by the inevitable damage that has to be accepted.

Running serves as an example representing all other sporting activities designed to enable people to satisfy essential needs close to nature, alone or in company, by physical activity and performance. Since "Chernobyl" this is apparently tied to risks. Attempts at justification, as still undertaken by sport organizations, which emphasize the significance of sport for good health, have become fragile in at least one respect. Just as in medicine, where the question regarding the effects is inevitably accompanied by the question of wanted as well as unwanted side-effects of medication, we now also have to distinguish in sport between effect and side-effect, usefulness, damage and cost. What was supposedly secure knowledge in sport all of a sudden turns out to be only temporary and uncertain, and the statement, "long-term damaging effects may occur", is also valid in sport. Sport, as a product of modern industrial society, is threatened by polluted nature, and it is nature that exactly this society tried to master, command and control. Thus nature endangers sport, and it looks as if nature will eventually triumph.

When talking about the risks people take in practising sport, we can pin down these risks by taking Chernobyl as an example. When examining the effects sport has on nature one becomes aware of other apparent risks; we have to realize that certain types of sport are to be regarded as interferences with our ecological systems, polluting, damaging and destroying air, water, soil and plants and endangering animals. Skiing, for example, may cause, the following ecological problems:

- *destruction of natural vegetation*
- *changes in the variety of plant species*
- *shortening of the growth period of vegetation*
- *deterioration of root quantities*
- *disintegration of protective forests*
- *soil compression*
- *chemical pollution of soil*
- *desiccation of moors*
- *increasing surface drainage*
- *growing landslide, soil erosion and avalanche hazards.*

Off-road driving, but also a whole variety of other motor sport, causes similar damaging effects. Furthermore, water sport like canoeing, rowing, sailing, wind-surfing as well as mountaineering and climbing are subject to accusations. From this point of view, sport is becoming a danger to nature, and thus has become a twofold social problem. The prospects evolving from this second aspect are congruent with the first. The endangering of nature, as caused by sport, together with other threats will eventually result in nature triumphing over man, however in a manner such that we can hardly imagine - in the fact of man's total absence from this planet.

The relation between sport and nature - characterized as a correlating problem with social effects - suggests questions concerning the causes, the responsibility and guilt for the problem, its depths and significance as well as our concerns, means of handling this problem and, not least, possible solutions.

3.   "Sport and the environment" - An exemplary problem of a risk society

For quite some time the phrase "sport and environment" has been used to label a topic which has been the basis for conventions, guidelines, hearings and publications, yet also for polemics. It usually focuses on the relatively simple fact that sport can have a positive influence on the environment, that sport, however, may also puts strains on or destroy the environment, and that practising sport can be jeopardized by environmental influences.

Let us investigate the problem that large segments of a sport-enthusiastic public may be deprived of the basis of their sporting activities due to the progressive pollution of their natural environment. This problem has not been caused by sport; sport, rather, seems to be a victim, and damage is inflicted on it. Man, in his role as jogger, skier, rower and swimmer, is being caught up by the other roles he must also play in modern society. The sporting individual suddenly finds himself in a cobweb of producers of energy, chemicals, cars and of the clients and consumers of these products. Suddenly he is deprived of the illusion of being able to enjoy sport in what has been assumed to be the one healthy environment of our society (an "external" area, so to speak).

We know those who have caused these environmental dangers and are responsible for them, the respective people as well as the institutions. Trying to force them to take responsibility for their actions, however, seems more difficult. The hazards we are exposed to are to some extent results of the highly differentiated division of labour; its consequence concerning the risks and side effects of industrial production is the phenomenon of "general companionship", merging into a "general absence of responsibility", thus making the "game of mutual accusation" inefficient. This is used to impose on the individual citizen the belief that each cause can also be effect and, therefore, is no longer a cause. The idea of an impenetrable system, of cause and effect, becomes a familiar metaphor for the "little man", too. The accusation of having caused damage is always accompanied by a relieving and exonerating argument (cf. *Beck* 1986, 43).

This phenomenon becomes apparent in our continuing to ski, knowing perfectly well that mass skiing has already caused great environmental damage in the Alps.

The publicly discussed argument that the cause of dying forests and erosion in the Alps includes factors other than skiing: toxic industrial fumes, long-term climatic changes and, above all, the lax legislation concerning environmental pollution in the eastern European countries may at least be an equally likely cause for the damage to the Alps. Such arguments result in the fact that even an enlightened and environmentally conscious citizen may continue skiing without a guilty conscience. That means one can act in a certain way again and again without being personally held responsible for it. One acts, so to speak, in personal absence, physically without acting morally or politically. The generalized "other" - the system - directs one's actions entirely. This is the slave mentality of civilization in which we socially and personally act as if we were subject to natural fate, the law of the system. We thus pass around responsibility in the face of threatening ecological disaster (cf. *Beck* 1986, 43). What causes our lack of commitment is primarily that our actions are orientated towards short-term yet well-articulated interests of directly affected people, and these interests are in their short-dated relevance also legitimate and justified. The long-term, and also legitimate interests of indirectly affected people, however, are not expressed. Thus, responsibility for future generations, as demanded primarly by *Jonas* in his "ethics of responsibility", still seems to be a long way off (cf. *Jonas* 1984).

The present risks of our society show another aspect which helps to support the arguments of sport organizations in the dispute with environmentalists. The fact that the risks of modernization, with regard to those who have caused them, can rarely be defined clearly, also corresponds with the ways in which risks appear today. Contrary to earlier risks, which could mostly be personally experienced, modern ones are often invisible and threaten us on a global scale, not only as individual people, social classes, groups, the poor or the Third World. They threaten all humanity, all animals, all plants. The central characteristic of the risks attached to modernization is its global aspect. These risks also evidently backfire on society, generating insecurities even for the rich and powerful in this world (cf. *Beck* 1986, 28 - 31). The global aspect, universality and invisibility, however, only seldom make us feel threatened by these risks in our "microcosm", the little world of our direct surroundings. These aspects, rather, provide relief and contribute to the suppression of the problem. This is aided by the fact that the present risks are relatively abstract phenomena, usually experienced through words and arguments. It is to be pointed out that, in the past, dangers were sensed by the nose and eyes, whereas today, they can only be visualized by means of chemical and physical formula. The dangers of mass skiing hardly ever become visible to the skier in the actual exercise of his sport. Wildlife does not die as an immediate result of ski-trekking, the lungs of joggers are not damaged by the polluted air of the city to an extent immediately realized. Often times the effects may be so far removed from their root cause that within the lifetime of affected people - as well as those responsible - there may not be tangible evidence at all. Consequently, the presently living people are not cognizant of the necessity of taking responsibility for future generations. Nor do we press science to fulfil its essential functions of providing information and promoting the enlightenment of the public.

All this proves the validity of the slogan that "what we cannot experience personally and physically does not count", and since the discussion about risks is taking place on unsafe grounds, we still follow the motto, "in case of doubt, in favour of sport" and, "in case of doubt, in favour of progress", which means "in case of doubt, look away" (*Beck* 1986, 45).

Those committing themselves on behalf of nature must soon realize that only a few of their arguments can be substantiated, and even substantiated ones can hardly succeed over permanent systematic doubt. It is, in fact, a major characteristic of a complex and differentiated society or of industrial modernization with its damaging side-effects that anything can be related to anything else. Besides skiing, as long as bark beetles, red squirrels, misguided forestry policies or logging techniques, and smokestacks in the valleys can also be blamed for causing damage, we are relieved of our responsibility. Tourist boards, cableway companies, skiing associations and, even less so, individual skiers will not be convinced of any reason to refrain from skiing. The lack of responsibility among sportsmen and sport organizations is also related to another aspect: even if we accept the supposition that dying forests are a result of industrialization, the disputes among experts provide us with suitable justifications for the continuation of our activities.

Are sulphur dioxide, nitrogen and its photo-oxides, hydro-carbon and other substances we have not known until today the cause of the last and eternal autumn, the final falling of leaves? Is the car in fact the nations' primary pollutant and therefore the main forest killer, or do we have to install high grade and state of the art desulphurizing devices into our coal power stations? Or will that not have any benefit either, because the toxic substances killing the trees are supplied "free of charge" by the different winds from the smokestacks and exhaust pipes in our neighbouring countries (cf. *Beck* 1986, 42)?

This line of questioning could be easily extended; its function is to point out the most common patterns of arguments also used in sport whenever they are accused of causing damage. "I hit you" and "you hit me", each side assisted by so-called experts, has become a game determining ecological debate in the field of sport. We order studies proving the ecological compatibility and harmlessness of a sport facility or a specific technique in a particular sport.

At this point it seems appropriate to make a special reference to the distinction between scientific counselling and sport policy, between preparation on the one hand and political action, as well as decision-making in sport policy, on the other hand. Science has its own responsibility as does all policy concerning sport. Moreover, what is scientifically correct need not be socially desirable. What is ecologically adequate, suitable for mankind, human or natural, cannot be clearly defined by science. We need a process of forming political opinions in order to decide which sport is acceptable in a particular location, in this respect revealing the consequences of science, thus enabling the public to discuss this matter. The question whether science in general or sport science in particular is capable of doing this today, must, however, be doubted in the face of the experiences made with science in this field up to now.

4.   The search for solutions

When looking for indications regarding suitable solutions, we can certainly maintain that the problems mentioned here cannot be solved by means of warnings and appeals; appeals can only serve as impulses for further-reaching solutions. What we need are institutionalized solutions and legal regulations, higher moral standards, a more suitable economy, science with a better sense of responsibility, perhaps a new form of religious thinking, and probably also a new and different concept of democracy; hence, we need a different society. "Learning", "new attitudes", and "change" are the terms which will form the basis of urgently necessary new concepts.

The achievement of this objective primarily requires a philosophical, ethical and legal discussion certainly not to be initiated solely by sport organizations. In this respect we ought to expect from sport that - in due self-interest - it begins going about solving the problems affecting its system directly. Consequently, sport itself should take advantage of the opportunities opened to its institutions and to the people practising sport. Money as a guiding instrument, but also education and the development of new rules by the legislative powers provide important opportunities for solutions.

4.1 Ethical means of regulation

To me it seems to be a key question in the controversy between sport and the environment, if, and to what extent, we succeed in finding an ethical foundation which has the power of regulating and at the same time serves man's, as well as nature's, interests. In the course of the last ten years, a number of important ethical constructs have been publicized, all having the same objective of offering solutions for the pressing ecological crisis. Hans *Jonas*'s concept can serve as a model in this respect; his criticism aims primarily at the previous discussion, in which man is the sole subject of ethical considerations. In contrast to that *Jonas* focuses on the metaphysical, comprehensive interest of mankind in its natural environment, which comprises the whole variety of species. According to him, nature possesses its own dignity and demands our loyalty. Consequently, *Jonas* does not start from the principle of man's primacy but from nature's equality. In another step he criticizes that the ethical discussion has so far only referred to singular or single actions; however, it has failed to address the demands of the challenges of modern technology. Ethics always have to consider the cumulative effects of technological progress and the actions related to it, which have the effect of making technological action irreversible and permanently creating new starting points. These new facts have to be the focus of attention in the search for a new set of ethical values in our technological age.

The specific problem concentrates on the question who is responsible for the cumulative effects, for the respective actions and their consequences. The real danger of our present situation lies in the fact that the direct short-term effects of technological progress may be manageable but not the long-term ones. Particularly the long-term effects, however, have the potential for the destruction of the biosphere, the over-exploitation of raw materials and energy resources. This is what endangers the existence of humanity itself. *Jonas*'s suggestions are guided by his conviction that man should continue to exist in the future, an imperative expressing our responsibility for our descendants. Our actions must not threaten the future of mankind (cf. *Jonas* 1987 a, 983 - 1002, 1987b, 103 - 115).

In his writings *Jonas* supports an ethical discussion of problems concerning sport and its impact on the environment. He questions our traditional anthropocentric world picture and defines man's responsibility towards nature in a new way (cf. *Schönherr* 1986, 687 - 698). The central question he focuses on is especially significant for sport: Do we have to refrain from an action in case of doubt?

As we know from chemical production as well as from skiing, actions in general and in sport in particular are principally determined by the fact that not all side and future effects can be considered in an instant decision. Consequently, we'll have to ask, as a matter of principle, for the responsibility concerning effects and side effects. Decisions must be made to the best of our knowledge, considering all calculable risks. Responsibility, however, is not to be understood as personal or collective, it should not be delegated, e.g. from scientist to politician. All individuals but also all collective institutions have, in the specific situation, the means to decide freely in favour or against something, however pressing the forces of reality or fact may be. The same applies to athletes and also to sport associations.

In the present situation the challenge for the individual is at the same time comprehensive and unique: "The singular aspect of our present crisis is the possibility of self-extermination of the human species and of irreversible damage of the whole eco-system" (cf. *Treml* 1985, 63). This characterization of our situation clearly indicates our need of an "ethic of survival" (cf. *Treml* 1985, 64 - 73). It has to be an ethic of not doing, of refraining, which also demands validity in the field of sport.

Both, 'not doing' and 'being committed' are necessary attitudes in sport, and what we need is a "homeostatic unity for survival", recognizing motives like "good health" and "the pursuit of happiness", which people want to satisfy by means of sport. To simply and unreflectedly continue growing and acting would - in sport as well as in other subsystems

- finally lead to self-destruction. Trying to find "stop rules" in sport therefore means helping to prevent their self-destruction (cf. *Treml* 1985, 71).

4.2 Legal regulations with effective and severe sanctions

If it is correct to say that at least in some areas of sport, like for instance, motorsport, a variety of water sport and almost all mountain sport, an organized retreat is required, we will have to realize that such a retreat will hardly be achieved on a voluntary basis. Mandatory limitations of the liberites exercised today will be necessary. Therefore we need a fundamental framework of political decisions, which can form the basis for the individual citizen's sensible and socially desirable behavior in his private sphere. Only then will he be in a successful position to meet the desired ethical standards. Thus, we need legal prohibition in terms of stop-rules preventing dangerous growth in sport, protecting natural areas and truly enabling their regeneration. Sanctions will be necessary to ensure and enforce obedience to the laws, and they will have to be sufficiently severe to provide an effective deterrence. In the interests of sport organizations, the number of sport intensifying the conflict with our natural environment must not increase in the near future. With due self-control and on a voluntary basis sport must be willing to refrain from organizing sporting events in areas declared nature reserves. In another step the use of nature reserves for sporting activities should be prohibited altogether. Simply pointing at other users of these areas, who demand in the same incomprehensible manner to continue their activities there, is more than questionable. With due self-interest sport organizations should take the initiative to freeze skiing tourism nationally and internationally on a quantitative level close to the numbers of the 1970s. To achieve this objective requires, for example, the prohibition of all further advertising for skiing including mass media commercials of the ski industry as well as advertisements of skiing organizations. The least requirement would be to connect advertising with information as it has become common for cigarette ads.

The sport associations would have to dissociate themselves voluntarily from motor sport organizations, since they are not to be justified any longer on the basis of an ethic taking ecological problems into consideration.

These changes require more than just appeals; what we need are decisions which change structures and foundations, which generate obligation and are tied to sanctions in cases of violation.

4.3 Money - A medium everybody understands

In a world determined by economic principles we can assume that money is the directing instrument which can count on the strongest response. Searching for solutions for the ecological problems caused by sport suggests special financial contributions as particularly suitable means. From an ecological point of view undesirable behavior is sanctioned by fees in order to change attitudes of sportsmen by economic measure. These contributions may also have another function like, for example, securing the funding of specific measures to protect the environment, where it is endangered by sport. Both types mentioned here are in conformity with free market policies and most suitable for our system of society. However, as long as these contributions are lower than the ideal or non-material profit gained by behavior that goes against ecological requirements, they are obviously inefficient and insufficient. High contributions or fees in the field of leisure and sport may be efficient, but they are also problematical. If the exercise of sport in nature was regulated through a concept of fees, environmentally harmless sport would be promoted and damaging sport would be made more difficult. It is, however, questionable, if sport can be regulated justly by these means, if, so to speak, ecological problems can be solved by putting up the price for sporting activities. There are signs that some ski resorts in the Alps are going this way, which only allows a few really affluent people to go skiing there. This example shows that following those economists who see the sole solution for environmental problems in the free market system, would very likely be problematical. Money is certainly a means everybody understands, yet it can be an extremely unjust means as well. Urgently necessary renunciation of human desires requires as a pre-condition a just balance of interests, if we want to avoid falling back to old pre-democratic class structures. The price as an instrument of regulation therefore can only be sensibly used if it is tied to political and legal regulations, and if it is based on an ethical foundation.

4.4 Education - A doubtful instrument

Among the numerous suggestions for the solution of sport-related environmental problems there seem to be only a few that are likely to promise satisfactory results in the long run, and some of these doubtlessly see education as a suitable means for the solution of the problems.

Such concepts, however, can only bring positive results, if education in sport, above all, is considered as political education, and if sport educators regard themselves as politically conscious people. This requires the realization that, in the same way as our relation to nature is socially determined and thus politically changeable, any action in sport is also related to society and, hence, is no less changeable (cf. *Digel* 1982). The principle that change is possible, is the key to overcoming the paradoxical relation between sport and the environment. Change provides the opportunity for "liberation in solidarity" (cf. *Winter* 1986, 4), which includes refraining from excessive consumption, intellectual apathy, opportunism, as well as, renouncing internal and external imperialistic dominance in politics and the economy. This is certainly a desirable educational objective, it is, however, so comprehensive that its practical realization is hardly ever achieved. With regard to our hopes for solutions within the field of education we should, rather, set more modest standards.

On the one hand focusing on education is popular, and the respective arguments basically make sense, relying on the "reasonable subject" and accepting the undeniable integrity of schools, which supposedly educate these subjects.

On the other hand this approach is to some degree part of a process of individualization typical of our society. Here, education has only short-term relieving effects; in the long run, however, it seems a rather inefficient instrument. The concept of environmental education is subject to dangers, which becomes particularly apparent, when we realize that it only serves a privileged group. Information and education can at best be favorable pre-conditions for effective measures. If they merely take place in an intellectually "free space" of those who, of course, do not want to give up their exciting pleasures and activities in nature, both are used as alibi functions, thus increasing indirectly the conflicts between sport and ecology.

Proposals for "environmentally sound skiing, hiking or walking" and the reports about it are extremely naive in this respect. They consider it an educationally important practical experience that people, who are privileged anyway, see with their own eyes dying trees, feel with their hand garbage disposal sites, take pictures of ski runs in nature reserves, and discuss these problems with tourist board representatives.

Stop rules cannot merely be introduced from inside, by the individual, they also need to be imposed from outside against the system of sport. Only then we will be able to realize the possibilities for lasting solutions of the ecological conflict between sport and the environment.

Concepts regarding environmental education subsequently have to be evaluated on the basis of this demand.

4.5 Relief through the development of community and neighbourhood leisure facilities

Scepticism and pessimism are both dominant aspects in the discussion of the potential of ethical constructs for solutions, legal regulations, financial fees and contributions as well as the free market and education. Important structural changes concerning the particular ecological problems caused by sport have been hardly recognizable up to now. For this very reason we do indeed also need singular measures, even if these are not far-reaching.

They should, however, be orientated towards those desired structural changes which, so far, have not yet been successful, but which nevertheless are still to be considered relevant.

In the field of sport we can recognize singular means serving the interests of sportsmen as well as meeting the demands of environmental protection. Sport organizations, and especially sport clubs, can possibly achieve the most by providing sport facilities in the direct neighborhood of their members. The opportunities offered should be attractive enough to keep large numbers of people away from areas distant from their neighborhoods, thus enabling endangered regions to start the process of regeneration. This could help to replace uncontrolled differentiated use by organized partial canalization.

Putting a concept of neighborhood sport and leisure facilities into practice requires a large number of singular measures, such as:
- the extension and maintenance of unenclosed green spaces in populated areas,
- the extension and maintenance of playgrounds and playing fields for children and adults,
- making play, sport and other club facilities accessible to the public,
- allowing parks to be used for sun-bathing, relaxing, for sport and games as well as for neighborhood parties,
- planting trees in residential streets,
- the further development and promotion of public transportation in order to provide easy access to leisure and sport facilities in urban areas,
- the extension of traffic-restricted zones in residential areas,
- the re-development of unused industrial estates and factories into sport facilities.

5.   An attempt to strike a balance

Today, two contrasting patterns are prevalent in the ecological debate. They are contrasting in so far, as one side speaks about an overall crisis whereas the other one regards ecological problems merely as temporary symptoms of an otherwise natural process of social transition. For one side, the ecological problems are an expression of the comprehensive crisis of western thinking, a profit- and growth-orientated economy accepting no limits and no goals of saturation. For the other side, however, ecological problems are of a technological kind, and we have always been confronted with them. They are regarded as results of bad technologies, and we have to overcome and master them by means of better and newer technologies. Technology, which is responsible for the crisis has to help to overcome it. Agreeing with this view implies the necessity of economic growth and profit in order to secure the funding of urgent measures concerning environmental protection. The other side makes completely different proposals, pleading for a new way of thinking, for learning to think in nonlinear cobweb patterns. What is demanded is an ecologically orientated alteration of industrial society, that is, a step-by-step, yet achievement-orientated change of our environment. The consumption of energy and resources has been geared towards the ideal of maximum conservation. We need an environmentally protective transformation of our transportation systems, and other fundamental sectors of our society must also be subject to change; this comprises energy, agriculture, housing development, as well as our leisure facilities and, of course, also sport. Viewed in this light, ecological problems are altogether cultural problems challenging the system of values prevalent in our society and questioning traditional patterns of thinking. The objective is the development of a "new model for our way of life".

Assuming that the latter characterization of predominant problems of our society is correct, we can answer the question raised by sport organization concerning the priority in the conflict between sport and environmental protection without the shadow of a doubt.

By no means can we argue in favour of a "balance of interests", as it is emphasized in many speeches and praised as a particular achievenemt in the 'art of compromising'. What we have to demand is an organized retreat and refraining from satisfying some of our desires which mean much to us, yet nevertheless, are not essential. Society as a whole but also each individual has to start withdrawing. Today, we have to realize that a large number of desires which our economy was orientated towards in the past are to be reflected upon anew. We have to find ethically justifiable "aims of affluence", and therefore our economic system has to comply with certain norms and standards. It has to comply with a "concept of affluence which is in harmony with the needs of both, man and nature" (cf. *Koslowski* 1984, 46). This requires a close examination of man's present desires. We have to reconsider the order of needs and answer the question if there are desires whose satisfaction must be made more difficult or even prohibited. In this process we ought to distinguish basic or existential needs from status-related or non-existential ones, and we should realize that the former are to be satisfied whereas the latter should not, and that therefore they are to be considered a particular danger of mankind. The slogan "higher, faster and further", interpreted as excitement, adventure and risk, has a specific significance for sport; needs and desires are projected on to it, whose saturation can simply no longer be permitted in the face of the ecological aspects which have to be our special concern.

Focusing on the efforts made by sport organizations in the conflict between sport and the environment, we recognize that this debate is largely to be characterized as a search for compromise. *Mayer-Tasch*, however, points out that the 'art of compromise' is presently the most menacing phenomenon with regard to the general ecological problems as well as the specific ones concerning sport. The continuation of the "weak policy of peripheral interference" signifies a particular danger of present policies. Authoritarian political conditions are almost inevitable consequences, especially in connection with policies promoting the establishment of big technological units, and those concerning the present handling of nuclear energy. Phrases like "everything is under control", as they are frequently used by politicians everywhere, will eventually lead to an ecological state of emergency, which might severely threaten our freedom (cf. *Mayer-Tasch* 1986, 1203). Sport certainly does not play any significant role in this respect, just as the answers to all the essential questions concerning environmental policies are not to be found within the scope of responsibility of sport. This applies, above all, to the question, which sectors of our environment are the most valuable ones and therefore need the most protection, but it also concerns the question regarding limits of acceptability in respect of dangers beyond which we need strict prohibition as a last resort. The strategy of compromising, common as it is in sport, however, bears the danger of being also a cause for the threats I have mentioned. When talking about compromise, officials in sport basically mean "carry on", and this is usually listed as a success in the dispute with environmentalists. "Unreflected and unrestricted carrying on", however, bears the specific danger of our time.

The Significance of Rules in Sport

1.   What are rules like in physical education?

From the moment when physical education was introduced into school it has been an almost unquestioned fact that physical acivity in class only is limited to sport activities and that it is orientated exclusively towards this direction.

These sporting activities are particularly characterized as being defined like the sport that is to be found outside school.

So a 'slice' of the world of sport is integrated into school in order to prepare students precisely for this world.

If we examine physical education - characterised by this generally accepted didactic concept - we see that the integration of sport into school forms causes difficulties. In forms you can hardly ever play football for twice 45 minutes, the basket in basketball has to be lowered to enable also younger students to achieve a successful throw. Taking into account the time limits and the necessary variety of sport disciplines in forms and considering the fact that physical education has to meet various different interests of different students then this kind of transformation of sport is necessary, and - from the educational point of view - sensible.

A closer look at different sports offered to students today reveals that it is especially the field of rules where limitations can be found. On the one hand physical education is orientated towards the closest possible adherence to rules in as many sport disciplines as possible. In this respect the codified rules of sport associations are taken as a guideline in education. On the other hand these codified rules are followed only to the extent the teacher considers appropriate. Hardly ever are, for example, the rules in basketball obeyed concerning dribbling, fouls or time. Nevertheless, it remains an unquestioned matter of course that only one ball is used, that there are 5 players per team on the field and that the referee starts the game with a high throw. This example can show the degree to which sport in school is rule-orientated and what generally is considered the educational significance of rules in physical education: An important part of the teacher's actions aims at the adherence to sport rules, and with this objective in mind, the students practise, play and are trained. This also reflects the significance applied to sport rules in the curricula. Accordingly, the most important rules of games and regulations for competitions are supposed to be introduced to the students to enable them to follow these rules appropriately.

In my opinion the educational opportunities provided by the rules of sport are taken advantage of to a very minor extent only. Of course it is an important and necessary task to teach students how to obey sport rules and to give them these rules at their disposal so that they can apply them in sport outside shool. However, if this was the only scope it would not justify the fact that they are taught in school of all the possible places. Sport clubs could meet this demand just as well. Which further educational opportunities can sport rules offer? Where is the specific chance that sport rules contain?

In order to be able to answer these questions it is necessary to analyse the significance of sport rules for people's behavior in general and acting in sport in particular.

2.   What is a rule?

Looking in an encyclopedia of sport science to answer the question which significance rules in sport have as far as sport activities are concerned we find that - surprisingly enough - there are no entries concerning the term "sport rule". Instead it is suggested to look up the term "rules of a game". This is a typical method in the discussion about rules in sport. As a consequence students are not the only ones who often think rule-related problems only exist in sport games. Such a restricted definition of the term rule is not very useful; above all the educational opportunities of rules in sport can be used only to a limited extent. This we can see clearly by having a closer look at the explanation for rules of games given in the encyclopedia of sport science: "A game's rule is determined by fixed patterns of the course of action and a standardized behavior of the players. Such a regulation refers to aspects of the game to a larger or lesser degree. It is either explicitly codified or implicitly established as a convention. It may refer to the technical procedure of a game or rather to the ethical aspects of the players' behavior towards their opponents or towards their team mates" (cf. *Röthig* 1977, 277).

You may find the language in this passage amazingly vague. However, this description - if interpreted generously - points out some interesting aspects which help to answer the question, what actually are sport rules? Together with codified rules there obviously are rules which are not recorded in writing. Of course, codification and convention do not oppose each other. But by mentioning the conventional character of rules it is suggested that they are based on conventions. Furthermore, the encyclopedia provides the information that rules can refer to various subjects. On the one hand, skills in a sport game are regulated; on the other hand, rules influence the ethical aspects of the behavior towards opponents or team mates.

However, this interpretation cannot obscure the fact that the definition given in the encyclopedia of sport science is contradictory, and in search for the answer concerning the definition of a rule in sport it is only of limited help. Therefore it is appropriate to consult scientific analyses which try to describe what a rule is in general and what it is in the special case of sport. We can name many social scientists who have written about the complex problem of rules, standards and values (cf. *Collet* 1977; *De Wachter* 1983; *Hermann* 1982 among others). But above all, discussion about rules referring to Wittgenstein's term "Sprachspiel", is especially suitable for my purpose (cf. *Searle* 1971; *Heringer* 1974; *Waismann* 1976; *Fritz* 1982; *Muckenhaupt* 1976; *Öhlschläger* 1974; *Wimmer* 1982). They have induced me to apply the term sport rule in a much wider sense than it is normally done in sport (cf. *Digel* 1982). I turn to all those rules which are of fundamental significance for the practicing of sport and which are important for its understanding. Thus I focus on far more rules than only those regulating motor actions in sport. First, the term refers to all kinds of sport. Furthermore it comprises a second, wider perspective if we introduce the term rule-guided action. The shake hands of two team captains, the congratulation of a loser to the winner of a game, the apology after a foul, manipulation by means of doping - all these are undoubtedly actions in sport though they do not keep or break those rules generally known as rules in sport. *Gebauer* points out correctly that even attack and defence are actions which are not defined in codified sport rules (cf. *Gebauer* 1983). These examples make clear that there are other sets of rules apart from sport rules which we follow. We are able to realize this if we understand rules as a pattern of actions whose function is comparable with that of a knitting pattern, serving as a guide line for our behavior in sport. Therefore the term 'rule' often is replaced by such terms as standard, norm, maxim, principle. I have chosen the term "rule" in order to be precise in terminology, implying that a rule, in my understanding, can be characterized as a social convention.

How exactly do rules determine human actions? This question leads to a rule typology, which helps us to understand the meaning of sport rules.

3.   How can rules be differentiated?

Searle especially has shown that rules can have very different functions concerning our actions. For example, if a sport rule says: "In shot-putting the shot may only be put with one hand", the existence of this rule guarantees two things. First, only due to this rule can shot-putting be practised in a way that is currently accepted in sport. Thus, rules constitute practice in sport. *Searle* calls those rules constitutive rules. Consequently, if the shot is put with two hands, it is no longer shot-putting but at best a sport similar to shot-putting. Regarding rules from this point of view, one can either deviate from a rule pattern or act according to the rules. The result of deviation is either a modified version of shot-putting or something completely different. However, if a shot-putter taking part in a competition suddenly puts the shot with both hands he acts against the rules and will be punished by a referee. From this point of view the rule does not only constitute a sport's performance but also regulates it. This shows that rules have two characteristics: They define as well as regulate (cf. *Hermann* 1982, 35-39).

In addition to these two aspects of constitutive rules, I think it is useful to add a second group of rules, which is indicated by the term 'maxim'. I am talking about those cases that are at our disposal like recommendations and which enable us to act with greater prudence, success and adequacy within a constitutively determined situational pattern. I have called these rules "strategic rules" (*Digel* 1982, 53-62). They are the rules we refer to when teaching somebody how to do something in the most effective way. In contrast, the constitutive rules are of importance when we intend to teach somebody how something is done and when we wish to define the performed action (cf. Table 6).

As to the consequences, the difference between these two kinds of rules lies in the fact that, if we disobey a constitutive rule, we do not do what we pretend or want to do. If we break a strategic rule we run the risk of failing provided that this rule is reasonable (cf. *Fritz* 1982, 60-69).

The fact that rules can, but do not have to be written down accounts for the distinction between constitutive, regulative, strategic and moral rules. Therefore it is important to point out that rules do not necessarily occur in the form of a sentence. Here we must distinguish clearly between a rule and its definition or explanation. A rule is by no means a sentence. We can follow a rule without explicitly defining it (cf. *Keller* 1974). Concerning sport rules this means that we must consider not only those rules which are laid down in codes of different sports but also those which - as informal rules - guide actions in sport. In sport they determine mainly the ethics, the concept of sport and the tactics used in the different kinds of sport.

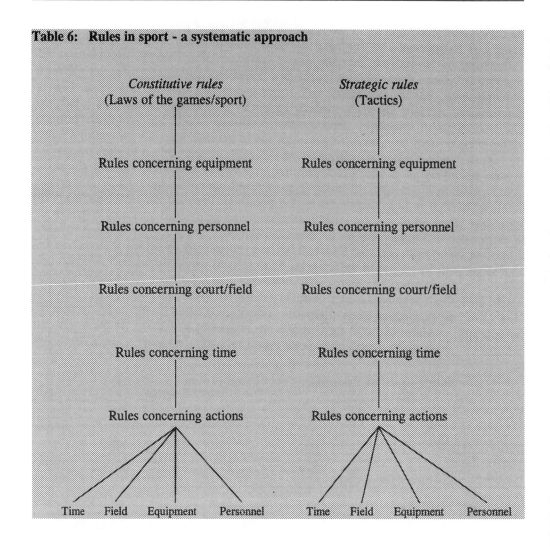

Table 6: Rules in sport - a systematic approach

Constitutive rules (Laws of the games/sport)	*Strategic rules* (Tactics)
Rules concerning equipment	Rules concerning equipment
Rules concerning personnel	Rules concerning personnel
Rules concerning court/field	Rules concerning court/field
Rules concerning time	Rules concerning time
Rules concerning actions	Rules concerning actions
Time Field Equipment Personnel	Time Field Equipment Personnel

Ethical-moral rules
"Be fair"
"Accept your opponent as a partner"
"Guarantee equality of opportunity"
"Mind your partners' physical and personal safety"
"Above all, protect the weaker athletes"
"Follow the accepted rules"

Rules related to the conception of sport
Rule concerning the lack of consequences
Rule concerning arbitrary obstacles
Rule concerning physical solutions
Rule concerning open result

Rule concerning competition
Rule concerning ambition and readiness to perform

Rules related to kinds of sport
"The goal is 2 m high and 3 m wide"
"The ball is made of a unicoloured leather"
"Duration of the game for men amounts to 2 times 30 minutes"
"A team consists of 12 players"
"It is allowed to use the trunk to impede the opponent"

On the one hand, rules constitute what is meant by the conception of sport as an idea. On the other hand, they also constitute the practice in the various sport disciplines. Above all they determine what is allowed and what is not. Additionally, they point out ways leading to a successful way of dealing with the concept of sport and of putting this concept successfully into practice. Rules can be written down, this is the case with doping regulations, the regulations concerning the different types of sport, and also with some of the strategic rules. But they can also have an informal character, as it is the case with moral maximes or the principal idea of competition.

Finally, rules can refer to very different aspects such as time, space, equipment and personnel in the same way as to the athletes' motor activities. They determine the moral aspects and the meaning which forms the basis of any sporting activity.

This formal description enables us to proceed to the next point and take a closer look at the significance of sport rules as far as our sport activities are concerned.

4. Of what significance are sport rules as far as our behavior in sport is concerned?

4.1 Sport rules guarantee the satisfaction of needs of those practicing sport, and they establish the basis of ethical and moral behavior in sport

The term constitutive rules is supposed to show the fact that rules are points of reference for the description of practice and the basis for its change. In terms of sport, this means that if there were no rules sport would not exist. In contrast to Volkamer I still assume that sport is constituted by its rules (cf. *Volkamer* 1983). However, - and I owe this conclusion also to Volkamer's critical remarks - we must not speak of rules of the different sport disciplines as the only possible kind of rules. They always constitute sport jointly with those rules that refer to the ethical and moral maxims and to the general meaning of sport activities. That is why the question as to what exactly sport is can only be answered because of the existence of rules which form the basis of sport. The rules existing in the different kinds of sport are usually artistically sophisticated patterns, which have developed and proven their efficiency, often throughout centuries. They have enabled many people to do whatever sport they might have wanted to do; they have been a guarantee for the satisfaction of people's needs and of what they expect of sport. This is one of the main reasons why we can by no means say that sport rules have simply a commanding or restrictive function concerning our behavior and activities in sport, as it is generally said. They are not merely arbitrary, either. They have rather an intersubjective character. Without their existence participation in sport would not be possible. Rules guarantee that we will be able to play football tomorrow exactly in the same way as yesterday - that we know whether a javelin has been thrown correctly or incorrectly - that we can explain what we have to do to learn a certain kind of sport.

I have tried to make clear that the main function of rules is to enable us to do certain things. This function requires that every sport participant follows the rules and that he can rely on the other participants to act accordingly. This shows that in sport our behaviour must be in accordance with the rules, otherwise team sport is not possible. An athlete taking part in a competition agrees without explicitly saying so to follow the specific rules of a specific kind of sport. This includes agreement to accept all those rules which refer to the conception of doing sport and the ethics of sport in general. If this agreement is refused, however, it results in a threat to the existence of the system of sport. This is the case when, for example, an athlete is doped, when, in soccer, a player of the opposing team deliberately touches the ball with his hands, or when devices are used which the opponent does not have at his disposal. These examples hint at the fact that - like in any other social organization - there obviously exist conditions of membership in sport as well, guaranteeing the ethics of these kinds of sport. Whoever participates in sporting activities has to virtually promise that he will follow the membership rules. The acceptance of further rules can be deduced from the basic membership rules. We can phrase the following as a previously determined rule: *every athlete has to assume that his partner is equally willing to follow the rules of sport just like he is himself.* This mutual acceptance has led to the unquestioned trust that forms the basis for the specific experiences we make in sport. We do not have to set up new rules day after day, we can rely on whatever was valid yesterday still being valid today. Trust and honesty on the part of the sporting participants are closely connected. These two terms "trust" and "honesty" refer to those unwritten rules which give sport rules the character of a social agreement. If the participants break this agreement, sport as a social system is in jeopardy. For the athlete this means that he as an individual supports the ethical basis of sport merely by accepting the demand for a general conformity regardless of his own preferences. This demand becomes even more important, if we consider sport rules as being of a quasi-universal nature. Like the codes of sport associations, the ethical-moral maxims of sport and the rules concerning the concept of sport and games are accepted worldwide; they have an intercultural basis and remain nearly the only system of rules in the world which can be interpreted in the same way in all cultures. The interpretation of the concept of sport as the idea of peace is therefore only comprehensible if we remember the intercultural aspect of sport rules.

These facts show the educational significance of sport rules in connection with the question of sport as a possible educational peace-keeping measure. The principle of peace in sport is based on the moral rules of fairness which comprise at least the following four aspects:

- *Recognize your opponent as your partner.*
- *Make sure that your opponents will not be physically or emotionally hurt.*
- *Make sure that there are equal opportunities for all participants.*
- *Protect particularly the weaker partners.*

The promotion of peace almost offered ritually by sport consists of the acceptance of rules and the appropriate sanctions in the case of violations. Both, the peace principle and the sanction are of course only useful if the principle of fairness in sport has been convincingly put into practice (cf. *Huber* 1983, 1-5).

Sport as it exists today is far from being a unique peace or human-rights-movement, as some conservative politicians and sport officials still believe. But it could be or become such a movement. To achieve this, however, it will be necessary to revise all those contradicting rules which have developed over the last years, and which do not agree with the ethical maxims, self-imposed by the conception of sport. If we want to achieve this we will have to realize the educational aspects of these rules and use them accordingly.

4.2 Sport rules have a key function for the training of skills and strategies

We can consider sport a sector which - like any other social sector - is constituted and regulated by its rules. This fact is pointed out in many analytic descriptions of rules. What seems to be less obvious is that, additionally, the constitutive rules are the main point of reference for all that is trained in a certain kind of sport and for all the possible skills and strategies that can be applied. As constitutive and regulating forces, rules determine the intended objective of movement in a specific kind of sport; they determine the object of movement, the performer of the movement, time, space and the equipment as well as the facilities necessary for the movement. The reason why for a team-handball match specific shots are practised for specific situations is that a shot at the goal is not precisely determined by the constitutive rules so that different shots are allowed in the goalarea. But also the question as to whether in a specific kind of sport, power, speed, or endurance require special training can only be answered with regard to the rules valid in the different sports. Even the efficiency of certain training methods cannot be assessed without taking into account the underlying system of rules. The importance of the rules in this respect often remains unknown to both, the coach and the athlete, the reason being that during training sessions rules are referred to only in exceptional situations. Sport and the skills they require are always seen as a whole. If a rule is altered, however, its importance for coaching becomes evident. The training methods have to be adapted to this new rule, for example, the technique of jumping has to be modified.

This example has shown the importance of rules for the skills and the training methods of a certain kind of sport. Rules play an even more important role in strategies, which we define as one of the possible procedures the sporting participant can choose from, on the basis of constitutive rules. Therefore, the constitutive rules limit the variety of tactical possibilities in sport. The less strict the rules are the greater the variety of tactical possibilities. This becomes obvious if we compare, i.e., different sport games with swimming or athletics. Thus the tactics of a sport are by no means arbitrary. They are rather influenced by unwritten rules determining what an athlete or a team - in keeping to the constitutive rules - should or should not do. These rules have an impact on the strategies pursued by the sporting participants. Therefore I have called them strategic rules. They are developed either individually or agreed upon mutually by the competing partners and the coaches as informal regulations and are applied according to the specific situations. The available scope of action offered by the constitutive rules is taken into consideration during this process. Some of these strategic rules have - due to their efficiency - come to be tactical sets of prescriptions and have thus found their way into books on coaching and methodology.

One example is the Fosbury-Flop, which is considered to be a technically optimal pattern for the tasks required in competition on account of the rules of high jump. The individual choice of technique can be understood as a tactical instrument. In team-handball some techniques have become standard defence-patterns (6:0, 5:1, 4:2). In soccer we speak of the 4:2:4-system. These examples show that there are strategic rules which on the one hand refer to the choice of technique and on the other hand to the methods used to approach the opponent. The dominance of the constitutive rules accounts for the phenomenon that sportsmen are mostly unaware of the fact that they also follow certain rules when they choose a certain technique. It requires the athlete's utmost attention and strength to learn how to do sport in accordance with the constitutive rules. Tactical actions are mostly left to luck. If the athlete, however, is aware of the relation between constitutive, regulating and strategic rules, and if he knows the strategic possibilities resulting from the constitutive rules, even a beginner can be expected to use the tactical scope of action more efficiently than it has been the case until now. If we accept that, for example, the ability to take part in sport games is defined not only as motor skill but also as the ability to interpret the rules (cognitive aspect) we understand the educational importance of this fact.

4.3   Sport rules are a dependent variable of human needs

As I have put specific emphasis on the necessity of a conduct which is in accordance with the existing rules, one could assume that the main function of sport is to instruct students to follow rules in the best way possible. In view of the methods in which sport is generally practised this assumption is easy to understand. For the further development of sport and especially for educational reasons (which still remain to be further explained) it would be disastrous if this was the only function of sport. Besides their facilitating function sport rules may very well become a threat to sport itself. It is therefore appropriate, to point out at this stage while maintaining - that sport rules are no laws of nature - the dangers that can be observed with regard to these rules (cf. *Öhlschläger* 1974).

In connection with the example of a soccer match I pointed out how skillfully sophisticated the system of rules for a game can be, which provides the satisfaction of many people. When we watch a children's soccer match or a match on the beach, however, we have to admit that the positive assessment of the official system of rules set up by sport associations can only partly be maintained. Often, it is even the case that the rules set up by the sport associations prevent us from taking an active part in sport. How is this possible?

We rigthly assume that sport rules, especially the codified rules for the different sport disciplines, have become socially accepted, because they are institutionally based on the agreement of a majority of a legislative body which has the competence to decide. We can further assume that if the rules had not been considered reasonable this body had not agreed on their acceptance. This, however, does by no means guarantee that the reasons which have led the majority to consent to the rules are equally comprehensive reasons for any possible situation in which sport is practised today (cf. *Lübbe* 1978).

This aspect becomes clear when we look at, e.g., the situation of physical education or at sport as a mere leisure activity with regard to the underlying reasons that have led to the specific rules. We notice that neither in physical education nor in sport practised as a leisure activity it is common to look for the reasons behind the rules. This is done outside the schools by the sport associations. At school we are normally confronted with already established and well-founded rules; the students are only expected to obey these rules. Thus, thanks to the various - more or less - reasonable forms of intertwinement of competitive sport and school sport, the schools have confidence in the reasonable legislative competence of their external partners. It can be seen at first sight that this procedure makes hardly any sense from the educational point of view, since the logic of the reasons depends on the assumption that the specific rules correspond with the central idea of sport outside school. This central idea of sport is that through the existence of rules an attractive, exciting and performance-orientated competition is generated, which is characterized by the participation of competing athletes and teams, which all have equal chances once the competition has started.

If physical education claims to be of educational value, it is immediately understandable that such a one-dimensional explanation of sport is not sufficient. Physical education remains heteronomous as long as rules are taken over from sport associations without reflecting them. This means that in school as well as in rule-setting committees the same process of consent-seeking between those people affected has to take place. Such a reflection leads either to an agreement that certain rules are suitable for school and therefore should be obeyed, or it leads to the decision that new rules suitable for physical education should replace certain extracurricular rules precluding that students accept rules only on account of the teacher's power to impose sanctions. This implies the risk that rules lose their ability-fostering function and are perceived as mere orders instead. The usual practice of determining rules is also dubious for those people who want to satisfy their need of being active besides school, but do not want to do competitive sport. Today, more people than ever want to practise sport actively. They want to experience their bodies, keep fit, practise sport with partners and in mixed groups, and not least, seek contact to like-minded people in order to communicate, which is often impossible in other areas of life. These examples show that people, with all their variing personal abilities, relate different needs to sport. These very different needs can hardly be satisfied if those kinds of sport with only one pattern, that is to say, defined by codified rules, are applied to cover all the various interests. Since it is the main task of sport to satisfy human needs it is not appropriate to adapt the people's needs to sport but the adaptation has to take place vice versa.

This is possible, because all rules bear the potential of being modified. Furthermore we can say that codified rules, since they are developed by human beings, can be changed or even abolished by human beings. Thus, rules are changeable in the sense that they are virtually chosen, which can be seen in the fact that there is the possibility of abolishing and replacing them. The possibility of departing from a rule is constitutive for social rules. The fact that rules in sport can be treated like this is the only reason why, e.g, soccer has developed in many steps to the game we know and appreciate today. This also means that, in the future, soccer does not necessarily have to be played in the same way as today, and that at present soccer can be played differently if the partners have agreed on it before. If we relate these observations to the comments on the importance of rules in sport given initially we can state in short that the possibility of departing from rules as well as the openness of the relation between rule and activity or obedience to the rule shows two controversial aspects: On the one hand there is creativity which can lead to new contents, and on the other hand there is the dangerous aspect of questioning the intersubjective foundation of rules. I have already mentioned the generally possible modification of sport rules. Thus, I have pointed out the way in which sport can be adapted to human needs. Taking the present situation into account we have to admit that human needs, like approaching sport in numerous different ways, are not always adequately satisfied; and that many people are still excluded from practicing sport. What are the reasons for this phenomenon? What should be done to change this situation?

There are two reasons perhaps: first, only few people seem to see the difference between a rule and a law of nature. This often leads to the situation that not only sport but many other fields of our society, which are defined by rules, appear like laws of nature determining human actions once and for all. Sport is seen as a biologically determined constant of nature. It is of special importance to reveal the error this attitude is based on because we notice that even P.E. teachers, sport scientists and athletes make this mistake.

A second reason could be that today the awareness of rules - for example of students - but also of adult leisure sportsmen is strongly influenced by the socialization agencies people prefer. These agencies present sport in an almost absolute shape. Television presents sport to children and young people that is characterized by constancy as far as rules are concerned. This is, of course, only a virtual constancy, seen as such, because nowadays the historical development of sport with all its variations is not particularly apparent. Furthermore it is experienced as constancy because people actively practicing sport are not encouraged to participate in shaping the future development of sport.

These are two very important reasons. Even more important, however, seems to me that, on the basis of these reasons and the discernments resulting from them, we develop a new way of justifying rules. In my opinion we can no longer accept that, in our society, sport associations still regulate how young people ought to realize their wish of practicing sport. The sport associations greatly exceed the limits of influence given by their rule-setting and rule-establishing authorities. Possibly they are unaware of this. However, they do so without contacting those people who then have to obey the rules. In the fields of physical education as well as leisure-time sport this coherence is alarming and dangerous. Accepting my evaluation requires the possibility of developing addressee-orientated, informal methods of examination, justification and enforcement, that is to say, need-orientated rule-finding processes.

5.   The significance of sport rules for education

The previous explanation together with the initially given rule typology indicate that the phenomenon "sport" can be exactly described by means of rules. However, this is a minor aspect in the rule discussion. It is much more important that an analytical examination of rules indicates the opportunities which affect sport education and the teaching and learning of sport in particular. I have already mentioned some of these opportunities.

Finally I want to examine the significance of sport rules for educational decisions in physical education. What experiences can be made by means of sport rules in class? In what respect are rules important for educational intentions in physical education?

In general we can answer that the teaching and learning of certain movement patterns have to be orientated towards rules which students are supposed to obey. The main significance, however, is attributed to rules against the background of those intentions which have induced us in the first place to regard sport as an aspect of education and to introduce it as a subject in school. Sport educators generally agree - by variing degrees - that a central task of physical education is to educate students to be partners who are competent as to their actions in sport as well as in other fields of life (cf. *Kurz* 1977; *Digel* 1977, 1982). The competence of students as well as other people acting in sport is characterized by their results they have achieved in sport, by the things they say about sport by their knowledge and understanding of sport and by their experiences and feelings. In class it is taken for granted that the student's capability of taking action normally is not sufficient in one respect or another. Therefore the necessity for development exists. Students are trained and taught in skills and strategies, and thus particularly their abilities in sport increase. Practical skills are usually restricted to the sport discipline exercised at a particular time. The possibility that these skills or interactions show any similarity to the skills and interactions of other sport disciplines or that there might be common structures is not consciously experienced - if experienced at all. If the only aim is to prepare the students for the practicing of a certain chosen sport or game, e.g. the mastering of volleyball, then the described teaching method bears no disadvantages. But if physical education is to enable students and future adults to practise a sport which did not yet exist or could not be taught when they attended school, if the student is to be taught how to practise sport with partners, how to perform exercises without any instruction, how to help - or teach - his partners to learn certain motions, if students are to have a better understanding of sport and are to be more competent as passive spectators of a competition - if all this is the case, then the previously described practice is a real disadvantage. It is a fundamental necessitiy in teaching to have a broad view of the various possible rule modifications. It is that view that enables us to simplify or complicate sport. This synopsis is also necessary if a game ought to become more interesting and exciting, if we want to increase the strenuousness in a certain sport, if the risk of a sport is to be reduced or if it is necessary to adapt oneself to a particular situation. The rules have to be adjusted to, e.g., the number of players available, insufficient equipment or inadequate facilities.

These examples point out the necessity to reflect the rule character of sport in class. The students have to be introduced to the rules guiding their actions. The planned use of rules should enable them to test the mentioned abilities in class. In such a way a second aim - equally important - might possibly be achieved at the same time.

I have already pointed out that competition-oriented rules meet the requirements of actual physical education and the interests and needs of athletes outside school only to a limited extent. Such rules sometimes cause conflicts between teachers and students and among students themselves. Some students are privileged, others are handicapped by official regulations. In order to solve these and other conflicts in class, rules, which are partly responsible for the conflicts, have to be altered. Nevertheless it seems to be hardly sensible for a teacher to introduce rule alterations without explaining their meaning to the students. It is even more important to explain to the students how the degree of difficulty in a certain sport discipline can be reduced by changing the respective rules. They have to find out the rules that have to be adapted to different age groups, and they have to learn how to make the complex structure of a sport discipline transparent by the systematic simplification of rules, and how the discipline thus becomes "teachable and learnable".

This is also a way of improving the social function of sport. Excluded players can be re-integrated in a game, experiences which the original rules did not allow are made possible. New kinds of sport can be invented by combining various types or rules of different sports; and after having made this experience it will become easier to create individual, new movement patterns. In terms of politics the rules discussion is of decisive importance for the modification of sport by human beings.

However demands that students should obey rules without questioning them - a claim that still exists among educators - does not meet these standards and prevents students from freely expressing their interests. Then sport is experienced in a reactive and reproductive manner; any self-initiative and creativity in physical education is subdued. Altogether it would mean a waste of the educational opportunities attached to sport rules.

On the change of values in society, leisure and sport

The industrialized societies of the northern hemisphere have been subject to fundamental and profound changes over the last two decades, and there is much indication that they are presently in a state of crisis concerning their future development. This also applies to German industrial society, which will be in the focus of attention here. Its future development as a "post-industrial society" (*Bell*) is in jeopardy, and it is also facing difficulties in respect of those prognoses describing the present transition as a "Second Industrial Revolution" (like e.g. *Schaff*). One thing, however, seems comprehensible for everyone, also for people who have doubts: the shortage or limited availability of some vital resources, the conflict-bearing north-south-gap, micro-electronics, biochemistry including advanced genetic technology, the civilian as well as the military use of nuclear power, the still considerable military potential in almost all parts of the world, man's ongoing over-exploitation of natural resources and the environment have generated a unique situation for mankind. It has become possible to exterminate the human species in a matter of seconds; yet, by applying presently available technologies we might, at the same time, be capable of solving many of man's essential problems such as hunger, the supply of energy and also the ecological problem. We will have to confront these questions and problems even in our private lives. They have caused changes in many people's attitudes towards nature, work, and leisure, but also towards their religious beliefs, their families and fellow citizens. These changes can be made apparent by means of a comparison: Germans comparing their present attitudes with those twenty years ago might realize that today they more frequently question the sense of their jobs, they might realize that they pursue more hedonistic enjoyment, eat better, drive faster and bigger cars, own more expensive furniture, have new preferences in terms of vacations, show more respect for nature, reconsider their abstinence from church-going, reflect more on world peace and are more concerned about their children's future. Such a comparison can be described as a comparison of values which guide people's actions.

Values are subject to change

In the social sciences we speak of a "change of values" in this context as a particularly significant partial aspect of a general social process of change. This change of values has been studied primarily with reference to a pair of contrasts and has been labelled "materialism" and "post-materialism" as suggested by *Inglehart* 16 years ago.

His theory of a change of values is predominantly based on empirical research undertaken in the countries of the European Community. By means of a set of empirical instruments Inglehart observed, over a rather long period of time, a fundamental change of political culture in the Federal Republic of Germany. In his view a part of Germany's population has undergone an epochally significant process of turning away from a originally religiously based and later increasingly bourgeois work and performance ethic. So-called material values like economical welfare, emphasis on performance, achievement and disciplines, external and internal security have been replaced by post-materialistic values such as the pursuit of participation, solidarity and self-fulfillment, freedom and equality, supplemented by new intellectual, social and aesthetic desires (cf. *Inglehart* 1977). Post-materialism means progress; values of self-fulfillment therefore are to be regarded as higher-ranking than material desires.

As far as I know the thesis of value change is being confirmed rather than questioned in almost all studies on the change of values since Inglehart. When considering the research of *Kmieciak* (1976), *Klippstein/Strümpel* (1985), *Noelle-Neumann* (1984), *Klages* (1983), *Klages/Hippler/Herberg* (1992) and others we can hardly ask the question at all, whether there has been a change of values in Germany. At the most its reach, its actual course and not least the question how the occuring change of values could be normatively evaluated may be debatable. The discussions about a solid theory of value change and its empirical relevance are still in full swing, and it is becoming increasingly difficult to distinguish those results from the large variety of available empirical studies that are the most likely to be consensual. For example, with reference to the general change of values representatives of otherwise very different scientific views almost unanimously agree the transcendental systems of belief have long lost their guaranteeing functions as higher values. In the last thirty years Germany has experienced a declining significance of "traditional work and performance values" (*Kmieciak*). Work is becoming more and more a means to an end, less and less an end in itself. Especially the values of a Protestant performance ethic as outlined by Max Weber seem to rule the world of work only to a limited extent today. Rather have value patterns evolved alongside work which refer to social sectors like family life, leisure, education and political participation.

The loss of values, their substitution and devaluation seem to be parallel processes. Some values are getting lost, like for instance, some religious ones, which is an apparent result of studies focussing on the attendance in religious services but also in terms of the change of views concerning values based on religion. Not only have the opinions about the dissolution of marriage changed, pre-marital cohabitation has also become normal in Germany.

Some values are substituted. So are values of performance ethic replaced by those of personal development and self-fulfillment, which has become obvious in the increase of desires concerning enjoyment and the parallel decrease of willingness "to achieve something in life" but also in the ranking order of the most important personal objectives in life. "An interesting life" and "self-fulfillment" rank very high among "post-materialists".

Finally, some values are being devaluated, like for instance, the sphere of work. It has lost its dominant position to other domains such as leisure, family and education (cf. *Engfer* e.a. 1983, 434 - 435).

Experts agree that such a change of values does by no means occur universally; nor are all sectors of a society equally affected by it, the reason for this being each person's different individual socialization process.

On the one hand, for those people whose professional career is still undecided a performance ethic still plays an essential role in their 'value budget'; on the other hand, the sense of performance-oriented behaviour is hardly comprehensible for all those who are alienated from their work or even unemployed, and who have to find a new sense of meaning in other areas than work.

The results of the numerous cross-section studies dealing with these questions lead to the conclusion that the conventional performance ethic has indeed lost some of its influence. Especially among the younger age groups we recognize prevailing patterns of values whose points of reference are located outside the domain of work. This result indicates the necessity of a group-specific perspective which has proved to be adequate in all other cross-section studies, too. Thus, for instance, the supporters of unconventional values predominantly work in service-related jobs; people successful in professional life, however, still support a conventional performance ethic (cf. *Engfer* e.a. 1983, 452). When asking about the significance of individual education standards for the respective value orientation, people with a higher education are more likely to draw back from a conventional performance ethic than those with a lower one (cf. *Fend/Prester* 1984, 60). A similar difference can be recognized with regard to different professional or vocational categories: people working in social services are the furthest removed from a conventional work ethic, whereas those having manual industrial or trade-related jobs are the most intensively oriented towards it.

Studies show that the older we get the more levelled such differentiations are again. Between the age of 50 and 60 - according to Engfer's results (1983) - the working population tends to readopt the value patterns of the conventional performance ethic.

Studying the materialistic and the postmaterialistic values from a normative point of view we might be led to the conclusion that post-materialistic values are more humane, more future-oriented and more adequate than materialistic ones. An evaluation of this kind, however, is out of place; a more precise analysis rather indicates that each value pattern contains contradictory values, and that - with reference to the respective individual and his or her value orientation - such a polarization seems hardly useful, because values become visible in real individuals, and the change of values occurs in the actual individual. Consequently values are by no means "mere inventions of wishful thinking"; they rather can be interpreted as the final and decisive determinants of human behaviour. Research on these issues has certainly not reached its end yet, but it already has brought about a large amount of material on the basis of which this statement is justified. Hence, people working in the scientific field of values presume that values or basic needs and desires are so-called "background determinants" of the majority of decisions concerning opinions and behaviours to be observed in social everyday life (cf. *Klages* 1981, 118). Considering this aspect we might well assume that the individual sometimes is orientated towards materialistic and at other times towards post-materialistic values. Klages calls this phenomenon "as-well-as presence" (cf. *Klages* 1983, 342). This situationally adequate use of value orientation seems to be typical of the presently occuring change of values, which consequently takes place as "mixture of values" (Klages 1983, 343) going right through people, developing independently of gender, age, social origin, and being continously influenced by a large diversity of external factors. As a consequence each individual possesses his or her own "set of values". Previously inflexible value systems are in a stage of dissolution. Problematical in this context is the fact that more and more people are having difficulties finding the right balance between their values, and that their value pattern may even contain unbridgeable discrepancies.

What causes the change of values?

What makes people change their attitudes towards social challenges? Why do they become oriented towards new value patterns? These questions can be answered only by referring to everyday experience, which does not seem insignificant at all. The following answer considers ten partial aspects:

1. *Firstly*: We assume, the presently observed change of values is related to a widespread process of secularization that has gained ground among almost all population groups in West Germany after World War II; this has resulted in the disintegration of rigid social roles with parallel development of affluence allowing almost all groups of the population to participate in consumption, which was a necessary basis enabling West Germany's "post-industrial society" to feature a pluralism of values and lifestyles. In this context *Strümpel* (1985) points out that - perhaps for the first time in human history - large sections of the population enjoy the freedom of decision in terms of their behaviour, which means that the individual is granted the opportunity to choose a lifestyle of independence, of mobility for the young, of work for females, of life in urban areas, travelling, having children, being a housewife, etc. (cf. *Strümpel* 1985, 4). Thus the emergence of post-materialistic value orientations is closely related to a large-scale economic boom in post-World War II Germany enabling society to overcome material want for almost all its members. Growing up in affluence leads to an increase of the "prince and princess syndrome" (*Fend/v.Friedeburg* 1985, 1) and to an attitude of passive demand. Therefore it is hardly surprising that in societies suffering from want there is, even today, no room for post-materialistic value patterns. However, as soon as problems of shortage and want decrease, a comprehensive social differentiation and thus a differentiation of value patterns is initiated.

2. Another reason might be rooted in the development of the education system and the parallel development of uncoupling education from the employment system and the demand for training and education. Today education is tied to vocational training. It refers to the preparation for conventional performance-oriented action to a limited extent only. Education rather aims at the development of personality, the teaching of comprehensive cognizant competence, the preparation for the successful coping with the multi-facetted situations of real life and, not least, leisure.

3. The change of values was probably also supported by the extension of social services and welfare, which has led to a welfare system predominantly oriented towards the principles of justice and solidarity. "Welfare for all" in this context means the comprehensive participation of all citizens in economic progress; in this process the required economic achievements are provided individually by the citizens. Thus attaching achievements directly to the individuals is no longer possible, which in turn, so we assume, supports a general devaluation of the individual's willingness for performance and achievement.

4. Furthermore we can see as another reason the increasingly visible conflict of interests between industrial production and the corresponding way of life on the one hand, and the conservation and long-term securing of natural resources needed for the maintainance of this social system on the other hand. The extraordinary superiority of man over nature as generated by enlightenment and scientific rationality has, in the past, led to a hierarchy of values which, should it be retained in the future, will obviously lead man to a conflict with the inherent danger of self-extermination. That most people seem to understand this more and more as a central conflict is an unanimous poll result of various recent studies. Beside unemployment

the ecological problem seems to trouble a still growing number of people. At the same time the number of those believing in "progress through technology" is continuously decreasing with the group of the "post-industrialists" being the frontrunners here too.

5.   The crisis of our employment system appears to have a very significant influence on the future development. In the face of scarcer opportunities, for example, for youths to be integrated into the labour market, in the face of continuously high unemployment rates, phenomena like resignation, alternative movements, but also new shades of delinquency are almost logical subsequential developments. Permanent unemployment does not only weaken young people's belief in objective justice in terms of achievement. However, personal work norms do not necessarily have to lose their relevance (cf. *Fend/Prester* 1985, 57 - 68; *Sinus* 1983; *Jugendwerk der Deutschen Shell* 1981).

6.   Another reason for the change of values might also be seen in the fact that the logic inherent in the field of work, that is, the principles of industrial production, will subsequently lead to a relatively independent sector of leisure, when people's real incomes grow. This sector has been generated by industrial production, which in turn needs mass consumption for its sustenance. Consequently, all aspects of consumption (reproductive, innovative, hedonistic) have become integral parts of the leisure domain. Thus, the regenerative function of leisure is overshadowed by more and more other leisure functions, which finally has led to the fact that leisure itself features different lifestyles.

7.   Moreover the change of functions of the family is likely to be causally related to the change of value patterns. The family quite often represents a place of emotional security and mutual enjoyment of life. Hardly ever, on the other hand, can children and adolescents really experience performance-oriented ethical values in their families. Child labour in the family is basically considered impossible, and helping with house and garden work are hardly ever experienced either as a result of widely available technical devices. The whole childhood is predominantly characterized by a lack of stability (the increasing divorce rate, for example, is among others an important indicator in this respect).

8.   The extensive exposure to and use of mass media seems to be a further significant motor of the change of values. Looking at the results of effect studies concerning this aspect particularly with regard to the use of television reveals that the cultural change in these times takes place, above all, on the screen, and that the trend towards hedonistic desires is supported by the large variety of channels and entertainment programmes offering such desires as models.

9.   Of a decisive character for the change of values we diagnose today is probably also the expansion of the service-related labour market during the last 30 years. This expansion has helped to create jobs which, due to their activity features, have been especially open to the adoption of unconventional value patterns (social services, the teaching profession, tourism-related jobs, etc.). *Offe* therefore calls them "reflexive(public) service activities" (*Offe* 1983), and Klages sees their specific position in the fact that these vocations are not required to direct values, "because the characteristics of the roles they can play permit a further-reaching value - fulfillment" (*Klages* 1983, 347).

10. Finally, we have to consider as another important fact. During the 1980's the situation of young people changed fundamentally. For the first time in German history all members of the young generation could participate in a real period of youth. Whereas in the 1950s most young people had to start working at an early age and had to be adults early, too, whereas only privileged upper middle-class children could live in an "extended psycho-social moratorium of self-research" and self-finding (cf. *Fuchs/Zinnecker* 1985, 23), today almost all youths are kept away from the process of work and artificially pushed into a space of sparing (post-adolescence). Over-schooling of youths has progressed further and further, the networks between young people in informal groups have become closer, and not least for this reason is the youth of the 1980s particularly able and willing to understand adolescence as a life period of growing, search for meaning and for one's self, consequently becoming a model motor for the general change of values. This function is additionally supported by the fact that the status of adults has increasingly been granted permission and freedom to learn. Life-long learning promotes the learning of new attitudes and values.

Summarizing the foregoing causes suggests the conclusion that the most important roots of the change of values are to be found primarily in the conditions of production and secondarily in the state and its institutions.

In more general terms, the reason for the change of values are rooted primarily in the process of functional differentiation of modern industrial societies. For this reason not all groups in society are directly affected by this transition, and therefore we cannot assume a comprehensive trend. There exists rather a greater pluralism today than ever before (*Klages* 1983, 341 - 352; but also *Engfer* e.a. 1983, 434 - 435).

Therefore we should say: No old value pattern is being replaced by a new one. Traditional value orientations will certainly be still significant in the future. In this respect, however, it is an interesting question to what extent the openness of value patterns has resulted in a re-positioning of the significance of individual value patterns.

The present change of values should be taken as evidence for our society's high degree of flexibility in terms of its situationally adequate handling of meeting challenges (cf. *Klages* 1983, 347). Nevertheless, the prognosis is not totally unlikely that our working society might enter into a crisis, when confronted with such value diffusions. The relatively conflict-free value balancing act of the majority of our society may indeed lead to polarizations, and it is not improper to think of a scenario where spirals of criticism, protest and dissatisfaction flush over from the political to the sector of work thus supporting the destabilization of the system as a whole (cf. *Klages* 1983, 348).

When turning towards the question what significance the general change of values to the same degree as our society as a whole or possibly even more, or maybe less, whether the system of sport reacts to changes in its environment at the same or at another time, than it has to be pointed out that empirical social research has not dealt with this question; nor can sport science present any results in this field.

The people's practicing of sport, however, is part of their leisure, which enables us to interpret empirical results diagnosing a change of values in our space time indirectly also as results concerning the change of values in the system of sport (cf. *Digel* 1986, 1990 a,b).

The change of values in leisure

On the background of the change of values we have to ask with regard to leisure and subsequently also to sport how the cultural opportunities determining our behaviour in leisure and sport have changed. Our society has been for at least two decades subject to a still continuing process of transformation concerning the reproduction of cultural resources. This process features the following characteristics:

1. The general qualification standard of the population is high, indicated by the increase of higher educational standards, the demand for eventing classes and the growing participation in professional training.
2. The virtually comprehensive supply of mass media for society has resulted in an increase of the general information and reflection potential of large sections of the population. Also significant is the growing circulation of magazines in general as well as publications catering for specific interests, consumer information and subject-specific transfer of knowledge.
3. New technologies, the diversity of symbols, the complexity of handling and ecological sensitivity in everyday life require the individual citizen's development and adaptation of sensible and appropriate behaviour patterns for which life-long learning is essential.
4. What used to be privileges of small bourgeois minorities in the past is becoming a matter of the masses through the commercialization of almost all cultural products (cf. *Lüdtke* 1989, 66).

The influence of these characteristics has apparently brought about a situation in which an increasing number of people have a greater and more differentiated repertoire of self-presentation, taste development and aesthetic enjoyment, enabling them to make use of their free time in ways contributing to a greater enjoyment and a better quality of life for more and more people, subsequently raising the general qualification and competence of large sections of the population in terms of devising their leisure and lifestyles.

In view of the present leisure activities on the background of these characteristics we recognize certain patterns of needs and desires which have existed for quite some time, which, however, are significant for the present with regard to their intensity. Five different patterns of needs can be distinguished, which in my view are still suitable means for describing today's leisure situation:

First, there is the desire of self-doing, being active oneself. This need is not only expressed in do-it-yourself work, it is also a feature of the willingness to get involved voluntarily, to take over self-responsibility in social, political and cultural matters.

The *second* desire could be described by the terms "spontaneity", "creativity", "self-development", "self-fulfillment". Accordingly, people look for unplanned, new, surprising things, they desire activities enhancing their imagination and creativity, and they try to spend more time pursuing their personal interests.

"Social contact", "togetherness", and "sharing" are terms characterizing the *third* desire. Tendencies of individualization obviously need to be counter-balanced by social contacts if they are not to become dangerous. Therefore we want to spend our free time with other people; what is demanded at present is sociability.

The *fourth* pattern refers to "relaxation" and "well-being", which characterizes a desire that probably is to be interpreted as a reaction to the strains of work. Stress and hectic times on the one hand require self-reflection and leisure on the other hand.

Finally, the *fifth* pattern is defined by the terms "fun", "happiness" and "enjoyment of life", desires expressed more and more frequently by many people who are striving for entertainment; distraction, simply wanting to have fun, laugh, live without annoyances and partying are descriptions characterizing this desire (cf. *Opaschowski* 1983, 77 - 78).

In the sociological research dealing with the change of values as well as in the so-called "lifestyle research" it has become common to attribute such patterns of desires to so-called 'value types' or lifestyles. *Gluchowski* distinguishes seven lifestyle groupings: the established successful professional, the young leisure-oriented consumer, the home- and family-centered person, the intrinsically motivated committed younger person, the passive adaptable employee, the norm-oriented average citizen and the withdrawn isolated older person; they all represent the pure, mixed and diffuse types (cf. *Gluchowski* 1988). The quantitative proportions presented by Gluchowski are probably debatable; however, it seems undebatable to me that they have to be taken into consideration in respect of the future development of sport.

Hinrichs/Wiesenthal (1983) distinguish so-called 'value types', focussing on their respective integration in the sphere of work. The first group comprises those employees with a traditional working-class consciousness; it is the biggest group of employees which has been touched by processes of value change to a very small extent only. For them work is still considered a necessary but self-evident evil, being a pre-condition for status rise in the sector of reproduction.

The second group is characterized by the term "the total maximizers"; it is a small group maintaining the values of an achievement and performance ethic, because their living and working conditions reward traditional work orientations. This privileged group features high social recognition and material security. Because their values can materialize inside as well as outside the domain of work they can be called "total maximizers". The third group represents the "optimistic enjoyers"; they are a growing group, and there are no consistent value patterns to be found among its members; the values of a performance ethic have been replaced by values of personal development and fulfillment or have been pushed to lower positions in the hierarchy of values. Depending on socialization background hedonistic-individualistic or expressive-emancipatory value orientations are dominant with life plans being uncoupled from professional careers. Finally, as a fourth group, we have to mention the "semi- or total drop-outs", who are a relatively small group, who are beyond the traditional achievement or performance ethic, whose members feature a high standard of education, have high demands and objectives and reject the pressures of work. In this respect this group has to be considered as a shade of individualism as well as a shade of a new movement of solidarity (cf. *Hinrichs/Wiesenthal* 1983).

These typologies help to give a differentiated picture of the needs and desires of the German population. They are supposed to serve as an aid in description and explanation. In terms of quantitative aspects, however, it should not be misunderstood, because recently we have not seen any evidence for the heavily and frequently criticized growing distance of people from their work. We rather observe a shifting of values within the domain of work.

Regardless of what interpretation of the value change in our society you may intend to follow, regardless of whether you share my optimistic views about the prospects concerning cultural resources for leisure, and regardless of which kind of differentiation concerning the development of lifestyles we might lean towards, the foregoing reflections can be used in our discussion on the present and future development of sport. They show that people practicing sport today can hardly be regarded as a homogeneous group if we consider the desires and interests these people associate with their sporting activities. Nevertheless, we also have to take into consideration the probability of the existence of a number of certain value patterns in the sector of sport, which means one characteristic of sport is possibly the fact that it is attractive for some lifestyles while it is being rejected by others.

How is the present situation of sport to be described on the background of the general processes of change as outlined before?

In my view it is hardly debatable that the large diversity of opportunities in the system of sport, as it has developed over recent years, are to be interpreted as evidence of a transition of values. Community sport classes, commercial sport studios, travel agencies, big multi-department sport clubs, small single-department clubs, churches, health insurance companies and business are examples of the diversity of agencies providing opportunities. Tai-Chi, deep-sea diving, breathing exercises, fun sport, competitive volleyball and senior citizen gymnastics represent the diversity of sport offered. The providing agents and the large variety of opportunities are indicators of multi-facetted desires.

Yet, it has to be considered that concerning this matter there may be quite large discrepancies between desire and reality. With regards to the question about the present as well as the future relation between supply and demand we should not think that everything still is as it used to be or that there may be only minor changes in the future. Over the past few years we have not experienced dramatic changes. However, we have to see clearly the three movements withdrawing from traditional sport. *First*, there is the individualistic one comprising activities such as meditative jogging, trekking, hanggliding - activities characterized by a particularly individual aspect. *Secondly*, we can recognize an alternative movement attempting to replace sport by a new concept of movement culture. Politically this concept leans towards the alternative scene, in terms of the activities it comprises it expresses its concept primarily through a new art of moving and forms of physical self-presentation and self-realization. This concept usually refuses to have anything in common with sport, whereas the first one makes efforts to remain a part of the sport system. *Thirdly*, there is a quantitatively significant direction labelling itself "fitness and health sport", "fun sport", and "leisure sport". It has emerged and developed alongside competitive sport in clubs. Probably it represents the most important challenge for competitive sport, also strongly influencing the idea of sport outside the clubs.

Thus our sport, games and play culture has not only changed outside the domain of organized sport; organized sport itself is indeed affected by this change just as intensively. In this process we are confronted with problems probably resulting from the growth of the organization, new groups of members, but also from the changed attitudes of old members. In organized sport, we can observe a weakening bonding and commitment ability of clubs and associations, which means that the members feel less loyal and less committed towards the organization. This is probably a consequence of those people's greater degree of independence who are increasingly getting involved in organized sport today, and who also show greater competence in criticism in respect of the contents and financing of the opportunities provided by the clubs. All this has led to the emergence of the social type of floating voter in the voluntary sport organizations, those members who work out account balance in terms of what financial and idealistic input will provide them with the best value in sport, and who turn to one or another department depending on the state of the account, who change the club, take advantage of a community sport class or buy their fitness in a sport studio.

The change of values in sport

The results discussed so far indicate a change of values in sport comparable to the one we have analyzed in other sectors of life in our society.

In this process sport has mixed its original structure of values, which were predominantly defined by training and competition, with new values. In terms of their significance for society as a whole they have - as a consequence - lost their clarity and some of their traditional symbolic strength. This is not only obvious in areas where sporting activities are becoming more and more removed from competition but to the same degree in competitive sport itself.

Some more recent features of sport can therefore be described as expressions of a hedonistically orientated society. In this context the increasing popularity of adventure sport (performance without competition) has to be mentioned. Finally, the emergence of new forms of body culture and health-oriented movement patterns has to be interpreted in the same way.

Further indicators of a change of values in sport are provided by statistics about the increase and decrease of active membership in various sport disciplines with sports like judo, golf, sauna, off-slope ski-mountaineering, cross-country skiing, squash and windsurfing being on the rise, whereas soccer, European handball, athletics, rowing and gymnastics are constantly declining in the popularity charts.

In these respects sport is following a trend towards modernization as it is to be observed also in other social sectors. These processes feature particular time-related dynamics set in motion by new desires that have evolved in our society. Initially these changes were carried by substructural currents endeavouring to establish a new movement culture beside sport in our society. Carriers of these "movements" were those groups which, according to Klages, are also important initiators of the general change of values. More simply expressed, they are people with a higher education, sympathizing with alternative lifestyles, yet also having had a socialization in sport which has generated their growing distance from high performance sport. Whereas the typical values of the traditional sport system used to be - and still are - youthfulness, success, performance and record, new values have been emerging, focussing on physical and body experience, social contact, happiness, well-being and health. Circus, pantomime, movement themes and clowning are being introduced into the world of sport. And "alternative" concepts of play are becoming an especially creative field of experience in sport. Through such initiatives and groups new values have entered sport, which are only marginally related to competitive sport. While they initially came to the surface mostly in connection with the traditional value patterns of the sport system, it now seems to be the case that through the new value structures the system of sport has lost its formerly rather homogeneous purpose structure. And through a process of value differentiation independent models of sport have developed. This process was promoted by people's growing health and subsequently, body awareness, which has made sport an institution of "general life assistance", thus becoming a "first rank integration factor" (cf. *Rittner* 1984, 45 - 46). This, in turn, meant that in terms of sport policies, sport was referred to all spheres of problems in our society. Consequently, today we have rehabilitation, resocialization and senior citizen sport, sport for foreigners and fringe groups, etc. This indicates an immense demand emerging directly from the problems of our complex society (cf. *Rittner* 1984, 46 - 48). All this is an expression of a process of differentiation of the sport system that is still going on. The greater the people's demand for sport the more the system of sport is functionally differentiated and tends towards a development of partial systems. Many of the functions now to be fulfilled by sport are almost completely removed from the nucleus of the old homogeneous system of sport, which used to be competitive sport. These functions rather gain their significance in the form of independent models of sport. The simple image of the pyramid with high performance sport as the peak and leisure sport as the foundation, which symbolized the system of sport in the past, is therefore hardly valid today.

This leads to the thesis that today we can recognize new models of sport apart from the classical one, each of them featuring its own value structures (cf. *Digel* 1984, 60 - 61; *Rittner* 1984, 44 - 46; *Heinemann* 1983, 37 - 38). With regard to the change of values this means, in turn, that the process of differentiation has, at least partly, taken place at the cost of a formerly rather homogeneous value orientation. The various sport models feature this change to different degrees. In the relationship between "professional" and "competitive" sport it becomes apparent in the fact that the amateur norm as the previously central instance of regulation in sport is no longer relevant. Concerning the relationship between "competitive" and "leisure" sport we recognize a separation of the health motive from the traditional concept of competition-oriented club sport. The usual connection between sport and health has disintegrated due to the functionally one-sided differentiation of the system of competitive sport in favour of commercialized supreme performance (cf. *Rittner* 1984, 45). At the same time this process has caused the devaluation of ethically responsible behaviour in sport. In a similar way as in the field of work responsibility and duty-related virtues have been on the decline for some time. With regard to the system of sport Klages' observation seems to be correct that "order/discipline" and "sense of duty" will not entirely disappear; yet, their directing power will diminish in concrete references to (real) life, and they will rather retain some of their significance on an abstract level like, for instance, as "fundamentals" in declarations and guidelines of sport (cf. *Klages* 1981, 83). The same applies to the frequently praised performance virtues of sport. In the same way as "performance tiredness" and the "resistance against performance pressure" are to be found among people in leading positions outside the system of sport, these attitudes can increasingly be recognized in "leisure" and "alternative" sport; this results in an upswing of all those hedonistic values in the system of sport which have been diagnosed for the transition of leisure.

Perspectives

The formerly rather closed system of sport has disintegrated in the course of comprehensive social demands it was confronted with in a mostly unplanned (and to some extent also unwanted) dispute with other politically relevant partial social systems, and that in this process sport has become subject to the change of values in a similar way as - yet a little later than - other social systems, we have to ask the question concerning the future prospects of the sport system.

The present conflict of values in sport suggests the assumption that organized sport is not likely to be able to agree on a homogeneous value pattern in the future. As a consequence, values will at best be consensual on the level of partial systems. In all other respects sport will have to accept a pluralism of values, which requires a high degree of value tolerance. Sport policies will probably be confronted with completely new challenges in the near future.

In political-organizational terms the consequence might be the necessity to reconsider the so-called "unified sport movement" and find new forms of organization. This prognosis is supported by the observation that - already in the past - processes of differentiation have promoted a differentiated institutionalization. With regard to sport this might lead to greater efficiency of the partial systems. However, a disadvantage seems to be the near impossibility of solving trans-institution and trans-system conflicts about value differences and distinctions.

In the face of such prognoses a shift of emphasis within the partial system of sport seems possible. No less likely, however, is the possibility that the presently noticeable accelerating process of differentiation might also catch hold of sport, assisting in the development of entirely new worlds of sport incomprehensible today.

Value patterns are conventions that means they are open for changes. New value patterns still unknown today might come into existence. They will determine activities and behaviours in the different fields of sport in the near future.

Consequently, the future of sport is open. The question whether this is to be considered a chance or a danger will be decided by the "people practicing sport" and the "agencies offering sport".

Chapter II:

Sport and Mass Communication

The Process of Mass Communication and Sport - from the stadium to the living room

"From Djakarta to London", could be the subject of a travelogue. The journey might go along many places - by train, bus, airplane, alone or with partners, interrupted by breakdowns and experienced with joy and anger. The way from the stadium to the living-room is characterized by a variety that is just as wide. If we try to describe this way in detail we find out that the significance of sport must not be underestimated in the process of modern mass communication in a positive as well as negative sense, and that we can point out a large number of problems at the same time. Today the process of mass communication can still be defined most appropriately by the classical *Laswell*-question of 1948:

WHO SAYS (WHY) WHAT IN WHICH CHANNEL TO WHOM WITH WHAT EFFECT? (cf. Table 7)

(The word "why" has been added by myself for the reason that by asking "why" questions of sport coverage, which are critical of ideologies, can also be considered.)

On the one hand the process of mass communication is defined by this formula in a very easy manner, and on the other hand, we can name those central fields of problems with this question, with which modern science of mass communication deals today. This area of science is, therefore, divided into the sciences of communicator, contents, media, recipients and effects.

In the following I want to present some scientific results referring to sport, and I want to ask which problems urgently demand a scientific description, explanation and solution. Before this can happen, it is, however, necessary to explain the term 'mass communication'.

1.   Mass Communication - what is that?

For quite a while the term 'communication' has been the subject of an unprofitable and therefore even more controversial discussion among numerous branches of science, resulting in a confusion of terms.

In order to point out what is meant in the following, when the term 'communication' is used, we should agree on the following definition:

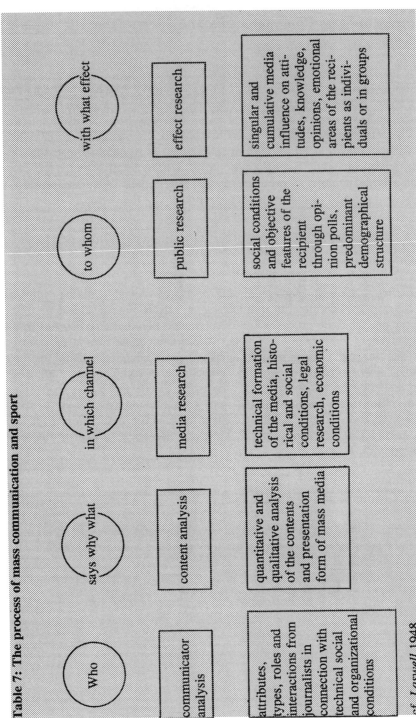

Table 7: The process of mass communication and sport

Who	says why what	in which channel	to whom	with what effect
communicator analysis	content analysis	media research	public research	effect research
attributes, types, roles and interactions from journalists in connection with technical social and organizational conditions	quantitative and qualitative analysis of the contents and presentation form of mass media	technical formation of the media, historical and social conditions, legal research, economic conditions	social conditions and objective features of the recipient through opinion polls, predominant demographical structure	singular and cumulative media influence on attitudes, knowledge, opinions, emotional areas of the recipients as individuals or in groups

cf. *Laswell* 1948

Communication is a phenomenon, which is possible, because persons start relations with each other by acting with a purpose. The actions of reference can take place directly from person to person or indirectly by the use of certain media, as it is for example the case in mass communication (in this respect, for instance, by radio, press or TV etc.). Communication between acting persons is secured by the symbolic character of their actions. If a TV-journalist shouts "Goal! Goal!" in a sport-report, he means something by it. This 'meaning' is understood because there is a regular reference to his utterance. The symbolism of our communicative actions is laid down in a language. The understanding of the utterance "goal" is the guarantee for our competence of the English language. In this context this is usually called verbal communication. If there had been a loss of sound during the TV-coverage, the act of scoring, that is, the ball crossing the goal-line, could have meant something equal to the reporter's verbal utterance provided that some particular conditions of comprehension had existed.

Here we also have a regular reference to the utterance, and the symbolism of the communication act of scoring is also laid down in a language, which, however, has to be defined as non-verbal. Facial expressions and gestures also allow acts of non-verbal communication. Because patterns of non-verbal communication are particularly frequent in sport due to the physiologically determined limitations of verbal communication, we will have to bear in mind their specific consideration when looking at the process of mass communication in sport.

Following this definition we can describe the problems of mass communication as problems of human (inter-personal) communication. In this respect, however, we must not forget the particular aspects of mass communication. Such aspects become clear in a definition of the phenomenon of mass communication:

Mass communication is organized communication. It is a differentiated and functionally specified sub-system in the process of communication of an entire society. The communicator in mass media works via a complex formal organization, which shows a high level of division of labor and expenses. As a consequence the communicator is yet only a part in the highly organized sender, at the same time the possibilities of access to mass media are restricted due to the high costs. The audience, at which mass communication aims, is relatively large, heterogenous and anonymous. In this context "relatively large" means that the audience is so large during a particular period of time that the communicator cannot enter into an inter-personal relationship with his individual members. Thus heterogeneity means that communication does not aim at an exclusive group but that it is to reach a variety of individuals holding different social positions. Anonymity means that individual members of the audience usually remain unacquainted with the communicator. The experiences of communication in respect of mass media generally are public, fast, and temporary; public, because everybody has access to the news; fast, because they reach a relatively large audience within quite a short time or even at the same time; and temporary, because they are consumed instantly.

Whereas on the one hand our everyday-communication is defined as face-to-face-communication, especially because individual persons who communicate with each other, see each other, and enter into intensive contact with each other, solve problems of comprehension directly, because there is the possibility of direct feed-back and because the partners derive from the same homogeneous socio-cultural environment. Mass communication on the other hand is generally determined by a larger distance of space and time, by a socio-culturally heterogeneous group of participants, by a low intensity of contact and by highly limited possibilities of feed-back. Therefore theories of mass communication refer to it as an anonymous disposing audience. These facts, however, do not consider that modern mass communication is becoming more and more dependent on knowing its audience well. Economic pressures force the communicators to adapt themselves to the wishes of the audience, that means, they have to be very interested in knowing how their communication is received. In so far it will be increasingly important in future to consider characteristics of inter-personal communication, and particularly the problem of feed-back in the process of mass communication, that is, it will be necessary to realize the energizing effects of feed-back processes, which could not be sufficiently considered by the traditional technical theories and models of the science of mass communication.

The agreed definition of communication, and also the references to the significance of the so-called 'feed-back', indicate that the problems of mass communication are by no means only of a technical kind, as it is suggested in a fundamental technical model (cf. *Shannon/Weaver* 1949). There, the central problem is that information going from the source to the receiver can be changed by disturbing influences: A picture does not arrive, there is a loss of sound, picture and sound are not synchronized, etc. These are technical problems of modern mass communication, and it is not surprising that, as a result of technical progress, the question referring to the channel or medium of communication has gained more significance, and that this question is becoming qualitative in respect of "new media".

The meaning of communication, as defined above, makes clear, however, that these are problems of mass communication which basically are relatively easy to solve and relatively unimportant. The major problems are not technical ones. They are rather problems of action theory - or more appropriately expressed - human problems, and they begin with sport practised by people. They range from the question about which sport they will report, to the largely unanswered question, what effects the selected and presented kind of sport has on their partners, who consume media-processed sport in their living-rooms. This and a number of other questions have to be asked if we look closely at the process of communication.

Table 8: Conditions influencing the selection of news

Structural conditions

- production conditions
- alloted space and/or time
- alloted lay-out
- pressure of time (obligation to actuality)
- financial possibilities
- editing equipment
- number of staff

Editing condition

- attitudes, values, objectives of the publisher
- analysis results on recipients' attitudes (opinions)
- political climate within editor staff
- political and journalistic position of editor-in-chief
- sales strategies

Personal conditions

- professional experience of the journalists
- style of perception
- observation (stereotyped forms)
- degree of conformity with the editorial staff
- degree of diversity of interest
- self-image
- image of profession
- general knowledge about sport

2. Sport journalists as conveyors - Communicator Analysis (Control Analysis)

Looking at the model of communication we can see that the sender has a particularly important position (cf. table 7).
In our context that group of persons will have to be defined by the term 'sender' communicating indirectly with viewers. There the role of the communicator in press, radio and on TV is taken by persons, who call themselves sport journalists. Their occupation is primarily that of a transmitter, that means, their work is characterized by intentional selection and transmission of news and information from a sport universe.

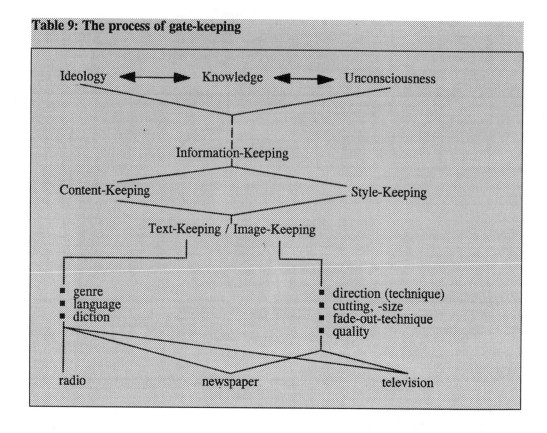

Table 9: The process of gate-keeping

If you want to get an impression of the quality of the work of sport journalists you have to look at the sporting events and objects as a whole about which sport journalists basically can report. In this connection, however, it has to be considered that the selection of what is reported is not only determined by the intentional decision of sport communicators. A selection, which is not intentional either, also takes place in the technical and bureaucratic institutions of sport media. In this context we speak of the "gate-keeper"-function (gatekeeper of the channel) (cf. *Breed* 1973, 356 - 387; *Robinson* 1973, 344 - 355).

The facts, explained here in short, are the central subjects of the so-called control-analysis, whose function is to find out sociological and socio-psychological constellations determining the development of statements made in the media. As far as the sport communicators are concerned this kind of research is still in its infancy.

Identifying the term 'communicator' with the journalistic institution of the genesis and development of statements, provides important hints about origin, school education and vocational training, as well as about the professional experience of sport journalists. But their social standards and references in relation to athletes and sport associations, their relationship to sport and their theoretical knowledge about sport also become obvious. In many ways, however, we are informed only about one aspect of the genesis of statements, and furthermore, this aspect needs permanent scientific observation. The role of sport journalists differs increasingly in relation to the various media (think, for instance, of the star-role which communicators take, especially on TV). Additionally, sport journalists are also not excluded from a generally observable social change.

All in all, we so far still know very little about the communicator role of sport journalists; this is probably a result of the fact that over a long time the science of journalism agreed to the supposition that you have to be a so-called "born" journalist.

The journalist used to be considered an individual quantity. Only American studies, which pointed out the gate-keeper-function in the field of genesis of statements, have brought new facts to the surface, which seemed worthwhile examining, also in relation to sport journalism.

There is, for instance, the question of the pressures which the sport-"gate-keepers" are subject to. Special attention has to be given to the sport news agencies in this respect. Meanwhile they have a position of monopolys as far as the communicators are concerned. In connection with an uninterrupted tendency towards a concentration of media (in Germany), we therefore have to ask if sport, which is determined by an extraordinary variety of patterns of movements, is still presented in a pluralistic, that is, in a factually appropriate and critical way by sport coverage.

If you accept the American studies on the problems of gate-keepers, the gate-keepers have no longer the freedom of decision in the press, they are rather subject to total control and dominated by factual pressures. The question, whether this also refers to sport journalists, demands an answer. Just as important though, would also be sociological research in staff quarters about the relations among sport journalists, about their own relationships to other departments and about their everyday lives. Another important question is: what influences the system of values of sport journalists? What happens to freshmen in staff offices? Which role do the so-called senior responsible journalists and the heads of sport departments play? In what way are freshmen integrated into the system, so that the structure of values remains unchanged. Another important question is to what extent sport journalists are politically patronized by other departments. Studies dealing with several problems of communicators from the point of view of people directly involved, confirm these facts, at least from the time of discussion about the boycott of the Olympics in Moscow in 1980. In Germany, for example, this discussion did not take place in the sport sections of newspapers because sport journalists considered themselves to be incompetent, and because their colleagues from the political department quickly monopolized the subject as a result.

Table 10: Ethical guidelines for sport journalists

Sport journalism wants to play a role in education. Guided by a common intention the sport journalists of all countries want to cooperate for the defence of ethical standards in their profession.

Sport journalists see the cultivation and advancement of all, of understanding and peace among nations, useful progressive and educational aims as their main purpose.

Reporting and criticism should always be guided by utmost responsibility and the love of truth.

In particular sport journalists endeavour to set a positive example to young people through impartial and unbiased judgement. While opposing frequent subjective and unfair rivalries, caused by excessive athletic zeald, they want to serve the promotion of the ultimate objective of sport: bettering the people and awaking a feeling of common interest.

Sport journalists oppose place-hunting and favour the sense of responsibility and dignity.

Despite every journalist's love for his/her native country, they see themselves as paying the way for cultural cooperation, as it is realized in sporting competitions.

The sport journalists bind themselves to the principles of companionship in sport suited to promote the spirit of harmony, fairness, and mutual respect in human society.

Written in 1924 by European sport journalists, endorsed in 1968.

More detailed descriptions of the connections between sport journalists and top-performance athletes, their coaches, officials and sport associations would also be desirable. In this context, as in all other topics of research mentioned so far, an analysis differentiating between the media has also become absolutely necessary. The criticism which up to now has been expressed in this context especially aims at the existing companionship between sport journalists and outstanding players and coaches. TV sport presenters are the ones who are most frequently exposed to such accusations. This has been quite appropriately characterized by one author, who observed that athletes are treated like children by TV-presenters, and that they therefore are addressed informally and by their first names: "Their age does not secure them from being patted, only their social reputation" (*Jens* 1973, 175). Especially on TV it seems to be the case that the presenter himself is the star of the programmes, and that he degrades his guests to super-nummeraries. In such programs sport becomes a product of a show-business, and their independent reality is lost. Of course, companionship between sport journalists and athletes often has downright material reasons, as many book publications show. Almost every fairly well-known TV journalist today is also an author and often cooperates extremely closely with coaches and athletes. Even though the communicators themselves are the ones to blame in the first place, we, nevertheless, must also realize that the dependence of communicators is created by sport organizations and associations themselves. Sport journalists today are confronted with an information monopoly of clubs and coaches. Every journalist is dependent on exclusive information, which, however, he/she only gets if he/she writes favourably about clubs and associations. Local patriotism is not seldomly the price for such involvement. How far such problems have developed meanwhile can be shown by means of the example of sport news agencies, where independent sport journalists work for sport associations and thus are in danger of losing their independence.

A particular communicator problem in dealing with athletes seems to be the athletes' private domain. There obviously is a sport reporter-syndrome, characterized by incompetence and lack of imagination; this lowers the standard of sport journalism down to that of the much abused rainbow press. Because the reporter has no other ideas, he invades, as a 'chatter-box' of the writing profession, the private spheres of athletes disregarding with great coolness all barriers of decency and good manners. The financial situation of athletes is investigated, sex-related stories are brought up and processed with great delight, and silly questions are also asked about hobbies, feelings and family life, which also contribute to the fact that interviews with athletes are so unbearably monotonous and, above all, meaningless. This criticism certainly is generalizing, but it also corresponds with the criticism of some athletes. Checking the range of such criticism would, irrespective of this, be an interesting field of research.

The TV-role of women in the field of sport journalism is another subject of research, which is hardly worked on at all. Here too, it would be the main point to describe the pressures and limitations preventing an adequate participation of women in this field.

Table 11: Reporting about high performances in sport

Phase 1

Prior to a competition the athlete is evaluated, and the expectations regarding his/her performance are expressed.

- Development of expected achievement
- Establishment of public opinion with regard to the expected achievement
- Development of achievement pressure for a team, coach, athlete

Phase 2

The event is presented through reporting. The actual achievement is assessed by the alleged expectation.

- Evaluation of achievement
- Diagnosis of the achievement "success" vs. "failure"

Phase 3

Further use of "success" vs. "failure"

- Success - human-touch-story
- Failure - story about the crisis

Individual-psychological, socio-psychological and sociological factors, such as the personality of the communicator, his self-image, his ideas about his job, his position and his duties, his opinion about the institution he works for, and about society in general, pressures which are entailed in the media and also the image the communicator has of his clients would have to be integrated into such research.

Specific attention very much should be given to the question concerning the relationship between communicator and audience. There is much indication that with regard to this relationship, sport journalists act with the presumption that they exactly know their "consumers" needs and interests, and therefore are able to orientate themselves accordingly. However, examining these facts, we discover that sport journalists often declare their own interests as the ones of their clients.

Thus there is the danger that complete sport departments domesticate themselves and produce their programmes not according to the actual interests of the audience. The surprisingly high ratings of some good sport programmes show that the audience is not interested in superficial entertainment about sport, as sport journalists often arrogantly claim, but that people actually are interested in a problem- and background-orientated coverage of sport.

Furthermore control analysis (communicator analysis) should also include socio-historical questions; focussing on relations between industrial production and social utilization on the one hand, and between show-business and sport coverage on the other hand. The analysis and description therefore should not be carried out in the usual manner, which constructs history as a result of present aspects; mass communication is neither separated from political nor from social history, it is only understandable in this context. The same applies to sport coverage.

Finally, the science of communication also has to turn towards the question if training and further qualification will be the right way to improve the situation of sport journalism. This can rightly be doubted. Today there can hardly be any doubts, however, that the patterns of qualifications, which ought to characterize a kind of sport journalism, that is more appropriate for sport, have to be described in more detail.

The problem of training of sport journalists is realized by the sport journalists themselves. 81 % of all German qualified sport journalists consider their training outdated and lacking any theoretical background, but only little has changed since this inquiry (cf. *Weischenberg* 1976; *Digel* 1992). One reason among others for this could be the union of sport journalists. Sometimes the unions of sport journalists are called "sects" of journalism. This position does not only become clear in questions of trade union representation, but also with special regard to the training and further qualification of sport journalists, which becomes obvious if you analyse the journals of these unions. As to the German one, the election of the athlete of the year, kind letters of gratitude and nice reports on journalists' soccer tournaments seem to be more important than questions concerning their training and further qualification. In connection with this, the important question concerning the role sport journalists have been playing so far with regard to the analysis of the process of communication has to be raised. An increasing scientific interest for several aspects of sport coverage has been noticed for some years; this can be seen as a positive development. Mostly, however, non-representative case studies have been the result. They are rejected by the people concerned with them, namely sport journalists, on the grounds of their lack of representativeness. It seems to be doubtful, however, whether interdisciplinary representative studies will have a different effect. It would probably be unjust only to blame the sport journalists for the extremely inappropriate state of knowledge about sport coverage today.

Table 12: Partial systems of the communication sector of sport, participants and localities

Partial system	Participants	Localities
Spectators	direct spectators indirect spectators (TV, radio newspaper) etc.	home public facilities etc.
Sport journalists	TV-, radio-, newspaper-journalists reporter, camera crew etc.	stands, stadium sport facility, studio editor's office publishing house etc.
Actors	athletes coaches, assistants officials referees etc.	Facilities of sporting activity locker rooms training room (gym) pub etc.
Commercial profit making	producer media, salesmen publishing companies consumer goods industry etc.	sport shops exhibitions restaurants/pubs stadium etc.
Officials	department chair person board of directors presidents association officials etc.	club homes administration buildings stadiums etc.

. Up to now sport journalists have proved to be - to a small degree - willing to cooperate, whenever a scientific investigation of their work has been concerned. Only in exceptional cases have scientists been able to take advantage of the journalists' cooperation, and it does not seem to be the opinion of just one official of the sport journalists' association that university departments obviously consider sport journalists as "fair game" and thus impair this profession from a wrong point of view.

The necessity of scientifically well-based information on the phenomenon of sport coverage must, however, not be interfered with such rejection. Moreover such an opinion does not help the journalists. Control analysis is not easy, as the mentioned subjects show. But its necessity, as well as its interesting questions, suggest that in future analysis of sport science in this field, the large variety of determining factors of the role of the communicator, will be considered. This means on the other hand that sport science must turn towards the problem of control analysis on an interdisciplinary level. One-sided advances will be out of the question in the future.

The way a control analysis connected with sport in the science of journalism is given from individualistic research designs of the gate-keeper analysis via institutional analysis, which turn towards questions of organizational sociology, to cybernetical models. In the cybernetical model the communicator is no longer an independently deciding authority, but he is subjected to permanent control by numerous institutionally internal and external feed-back circuits; this control makes his own preferences and constitutions appear relatively unimportant. This model can be the theoretical starting point for control analysis in sport science. However, it requires creative supplementation, in the cause of which it should especially be open for methodical creativity.

3.   Contents of sport journalism - Content Analysis

Dealing with the communicator problem in sport has already pointed out that this aspect cannot be described independently of other aspects like media - audience and effect analysis. The individual aspects determine each other, and only an analysis of all of them truly may ensure that the process of mass communication is appropriately characterized. This also applies to the second aspect of analysis, the so-called "content analysis" of sport coverage. In contrast to the control analysis, an extraordinary variety of scientific approaches has been developed in this sector. This subject seems to enjoy extraordinary popularity, although most studies suffer from a lack of quality. Almost all analyses, presented so far, result in almost the same accusations now being almost 50 years old. They are based on the analysis of selected daily papers, TV programs and radio reportings and refer to a mostly unexpressed normative idea of so-called "better sport coverage". Sport coverage, and thus indirectly sport journalists, are accused of having a general tendency towards sensationalism and star cult, of being orientated towards the taste of the masses of over-representing top performance sport and especially soccer, of nationalistic and chauvinistic tendencies, of limiting sport coverage to ostensible features of sport, and of upholding the ideology of high performance (cf. Table 13). The opposites of these aspects allow the notion of a kind of sport coverage which the critics of today's sport journalists may have in mind. Such a kind of coverage seems to be desirable, although the critics themselves have to accept some accusations, too. Up to now it can be seen on the side of theory as well as on the side of methodics that the scientific content analysis of sport coverage only to a small extent corresponds to the standards of quality, which have been developed for content analysis (cf. *Berelson* 1952; *Ritsert* 1972). This problem can be seen in respect of content analysis referring to sport, especially if quantitative statements are analysed.

Table 13: Communication rules for media sport

1.   Proximity

2.   Records, victories, elites

3.   Conflicts, violence, action

4.   Personal touches

5.   Human interest

Before looking at the results of such reflections on content analysis in greater detail, it is useful to focus our attention on some methodical problems of content analysis. Some scientists see content analysis as a kind of statistical approach to the description of contents of newspapers and magazines. Similar approaches already existed about the turn of the century, and they were based on the intention to overcome philological textual analysis and achieve the new objective of making interpersonally controllable and valid statements about certain quantities of texts within an explicit frame of analysis.

The method of content analysis is based on the assumption that a text, which can be called a specific form of symbolic behavior, does not only allow references to the producer of the analysed text - as it is certainly possible in the traditional text exegesis; - but also that it should allow references with regard to political intentions and effects in respect of the recipients of the text. Language is also considered as a means of politics to spread and enforce contents, values and norms, enabling one to draw conclusions from the quantitatively varying appearance of, for example, certain political symbols to corresponding changes in the outward political behavior and actions of governments and nations, etc.

This assumption, however, is problematical, and today it seems to be more sensible and realistic to consider texts as open, in so far as it is possible that intentions of authors are not realized by the recipients, or interpreted in a different way than it was perhaps intended, and a methodical observation of verbal expressions will possibly convey different statements and contents than the originally communicating persons themselves intended.

It is another aspect of content analysis that not single texts but a dispersed quantity of texts is analysed, whereas the quantity of texts is defined by the question of analysis. In contrast to the philological analysis of texts, where a statement about the whole of a text is made, the answer of text-externally formulated questions of analysis is sought in content analysis with the help of certain characteristic features of texts and under consideration of their change during the analytical process. The application of the method of content analysis still causes extreme difficulties in the science of journalism. The content analysis shows some weak aspects; naive and often very stereotyped procedures, as they are seen in most content analysis, lead to an undifferentiated, and hardly sound and valid, instrument for analysis.

When looking at the results of content analysis referring to sport on the basis of this methodical discussion, only few analyses of sport coverage can be rated positively. One of the exceptions worthwhile imitating succeeds in proving, primarily in respect of quantitative aspects, that (in Germany) sport coverage is one-sided, and corresponds by no means to the principle of pluralistic coverage. This analysis refers to the use of journalistic stylistic devices, asks what importance local sport has, distinguishes between sport branches, and states the negligence of sport at school and recreational sport, of sport policies and sport science by means of empirically secure data (cf. *Binnewies* 1975).

In contrast to the quantitative recording of contents, qualitative content analyses have been published only seldomly up to now, and the few impressionistic studies only have limited representative value. This applies to the ideologically critical question of idolization by the rainbow press as well as to the large number of comparative analyses, in which, for instance, the sport coverage of a West German newspaper was compared with that of an East-German paper. The fact that by means of such analyses interesting aspects of a society-related coverage are made apparent, remains untouched by this criticism.

Contents of sport coverage have been analysed much more completely by philological principles than by means of the method of the content analysis of social science. It has to be considered, above all, as a matter of course, that the analysis of sport coverage deals primarily with linguistic products. Sport-related communication, just as any social communication, is, above all, linked to linguistic articulation, and therefore to a system of language in a society. Visual communication also refers indirectly to processes of communication, which have been agreed upon in verbal communication. This applies to the pictures on TV as well as to gestures, facial expressions and other kinds of non-verbal communication. They can be understood as supporting independent factors in the process of verbal communication. Possibly, however, it is just due to our natural way of dealing with language that in reality we know very little about the linguistic usage of coverage, although this use has frequently been exposed as a problem. With regard to the analysis of the so-called sport language, scientific precision is also only occasionally spotted. In most cases, sport journalists are labeled as "linguistic fecalists". They are accused of having an emotional linguistic style, of tending toward linguistic exaggeration, of creating idols by means of language, of supporting or promoting unreflected performance orientation, of evaluating in a stereotypical way and of using superlatives, of using clichés and of being careless in their use of words, of preferring dynamic and emotional images and martial metaphors, of avoiding problems and of neglecting the playful elements of sport.

Such criticism is not wrong in principle. But it is always problematical when critics do not even marginally take account of the conditions successful human communication is subject to. Furthermore, sport journalists work under writing- and speaking-conditions which are specific to their profession. Sport journalists do not speak and write for an elite, the comprehension of a large number of recipients rather is a necessity of their media. Besides, they have to articulate fast, and in connection with always equal or similar events they have to create excitement. The frequently abused superlative, and the often criticized metaphorical devices, therefore are almost a logical necessity.

Nevertheless, this does not excuse the use of meaningless metaphors, violations of good taste, the use of terms the recipients do not understand, and the monotonous preference of selected journalistic devices. Still, it is correct that the language of sport journalists is an "evergreen of cultural criticism", taking place mainly in a pre-scientific area, at least from the point of view of a modern understanding of language. In this respect philological linguistic analyses are only helpful in a few cases.

Approaches which use the terms "special sport language" or "technical sport terminology" are just as suitable.

What is missing, however, are analyses which have as a subject the linguistic behavior of radio reporters and TV-journalists, of TV-presenters, interviewers, the language usage in sport reportings, in features and commentaries, and which consider the character of linguistic utterances in respect of actions, as well as the functions and effects intended with regard to the recipients. So far there have been only initial experiments. Particular criticism must increasingly be faced by TV-sport. Critics see sport in the danger of trotting like a circus-horse at the longue of TV. And many critics hold the view that TV might have negative effects on the sport movement.

As far as content analytical aspects are concerned, however, criticism of TV sport is not sounder than criticism of the production of the sport press. Apart from a few expectations this criticism consists of feuilletonistic statements, referring to single programmes, or making big sporting events the objects of criticism. Justified as such criticism may be, we still have to state that qualitative and quantitative content analyses of sport coverage are nevertheless linguistic fallow land. This will be an interesting area of analysis for future science.

By differentiating between different types of press in sport coverage, it becomes obvious that up to now the interest in content analysis has been primarily focused on the national and the rainbow press. In this respect a change of orientation would be desirable for future analyses. Particular attention should especially be paid to the local press, because the local section of a newspaper is the most popular one with the readers, its popularity still growing. If we analyse local papers, e.g., in Germany, we can point out the deficits of sport coverage, which are sufficiently known from the national papers (local patriotism, dominance of soccer, deficits of qualification etc.). This attempt, however, only marks the problems of local journalism; an empirical and statistical subsistantialisation would therefore be welcome in addition to a sport-related media analysis. The same applies to sport magazines, which have been spreading recently, and for the so-called sport movies.

The question which role the sport picture plays in sport coverage, has up to now also been totally neglected. The connection between picture and text, however, seems not only worth while analysing with regard to the medium of TV. In this respect it becomes clear that the understanding of pictures hints at the question to which there have not been any answers yet. Because journalism in general shows a similar deficiency, creative initiatives with regard to analysis will be particularly important.

4. Sport as an economic factor in media - Media Analysis

Not later than the Olympic Games 1972 in Munich it has become obvious that sport plays a central, even extraordinary role in West German media. TV, radio, newspapers, illustrated papers, and scientific journals almost daily report on events, athletes and teams in sport. Live-broadcasting, studio-programs and entertainment shows are dedicated to sport. In political news the attention of the audience is paid to important sporting events, political programmes present information on backgrounds and conditions in sport. Books deal with big sport associations, with athletes and sporting events; they are written by sport journalists and sport stars who appear as pseudo-journalists. If we add the market for special sport books the mass media apparently seem to have increasingly been profiting from sport over the last years. On the other hand, however, this also applies to sport itself. What sport is today, it primarily is because of mass communication. It has made them fit for good society, business and politics. As a consequence sport has become a mass phenomenon, and sport organizations and associations have risen to factors of political power of social pressure groups.

When talking in this manner of the relations between sport and media, and pointing out the importance of sport in mass media, people normally do not make any particular distinctions. This derives from the fact that up to now there is no sport-related media analysis in the true sense of the word.

Table 14: Share of sport programmes in minutes and percent on German TV-channels in 1990 and 1993

Channel	1990 %	1993 %
ARD	11,2	9,71
ZDF	9,3	9,91
3 SAT	5,5	4,90
SAT I	7,8	7,95
RTL	5,4	3,44

A differentiated analysis of sport media, however, seems to be urgently necessary today, not least on the background of "new media", which in the future will define the relationship between sport and media anew. Which role does sport play on the radio, on TV, in the sport sections of daily newspapers, for instance, with regard to economic aspects? Does sport help to increase circulation or does it influence ratings of media positively? How can the still increasing demand of regional and local coverage in the field of sport be met by means of old or new media? Which role does sport play for the relationship between the reader and the newspaper, or between the TV or radio station and the audience?

These exemplary questions point out that in the area of media analysis the necessary studies cannot be seperated from the area of audience and content analysis either. Depending on interest, however, media analysis can feature its own priorities. As far as sport in Germany is concerned, the role of news agencies especially seems to be worth while analysing. The Sport Informations Dienst (SID) and the sport department of the Deutsche Presse Agentur (DPA), the two biggest German news agencies, have a specific function. More than 18 % of DPA's work is related to sport, and sport - behind politics - provides the second largest part of news. As far as SID is concerned, we can speak of a monopoly of information in relation to the rank of the output of information. Sport coverage today is - not only in daily newspapers - almost completely determined by these two agencies. A particular problem from the point of view of media criticism is the SID-sub enterprise, "prosport-press-service", which does the publication work for the sport associations and manages the public relations of big sporting events. There journalists are at the same time organizers of sporting events, on which they are supposed to report; in this respect they, as members of the press, become dependent on their sponsors not only in financial terms. Whether this leads to "good behaviour" of sport journalists, and whether they thus lose their journalistic independence, is more than a justified question.

Table 15: Share of covered sport on German TV-channel ZDF in 1991 and 1993

Sport	1991		1993	
	Min.	%	Min.	%
Tennis	6.023	39,3	7.464	42,4
Soccer	2.236	14,6	1.490	8,5
Athletics	1.762	11,5	2.066	11,7
Ice Hockey	679	4,4	523	3,0
Alpine Skiing	998	6,5	2.201	12,5
Figure Skating	429	2,8	436	2,5
Ski Jumping	247	1,6	352	2,0
Motor Racing	---	---	115	0,6
Handball	200	1,3	275	1,6
Dancing	137	0,9	213	1,2
Riding	209	1,4	114	0,6
Swimming	434	1,8	155	0,9
Fencing	---	---	117	0,7
Basketball	20	0,1	342	1,9
Bob Race	29	0,2	35	0,2
Others	1.956	12,6	1.694	9,7
Total	15.319	100,0	17.592	100,0

cf. ZDF-Yearbook 1992, 1993

.... Media competition

Another topic of media analysis is of specific socio-historical and contemporary political importance. It refers to the change in the media scene, and in this context especially to the role of TV. Whereas radio sport reporting was of particular importance with regard to current affairs in earlier days, today TV has a decisive influence on the function of the radio. Radio sport reporting today can only count on limited success with the audience, a fact that has led to a change of concepts of radio sport programs. Together with modern light music they try to come up to at least two interests and futhermore, they especially use the gap which cannot be filled by other media. We are talking about the short and fast coverage, as it is, for instance in Germany, typical for the first division soccer programmes on Saturday afternoons. There is much indication that radio sport programs are an appropriate and suitable kind of coverage for a specifically mobile audience. The car radio seems to be the most suitable receiver in this respect.

The aspect of media competition becomes clearer when looking at the relationship between TV and newspapers. TV is superior to the press in two ways. It presents information faster, it can illustrate events not only by means of words but also by means of pictures, and it can repeat results as often as it is desired, even in slow motion. This implies that the structure of press coverage of sport had to be changed. Journalistic stylistic devices as the feature, the gloss and the commentary have become increasingly important, and the mere reproduction of results has been pushed into the background. Therefore today, writing journalists are primarily expected to produce background reports, and the element of entertainment should not be neglected either. The dangers, which have developed in the course of this change meanwhile have become obvious everywhere. The idolization of athletes, artificially created excitement and the undetached presentation of sport associations, athletes and teams are the results. The style of the rainbow press thus, has become somewhat the "ideal" of the whole press.

.... Media change sport - sport changes the media

The question, to what extent sport coverage changes sport as to its practical aspects and its organizational structure, refers to an interesting aspect of media analysis. The relationship between sport and media is becoming more and more determined by the conditions of TV, especially with regard to organizational problems, and the danger that consequently a fundamental change of rules in sport might develop, does not seem impossible. It is mostly unproblematical that, in terms of commencement, sport has to be orientated towards the schedule of TV sport programmes, if sport wants to take advantage of financial sources made available for the sport associations by TV. Even the colour of the player's T-shirts has to be selected according to the fact that TV broadcasts are in

Table 16: Interrelation between mass communication system and related systems

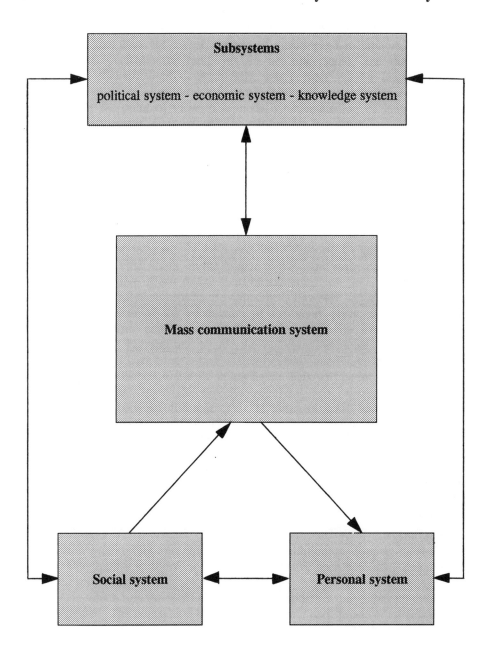

color. More important, however, is the fact that sporting events can only be telegenic under particular circumstances. In this respect the changing of rules seem to increase the telegenety of action patterns in sport, which, however, will lead to general changes in sport, and in some sport branches such changes can already be observed (e.g. team handball, volleyball). The competition between private and public TV channels is becoming especially problematical from the point of view of sport. Their competition causes the problem that sport coverage is not orientated towards the concerns of sport but towards the programmes, and therefore the pattern of competition between the channels. There is much indication that during the last few years TV has undergone changes caused by sport, and thus it has to be pointed out that those responsible for the TV stations today ask themselves, whether sport coverage has become a strain for the whole structure of TV programmes, which means that other kinds of programmes and target groups are possibly at a disadvantage.

.... Sport coverage is inexpensive, but not always profitable

One part of the analysis of media must, after all, be the question concerning the importance of commercials, and in connection with this, the question concerning the costs of sport media production. Especially in connection to sport coverage there seems to be a direct relation. Sport coverage over the last few years has increasingly taken on the function of commercial areas, and the advertising business has become a sponsor of sport programmes. The publishers of newspapers offer their results to advertisers as a target-group, whose purchasing power can be exploited via the media products which stimulate consumption; and the publishing companies try to prove in their advertisements that the costs of commercials are profitable. This points out that the readers, who transfer their confidence to the editorial section, also transfer it to the advertising section. In this respect sport often is used as a striking example. That kind of press, however, only feels bound to the principles of freedom of the press to a limited extent. There rather is an orientation towards profitability and a dependence on materialistic values. Up to now we can only speculate upon the role of sport in this. At least in respect of the cost and effect-relation it seems to be the case that sport programmes and sport coverage show high profits as far as the costs of production as well as the advertising value are concerned. From the economic point of view, the question of the economic role, sport coverage plays today, is also important.

The two big German stations, for example, telecasted more than 100 hours of the Football World Cup in Italy in 1990. This event became the permanent sport hit over four weeks - and it worked as a brake for all other TV programs. But from the economic point of view those weeks caused a loss of production, which supposedly almost reached one billion DM. This figure points out that politically it is hardly acceptable that sport associations expand their own sporting events and need international championships more and more without comprehending socio-political implications.

Table 17: Television rights costs (in US $)			
Summer Olympic Games	Television Rights Costs	Winter Olympic Games	Television Rights Costs
1960 Rome	394.000	1960 Squaw Valley	50.000
1972 Munich	7.500.000	1972 Sapporo	6.400.000
1976 Montreal	25.000.000	1976 Innsbruck	10.000.000
1980 Moscow	87.000.000	1980 Lake Placid	15.500.000
1984 Los Angeles	225.000.000	1984 Sarajewo	91.500.000
1988 Seoul	402.000.000	1988 Calgary	309.000.000
1992 Barcelona	750.000.000	1992 Albertville	243.000.000
1996 Atlanta	1.000.000.000 *	1994 Lillehammer	300.000.000

* = Estimation

.... New sport in new media

The question which role sport will take in connection with the development of new media seems to be of particular explosiveness. Video-text, screen-newspaper and cable TV seem to provide TV with interesting possibilities and opportunities in the near future; in this respect, especially local events might gain a completely new publicity. It is already absolutely certain today that sport will be a potential supplier of programmes for the new technologies, but whether the so far neglected areas of sport, for example, leisure and recreational sport, will bring the various sport associations into the game, is very doubtful. It also seems to be doubtful whether those carrying responsibility in politics, media, and sport are fully aware of the dangers the new media might cause for children and adolescents, for familiy life and for the education of the recipients.

5. The clients of sport coverage - Audience Analysis

Looking for an answer to the question as to what kind of people primarily take notice of the media, almost all experts on mass communication agree that the audience for mass media, as to its social composition corresponds to that of the population of a country. That means especially in respect of the press for the masses, and of TV, that the major part of the audience consists of members of the lower and middle classes, of the class of wage-dependent people. The communicative needs of this audience (according to some scientists) can be deduced from their working- and reproducing-conditions. The living conditions of working class and employee families determine the specific demands for utility value of the audience towards the media. A large number of empirical data fit into these hierarchical assumptions on the utilizing behavior, these data refer to the general consumption of media. In 1991, about 99 % of all German households had a radio and 98 % had a TV set. 81 % of the lower social classes watch TV daily (65 % of the upper class), and the daily quantity of TV consumption amounts to an average of 263 minutes.

Similarily popular seems to be the daily newspaper in Germany. It still is the medium users want to miss the least. The regional newspaper is regarded as most important in respect of the conveyance of news (84 %), although 74 % think that the best medium to form an opinion from is TV. In contrast to the newspaper, TV (76 %) succeeds most in making people forget their sorrows, troubles and problems. Sport media correspond only to a limited extent to such a general users' perspective. There is rather much indication that sport coverage is an exception within the media.

Table 18: Attendance at selected spectator sport, 1960 - 1987

Sport	Attendance (millions)			
	1960	1970	1980	1987
Baseball, major leagues	20	29	44	53
Basketball, college	--	--	31	38*
Basketball, professional	2	7	11	13
Football, college	20	29	36	36
Football, professional	4	10	14	15
Hockey	3	6	12	13
Horseracing	47	70	75	70
Greyhound racing	8	13	21	26

* Including women's basketball

Source: Based on Statistical Abstract 1989, p. 226; 1980, p. 249

.... The interest in sport media is overestimated

Considering the figures with regard to audience interest during the Soccer World Cup in Spain 1981 we may assume that sport enjoys a particular popularity with media consumers. A comparison of these assumptions with the few verified data about sport-related use of media shows, however, that this assumption is only partly correct. Sport apparently has an important position in the programme structures of almost all media, but in this respect the interest of the advertising industry, and not so much the interest of the audience, seems to be decisive. Apparently, it seems to be right that 65 % of the German population is interested in sporting events but only 45 % in politics. It also seems to be correct that sport coverage meets an audience ranging across all differences of class, education, occupation, age and gender, but there is much reason to believe that the quantity of media consumption is overestimated to a large extent. Considering the ratings of the weekly routine sport programmes, we find out that the audience interest is increasingly defined as "medium". The same applies to the sport section of newspapers. Thus, it is hardly surprising, that in Germany, in contrast to France, Italy and Switzerland, there is no daily national sport paper, quite contrary to former times. In

1899, the first daily sport paper "Sport im Wort" was published. Today the headline of an article may rightly state: "Sport is only a subordinate matter for newspaper readers". Reader analyses, which are carried out by the majority of newspapers, emphasize this opinion. In a comparison of 17 different areas of interest, local sport rank eighth with 57.9 %; the rest of sport ranks tenth, and first division soccer ranks 11th with 53.1 %.

Considering this and similar data, it is astonishing to what degree sport journalists think they know the wishes of their clients.

As far as the use of media is concerned, we can only make speculations as to the present habits of users, due to a lack of empirical data. The only interest is orientated towards TV-sport. The interest in other sport media hardly exists. Fictional sport literature is only of very minor importance in the German book market, not only because authors still neglect sport to a large extent. If there was a demand, we probably would not have to wait long for a book boom. The same applies to the sport film. Full-length sport films have, apart from a few exceptions, not been produced in the last 30 years.

.... Sport media consumption is a matter of certain social groups

The TV-role of women in the field of sport journalism is another subject of research, which is hardly worked on at all. Here too, it would be the main point to describe the pressures and limitations preventing an adequate participation of women in this field.

Not only apologists of sport regard sporting competition, championships and first division games as social events, accessible for all people, where everybody can participate actively or passively, and where everybody has equal opportunities of communication. In contrast to the social inequality found in almost all areas of life in our society, the world of sport is, according to this opinion, a world of justice. With regard to sport media this opinion has led to the frequently expressed allegation that all social classes have an equal share in the sport audience, that among the sport audience, according to the normal ratio of distribution, lower social classes are even dominant (and that therefore sport consumers have a lower standard of education).

The small number of analytical results referring to this allegation show that in this respect, too, wishful thinking dominates the discussion rather than realistic evaluation. The lower classes are hardly better represented as readers of sport magazines than as readers of political magazines. The same applies to radio and TV. People without occupational and vocational training have a smaller interest in sport programmes than listeners and readers with a higher education. These results are altogether in contrast to usual cultural criticism, which today still is dominant in respect of sport. The consumption of sport therefore is by no means primarily a matter for aggressive and stupid consumers among the lower classes (cf. *Digel* 1992).

.... Those who practise sport themselves are interested in the sport media

Those people who very actively practise sport seem to be particularly interested in sport media. This applies, above all, to male juvenile members of sport clubs and male adults.

Girls and women, however, are not so interested in sport during their spare time, they more often read books, not quite so often newspapers, they reject presentations of violence on TV more strongly, and sport programmes rank only tenth on a popularity scale ranging from 1 to 12.

In respect of TV there also seems to be a sport branch-related interest. Some trends of sport are to a larger extent preferred by women than by men. On the whole, however, women seem to have a "sound" dislike against an unreflected area of dominant masculinity. Just as sport as an action field is primarily characterized by male youthfulness, this is obviously mirrored in the media audience. Younger age-groups show more interest, children and elderly citizens are hardly interested in sport coverage at all.

.... What also would be desirable

Focusing on the situation of analysis of audience and utility in respect of sport media from a critical point of view, it has to be stated that today we still know next to nothing about the needs and expectations of the audience with regard to media. If sport journalists rely on letter-to-the-editor campaigns, as they often do to justify their work, we must point out that the readers' letter cannot provide a representative survey on attitudes and expectations of the audience. It is also problematical that sport reporters (just as any other reporter) are oriented towards a fictitious coverage consumer; this leads to the fact that minority-groups cannot find their interests represented in the coverage. Such orientation, for example, takes place in Germany if sport journalists in their work only take into account an audience exclusively interested in soccer. They do this despite obviously knowing virtually nothing about the actual wishes of the average consumer. The question why a sport medium is used or not, also waits for an answer, and today we still know hardly anything about the process of use. How do children, youths, women, working people, shift workers, etc. use sport programmes and sport reportings? What do they do during a sport programme? What do the other members of their families do? How are childeren and adolescents educated "into" sport consumption? What causes people to switch off? What causes permanent watching? Can the phenomenon of double and multi-utilization be explained? Who multi-uses sport media?

The consumption of sport coverage takes place mainly during leisure periods. The question in this respect is, whether, for example, the consumption of sport programs is really chosen freely. Observing myself, I find that sport programs are so fascinating for me that other activities are interrupted or stopped by them. Because sport programs are integrated into a fixed or set program structure, I do not seldomly structure the course of a day or week according to it. Whether my maturity and independence is jeopardized by this, is not the question. But whether the spare time activities of many (and which) people are thus structured and limited, is a question of sociological importance. Is media consumption in sport practiced like a ritual? As the few verified data show we often speculate about the use of sport media today, and the importance of sport media is mostly overestimated. This would be enough evidence to make utilization analyses, which refer to the question asked here, an urgent task (cf. *Volknant* 1988; *Digel* 1992).

6.   Sport coverage as a multi-functional instrument

The usual questions of analysis in the science of communication are supplemented by the word "why" in order to point out facts in respect of sport coverage which have up to now been neglected (cf. Table 7).

In handbooks about mass communication the question concerning the effects of mass communication is frequently asked in order to define indirectly the functions of coverage as well, the ideological component is at best marginally touched. In content analyses the question of ideological effects is often focussed; but in this approach only the ideology-carrier function of a certain medium is explained. This mixing makes it seem reasonable to deal with the question of the functions of media separately from the question of their effects and ideological power.

This shall be attempted in the following. The question why sport coverage is, and must be, like we face it today, can, however, only partly be answered here. A direct answer can only be provided by the people involved, the communicator and his recipients. Because the following description of functions is based on such answers, this way seems to be appropriate.

.... Prestige-providing, norm-stabilizing, narcotizing

Reading critical social and cultural essays on the phenomenon of mass communication shows that the media are attributed, in a very generalizing way, positive as well as negative functions; the respective evaluation is dependent on the evaluation of the social system in which the evaluating person lives. So mass media are, for example, often blamed for a decrease of the audiences' cultural taste, for an increase of crime, for their contribution to a general demoralization, for the stultification of recipients in respect of their own consumption of mass media, and for the suppression of creativity. This criticism is opposed by a positive evaluation. According to this, cases of crime and corruption are detected, the plurality of opinion and information is guaranteed, and the masses are, for the first time, brought into touch with culture and pleasant entertainment. If we want to analyse such functions a little more systematically, we have to distinguish between the following functions of media:

Mass media collect and spread information, interpret this information, may provide advice as a consequence, socialize the audience according to norms and standards of the prevailing system of society, and entertain their recipients.

This relatively neutral description of the functions of media only allows a limited judgement of the degree to which, for example, such functions have a stabilizing or destabilizing effect on society.

By taking such an evaluating point of view, we can distinguish between *three central functions* of mass media. *First*, they give prestige, *second*, they strengthen social norms, and *third*, they have a narcotizing malfunction (cf. *Lazarsfeld/Merton* 1973). Prestige is generated by mass media in so far as the fact that something is considered or mentioned in mass media makes it an important thing. Persons who are mentioned in mass media, as a rule, enjoy an increase of prestige. Especially for the attitude of athletes towards sport coverage, this context is important. Having been an active athlete oneself, one knows the importance of reading the Monday edition in order to see whether one's own name is mentioned in the match report, and how the performance of one's own team is evaluated. Of course, sport coverage is also prestige-generating in sport in so far as without it the market value in professional sport would not be calculable. The fact that media strengthen social norms, and thus exercises the second function, is, for instance, mirrored in the statement that the press is too powerful. With regard to minorities we therefore often use the phrase: "the crusade of the media". This shows that not acting in accordance with norms becomes a social problem under the pressure of the media. The functions of generating prestige and of strengthening social norms usually are known to the producers in the media. They are not so well acquainted with the third function, which is called a malfunction (cf. *Lazarsfeld/Merton*, 1973), because we suppose it is not in the interest of a complex society that large parts of the population are politically apathetic and indifferent. But precisely this is caused by the media. The more time people spend using mass media, the more apathetic they become as far as the solution of their own problems is concerned. Whereas it may be right that the mass media have increased the level of information of large parts of the population, a stronger dose of mass communication, however, changes the opportunities of people according to many analyses; active participation develops into knowledge, but people remain passive.

Today, we still know very little about the degree of effectiveness of mass media in this respect. Undoubtedly mass media contribute to the availability of knowledge about the powerful existing norms in a society, and to the reinforcement of ideas concerning norms and values, which are accepted in society. Particularly problematical in this respect is the entering of individuals into an intensive relationship with the mass media, which leads so far that they consider the messages of mass media to be a reflection of social reality without realizing that thus in the end a new reality is created. What is presented in mass media can by no means correspond to the real basis of the presentation. This is a fundamental problem, and therefore the media producers can only be blamed for it to a limited extent.

But we have to criticize that in sport media the multiplicity of sport become the monotony of top-performance sport. But only those norms become associated with sport, which get their reinforcement from the media. On the other hand one can more positively interpret the fact that sport coverage is a welcome event for communication, and that especially talking about "reported sport" is a form of communication which allows equal communication. Sport coverage is an opportunity for shop-talk, and a good coverage of an exciting soccer match can by all means entertain a large number of people in a pleasant way. So it is quite obvious that sport, due to its archaic simplicity, is an excellent subject of mass media utilization. But we should not fail to see the darker side of these fact. The highly praised communication, supposedly independent of any class membership or status, can also present itself in a way that it confines itself to the mere reproduction of programme contents, and that therefore sport coverage rather causes a streamlining of large masses of the population than release for the realization of individual or group interests.

.... Media sport - an improved copy?

It is also possible to give a more positive comment on sport, especially on TV sport. In respect of TV sport programs we can see a qualitative improvement of sport. A televised football match is not a reproduction of reality but a qualitative alteration. In contrast to the classical reproduction characterized by the epigonious reproductions of sculptures and paintings, which are, for instance, evaluated according to the value of the original and therefore relatively lower - in contrast to this, the original loses some value to the copy as far as sport telecasts are concerned. Referring to sport we therefore can speak of the improvement of the original by the copy "TV succeeds in improving reality, even if it sounds paradoxical". The improvement, however, always means a falsification of the original too. In respect of the effect of the phenomenon we therefore see, above all, two changes: First, the active practising of sport might be pushed too far away for the consumer, because the real practising of sport in comparison to TV sport must always be disappointing. For clubs, however, this might possibly have incalculable economic effects. Only top competitions are still attractive for the audience and during periods of bad weather, passive TV consumption is preferred to going to the stadium. But it is also a disadvantage for the clubs if athletes become stars due to TV, and thus are, in an indirect way, supported in their exaggerated salary claims. This fact points out that, without TV professionalization to the degree we have now would never have been possible. The same aspect, however, can also be an opportunity for organized sport. Not least the TV-incomes of sport associations have guaranteed independent sport a certain independence over the last few years, and the development of leisure sport to a popular sport movement has been possible due to this financial support.

.... Media sport as an illusion?

In respect of the functions of sport coverage another aspect seems to be very important. Due to the fact that many people, and therefore also most critics of sport, rarely see a sporting-event live, their image of sport must necessarily be determined by second-hand information, which by no means meets the complexity of the system of sport. In reality sport is extremely complex and rich of social references, the reproduction in mass media, however, makes sport a myth of illusory simplicity.

In this respect sport coverage has a narcotizing malfunction, and in respect to the stabilization of current norm patterns parallels can be pointed out. The alteration or creation of new norms and values might be the decisive function of sport coverage. We may assume that our attitude towards sport and thus sport itself is influenced by it. Show sport has nothing to do anymore with our ideals of play, honesty, gallantry, respect of rules and opponents or competitors as well as the purposelessness of sport, and thus an increase of freedom of the individual. Some analysts believe that the new world hierarchy already determines to a large extent the attitudes of consumers and also affects the individual's practising of sport. According to this everything that is useful, or promises success, is allowed. This also applies to the willingness of people to act aggressively in sport. It is also believed that the language usage of sport journalists influences the actions of athletes and the audience. Sport journalists in Germany, for instance, define fouls of German players more seldomely as violations of rules, mostly they are understood as tactically useful means in the course of a match, and thus excused for the sake of the desired success. Fouls of opponents, however, are precisely defined as such and condemned. So the audience or the reader learns to evaluate equal actions by different standards, and sport coverage becomes an instance of double standards concerning morals. There are still some doubts as to this causal connection of effects, but we may well state it as long as the opposite has not been proved. Considering this double standard of morals we might come to the following conclusion:

"Educators are helpless against this influence of the media. Their efforts become a nostalgic confession of faith" (*Volkamer* 1981, 26).

We still could derive many aspects from the large number of single analyses referring to the functions of sport coverage, and still the basis of criticism from the point of view of sport science would not change. The quoted assignments of functions are primarily based on the method of plausible argumentation, as the examples have shown. A mere systematic and determined advance of the analysis of functions would therefore be desirable, and in the course of it, the solutions of the analyses mentioned in the following chapter could be taken as guidelines.

7. What effects has sport coverage on the consumers?

The search for an answer to the question concerning the functions of coverage has already shown that we can rightly proceed from the assumption that coverage has consequences and effects. The way in which something is reported is obviously responsible for the reactions of the recipients. This assumption is reasonable and accepted by almost all experts. The question dealing with the kind of reactions, the timing of reactions and asking which recipient reacts, can, however, not be answered clearly.

The explanation of the mechanism of mass media is a central problem of scientific interest since press, radio and TV came into existence. In most cases the question, to what degree the socialization process of recipients is influenced, is in the focus of attention. In respect of the socialization of adults the question of manipulation of political opinions by the mass media (election analysis) has been of specific interest. Besides, the problem of the effects on the behavior of children and youths is especially important today. In this respect TV deserves particular attention (cf. *Sturm/Brown* 1979).

Today we know that children are often confronted with TV contents and their personal experiences can hardly be a correcting factor. The primary period of socialization, mainly performed by the family, today is followed by a secondary socialization which to a high degree is determined by the contents of mass communication. Even two and three year old children start watching TV, and thus build a social framework determined by current norms and values, which the mass media themselves are subject to.

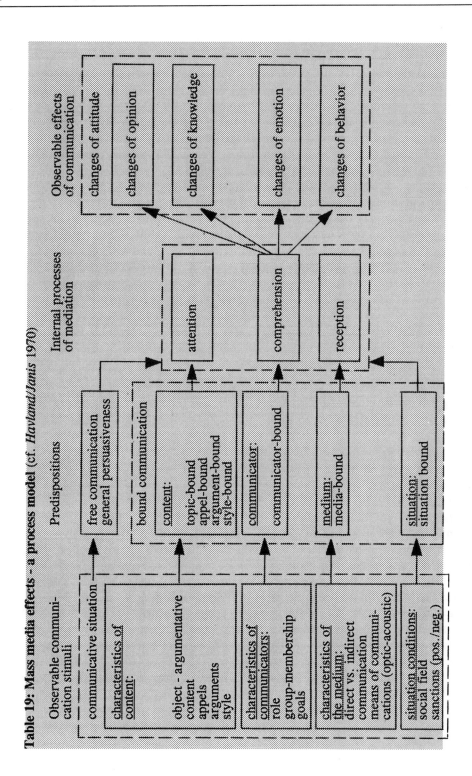

Table 19: Mass media effects - a process model (cf. *Havland/Janis* 1970)

.... Media are not omnipotently effective

Meanwhile there is a large number of competing theoretical approaches trying to explain the effects of mass media. In this context effect is mostly understood as all changes with regard to the behavior of the recipient during the receptive process and with regard to the behavior and experience after this process, provided that these changes are results of the persons' turning to the allegations of mass communication. It is also generally accepted that effects are distinguished with regard to their relation to observable behavior, knowledge, opinions and attitudes, emotions and the deep sphere of the psyche. Another aspect theories of effect have in common is the fact that the basic concept of explanation of all efforts is the so-called "theory of stimulus and response". This theory maintains that carefully designed stimuli reach every individual of society in the same way via the mass media, that every member of society receives the stimuli in the same way, and that, as a result, a similar reaction is achieved with all members. On the basis of this theory, media appear as omnipotent; in respect of the activation of passive consumers of sport coverage the media would be of downright outstanding importance. If the media have a positive function, which they were granted at the beginning of this century on a general level with regard to the humanization of society, this concept of explanation also suggests a pessimistic view. If the media were effective in this way, they would be a dangerous instrument of manipulation. Then sport programs, e.g., in Germany, provided they are designed accordingly, would generate or cause aggressions in the consumers, would create feelings of revenge and chauvinism, and they would, above all, press their clients to play soccer, because the stimulation of sport coverage is primarily coined by this sport branch. Many fears expressed in the last few years by officials, sport scientists and partly by media experts about sport coverage are based on such an assumption on the effects of media.

Today we know that people are different with regard to their personality structure and reception, and so it was fairly easy to point out that different types of people in an audience receive and interpret the allegations of mass media in a completely different manner.

Today it is still unquestioned that mass media have effects; considering the individual differences it seems, however, reasonable that the effects of mass media on different members of the audience are different. This statement also applies to the sport audience of mass media, and critics as well as supporters would be well-advised, if in future debates about the consequences of mass media, those empirical aspects are considered, which have been available for some years now in the field of mass communication analysis. This should, however, not be understood in a way that critics become victims of the argumentation of many media experts, who embrace the basic argument, according to which media are relatively ineffective, and thus justify their inactivity in respect of the problem of effects. So those from a large number of controversial results are selected which serve their own prejudices. It is certainly still true today that the analysis of effects cannot answer clearly a fair number of questions, as, for example, the question, whether the presentation of criminal und brutal behavior in mass media causes a higher crimerate. But to grant mass media ineffectiveness for that reason would be contrary to the effects we daily observe.

the behavior of children and youths is especially important today. In this respect TV deserves particular attention (cf. *Sturm/Brown* 1979).

Today we know that children are often confronted with TV contents and their personal experiences can hardly be a correcting factor. The primary period of socialization, mainly performed by the family, today is followed by a secondary socialization which to a high degree is determined by the contents of mass communication. Even two and three year old children start watching TV, and thus build a social framework determined by current norms and values, which the mass media themselves are subject to.

Table 20: The effects of sport coverage

There are five kinds of effects generated by sport coverage

- effects on knowledge
- effects on linguistic and social acting
- effects on social acting
- effects on attitudes
- effects on emotions

.... Media have limited effects

Wanting to summarize the most important results and agreements in the field of audience and effect analysis is a problematical enterprise, considering the variety of different analytical approaches. Because a beginning still has to be made in respect of analyses of effects of sport coverage, a simplified presentation, however, seems to be appropriate. In the following I will therefore try to point out views and results of some studies, which probably present the best-founded attempt of a localization of audience and effect analysis. Following these theoretical approaches and empirical results, we can state, on the mechanism and effects of mass media, that:

- Analyses have shown that information about events of average relevance for the population (e.g. about the events of the day) generally get directly from the mass media to the recipients (one-step-flow). If events reach a degree of attentiveness, as it might occur in periods of crises, interpersonal (mouth-to-mouth) communication gains more importance than the mass media as the primary source of information. The flow of information from the mass media to the recipients is, to a small degree, defined by opinion-leaders (two-step-flow), and even socio-economic class distinctions play a less important role in the first phase of the reception of information, as often is assumed. Regardless of this, recipients from upper classes are different, because they try to get qualitatively better further information.
- The assumption that recipients do not examine information which they like or reject (inconsistent information; selective-exposer-concept) is not confirmed in the available empirical analyses. On the contrary, the recipients actually expose themselves also to information, inconsistent to their attitudes and opinions, and therefore cause tensions in their cognitive systems. The selection of media by recipients furthermore is exercised independently of factors of opinion. Media can be

selected as substitutes for insufficient personal relations, as a means of control of the environment, as an opportunity to escape, as means to find personal identity, etc.

- The different motives for turning to mass media indicate that their possibilities of influence are nevertheless bigger than expected. Mouth-to-mouth communication and group-forming, as well as the influence of normative culture do not isolate or seclude the recipients from the penetrating mass media.

The variety of mass media and the resulting over-information rather supports this influence as well as the tendency of recipients towards the illusiory familiarity (para-social-interaction) in respect of the communicators. Here the medium becomes a substitute for lacking real opportunities of interaction (cf. Schenk 1978).

With regard to a direct change of opinions and behavior, the influencing possibilities of mass media must still be considered small. Changes of opinions and behavior are restrained and modified or sometimes supported by processes of mouth-to-mouth communication. The direct influence of opinion-leaders, however, has to be considered more limited than so far expected (two-step-flow). We rather have a reciprocal or mutual process of influence, in which opinion-leaders and opinion-seekers change roles as advisers and advice-seekers. Inactive or socially isolated people, however, are excluded from this mutual side-influence. People try to decrease the consequently developed lack by extreme consumption of escapist media contents. These media contents (e.g. dream world), however, cause additional deprivations. Inactive people limp behind in the process of change in society; they know less and do not participate in the process of forming opinions. On the basis of these features, described in empirical analyses, we can define more precisely the connection between mass media and recipients as well as their interpersonal environment of communication. Generally two functions and tasks can be assigned to the media. Recipients can be provided with information led by interest, and recipients can be entertained.

It is the recipient's choice to select from the large amount of offers of information and entertainment those contents which he is interested in. These might be contents orientated towards reality (e.g. information about important events or problems) or escapist contents (e.g. reality-distracting). Which contents, however, are considered worth turning to by the recipient, depends on widely differing factors, e.g. on his education and social class on his previous experiences, on the advantage promised by information, and on the gratifications offered by the contents. The recipient's openness as to inconsistent contents depends on his self-evaluation (the evaluation of the capability to cope with different social situations, his objectives and knowledge). But factors like credibility of the communicator, the way of argumentation and the kind of medium are also important. After the single-stage reception of information about mass media the recipients enter into interaction with other recipients (family, friends, colleagues etc.) in order to get background information about the particular event, or to interpret and evaluate the information. The probability of the recipient's interaction with others is particularly high if the allegations of mass media are supposed to cause changes of opinion and behavior, and if the recipient must decide whether he/she shall give way to the new direction. In this respect the recipient's discussion will be specifically dependent on his sociability, that is, on the degree of his social integration. Here it is also an important question how he is judged by others in respect of his social status and his standard of information. It depends especially on this, to what extent there is opinion-sharing or opinion-leading between two interacting partners. Inactive recipients will not participate in these processes.

.... We do not know what effects sport media have

The statements with regard to the state of analysis of effects by no means refer specifically to the so-called sport media. So far the general analysis of effects has turned towards the phenomenon of sport coverage. In the light of this fact it is difficult to answer the question if such general statements can be transferred to sport coverage and its effects. But since sport coverage is not excluded in the above mentioned statements, which are expressed in quite generalizing terms, at least part of these statements seem to be transferable. The presented statements are by all means suitable to be checked in respect of their importance.

Which role do sport programs play with regard to students or pupils imagination of sport? Does actually take place, what we can define as "structural" education, or what in a different context is called the "secret curriculum"? Which influence has sport coverage on a person's actions in sporting situations? Are the buying habits of consumers in the field of sport influenced by sport media? Which role do the sport idols, and the TV presenters, play in this respect? Which awareness and consciousness of rules develops due to sport coverage with regard to the consumers' own practicing of sport, or in respect of the keeping to rules of others? Are there so called opinion-leaders in the relation between sport mass communication and (interpersonal) mouth-to-mouth communication? What role is played by the phenomenon of permanently repeated monotony of sporting events in respect of the effects of sport coverage? (Compare especially the coverage of first division soccer.) The questions asked here are only a small selection from a large number of problems confronting us with regard to the effects of sport coverage. Answering them will not be easy, a difficulty not least deriving from an unsolved methodical problem. The existing available methods are only useful to a limited extent - as the first attempts of sport science in this field show - and so, new ideas in the field of methods are be needed in order to describe the relations or effects between sport and sport coverage. Today there is no doubt that this must be a central task of the science of communication and sport science. Its necessity derives from the sole reason that people, and not only scientists, talk almost every day in a speculating manner about the effects of sport coverage.

8.   Prospects

Sport coverage - as the presentation of the different aspects of analysis, outlined seperately for analytical reasons, has shown, - is a field not only neglected by sport science. Nor have media scientists themselves looked hard at sport coverage. This might be surprising considering that, all in all, media sport has gained a relatively high level of popularity. On the one hand this might be connected with the fact that for journalism there are also other possible and more important topics waiting to be analysed. On the other hand it might derive from the fact that sport science in its heterogeneous composition up to now has considered the problems of sport coverage as less important than other problems. The large number of unanswered questions concerning the communicator, the contents, the use and, last but not least, the aspect of the effects, in my opinion, make clear, however, that interdisciplinary cooperation with a common objective in the field of sport coverage is an urgent necessity. Only on the basis of such cooperation can we expect the development of sounder statements and more comprising results in respect of sport coverage than have been presented so far. The analytical separation of the process of communication, which has been carried out in this presentation, will certainly have to be given up. There rather must be more emphasis on an appropriate consideration of mutual and reciprocal relations between the single elements in the process of communication in practical science.

The so far neglected question concerning the "why" in the process of communication will also gain particular importance in connection with sport. It refers to the social relativity of mass communication, and thus to the dynamic relations of elements of further scientific work in the field of mass communication, which have been described here isolated from each other. Therefore it would be wrong to understand sport coverage as an isolated section of society. Sport coverage rather must be comprehended as an expression of modern mass communication, and this again as a phenomenon of social communication. Sport coverage as it exists today has no accidental character, it has only become possible and necessary at a certain state of productive powers and due to the development of certain social forms of interaction. Therefore the social context of sport coverage, from which the contents of coverage gain their determination, has to be included in future science. If we want to cope with this dynamic relation, we will have to develop new methods which contribute to pointing out the complexity of the problems of mass communication and to leading to a solution.

But sport science will also have to answer the supposedly most important question of what an improved sport coverage could look like. Up to now it has only turned to the deficiencies of coverage in a number of analyses, but has not made any contributions itself for the elimination of these deficiencies. The same applies to organized sport itself, which until today has not managed to present a successful concept for the media. For both areas it seems to be an urgent necessity to come up to the responsibility they have in the field of sport coverage.

Expectations About Sport Journalism

Expectations towards sport journalism from the perspective of sport science have to differ from expectations of other institutions, groups and individuals in two ways. First, such manifestations, which are to be defined as scientific expectations, should not be of any private character, they should rather be based on a number of intersubjectively controllable statements. Second, they should be based on theories, that is, by applying suitable scientific methods the facts these expectations are aiming at should be displayed in a scientific context.

To the present day, these two conditions have not been met by sport science with regard to sport journalism. So far, sport science has been dealing with journalism only sporadically and mostly in hardly representative case studies, frequently running the risk of transforming flat prejudice into unjustified condemnations in the course of initial scientific experiments.

If, nevertheless, I try to outline ten expectations towards sport journalism in the following, the unsafe ground my expectations are based upon should always be kept in mind. I will, however, refer to empirical studies carried out by other scientists or by myself.

The following expectations refer to functions and tasks generally to be performed by sport journalists if their own principles are taken seriously, and especially if we take into account the interests of recipients who daily consume their products (cf. Table 10).

Besides describing and explaining these expectations I will also try to outline how journalists can successfully perform these tasks.

1st expectation:
Sport journalists should take the recipients' wishes and interests seriously; sport coverage in the media should be based on democratic principles.

Despite many appeals and much criticism sport journalists still know very little about their clients' wishes, interests and needs. Hence, sport journalists ought to respect their clients' wishes and needs and go about their work with more critical distance. Their claims maintaining that they provide exactly what the public wants and expects are absolutely inadmissable.

The usual motto, "this is a hit" (i.e. soccer), or, "that doesn't interest anybody" (i.e. sport of people with disabilities) shows the journalists' patronization of the recipients and their autocratic attitudes rather than their competence.

In general, sport journalists discuss issues in 'in-groups', they decide among themselves what should be written or broadcasted.

These discussions in small groups bear the danger of self-domestication and self-manipulation, symptoms which frequently can be diagnosed particularly among journalists working for TV-stations. Disregarding the public's interests, sport journalists only marginally deal with the people and their ways of life with regard to such important fields like leisure and recreational sport, although the recipients declare that, especially on the local level, these sectors are the most interesting ones for them. Consequently, sport coverage appears to be in sharp contrast to its socio-political mandate as well as to the reality of sport. 98 % of all sport coverage exclusively considers high-performance sport, whereas, for example, more than 25 million German DSB-members in over 76.000 clubs mainly go in for leisure and recreational sport.

This comparison sufficiently indicates the wide gap between the objectives of media coverage and the socio-ethnic as well as educational objectives of sport. Hence, the public's interest in sport seems to be more advanced than that of sport coverage. Empirical projects investigating Germany's mass media strongly suggest the abandonment of some of their clichés. It is, for example, a widespread error to attribute to soccer a particular attractiveness among the lower classes. Scientific research rather indicates that the lower classes are, in fact, not over-represented at all, neither on the soccer fields nor as consumers of sport coverage. There is more evidence for the fact that the middle and upper classes are more likely to be over-represented. The same applies to sport on TV, which was generally assumed to be male domains. This may be correct to some extent, however, studies on the composition of media audiences show that the ratio between males and females is far less extreme than we would expect: The audience watching one of the major German Saturday night sport programs consists of 66 % men and 34 % women.

It is also interesting in this context that there is a reversal between the sexes in terms of their preference for different kinds of sport. Thus 81 % of the female TV-audience express their specific interest in figure-skating, whereas only 58 % of the males share this preference. With soccer it is just the other way round. The traditional notion of a purely male interest in sport on TV is no longer true and requires fundamental change. Empirical research has also shown that it is by no means clear that the sport section of newspapers is their most popular part, a presupposition frequently stated in order to justify higher to existing forms of sport coverage.

Extensive investigations have shown that about 75 % of the readers are interested in the sport sections, with regard to other sections, however, this figure rises to 95 %.

Among the various sections of newspapers local sport only ranks in 10th position, other sport even lower; politics, local events, crime and accidents rate substantially higher.

A closer look at the few published analyses of listeners', readers' and spectators' wishes and interests leads us to demand a profound democratization of sport coverage, because this has been - as all analyses unanimously and rightly criticize - largely undemocratic. As a consequence, the practical work of sport journalists needs to be reorganized, the objectives being decentralization, regionalization and sub-regionalization as well as a greater emphasis on local events. Considering the way in which local sport events are presented in the media at present, it is no wonder that they do not attract more people within the audience. In order to change this situation especially the big TV-networks would have to show more courage, and people responsible for regional programs would have to find ways of covering high-performance sport from a local (patriotic) perspective.

2nd expectation:
In their reports, sport journalists should give sufficient attention and the space it deserves to the world of physical activity and sport they actually come across outside their offices and studios.

It is unjustified to accuse the sport media of neglecting the world of everyday sport and physical activity or to blame them for the fact that it is only reflected in the media in a reduced form; rather are selection and the reduction of reality fundamental necessities of journalistic work. So the question hast to be: What are the sport journalists' criteria for the reduction of reality? In this context they are rightly accused of unbalanced reduction and selection.

The selection of contents in sport coverage is primarily based on the principle of spectacular performance. Simple, controllable and exciting sporting activities are in the focus of attention, and if these features are still insufficient the excitement is generated by means of technical tricks. As to dressage, for example, only the voluntary exercises are presented, and the same applies to figure-skating and gymnastics. The compulsory exercises are not interesting for the consumers, so the journalists think. This example indicates that - in the sport journalists' view - sport on TV can only be successful if it succeeds in generating excitement; sociability and human interest stories should possibly be added. However, this kind of excitement and entertainment is strange to sport, reducing supreme performance to its ritual aspects. Soccer merely consists of scoring and goals, athletics comprise only record and defeat. The process of performance, the generating of a supreme performance is usually ignored; consequently, a superficial and reduced impression of sporting performance is conveyed.

Particularly annoying is the electronic media dramaturgy, which has gained specific significance in so far, as the orientation towards world records now dominates all kinds of sport. During athletics events, for instance, the world record time is being screened, which inclines the audience to believe that the runners only compete against the stop-watch, whereas in most cases they simply want to beat their competitors, the time being of secondary importance only. Thus the sporting event is eclipsed by an artificial drama and the actual performance consumed secondarily.

Table 21: Questions concerning the evaluation of sport coverage

a) *The question of topics*
    What is the topic/subject of a report?

b) *The question of contents*
    What is mentioned or shown in a report?

c) *The question of functions*
    What is the meaning of a report? What kind of action is performed in a report?

d) *The question of form/structure*
    How is a report structured?

e) *The question of criticism*
    Are the contents of a report true, information, relevant, topical, intelligible, etc?

The media-mastered conditioning of sporting events has increased to the extent that the actual sporting activity is no longer left to the athlete, constant information regarding the positions in the race, comparisons, etc. prevent an undisturbed sporting competition. The informational value provided by parallelly screened running time is, in fact, very limited, since only intermediate times make any sense at all.

The fixation on figures and records therefore proves that TV-sport entertainment is based on something invisible, since the record cannot be experienced as a direct result of the sporting event but only through the clock, the measuring table or the scales.

Thus the primary features of sport coverage are, above all, records as to the number of spectators, records as to the number of yellow or red cards, records as to the number of goals, etc. All this seems to be worthwhile reporting, the true meaning of sport, however, is being distorted to a dangerous degree by the merciless principle of triumph and failure. Record fetishism and record-mania also have direct and negative consequences for the recipients: They can never enjoy a few details, they can never watch an event undisturbed and are only rarely allowed to explore. Basically, their concentration is permanently led by the nose.

Furthermore journalists think they have to 'polish' one and the same thing again and again, which results in the tendency towards double information, and considering the meaninglessness of this information, can only cause our astonishment. The multi-usage of media even reinforces this tendency, and today the overlapping of contents has become a normality for all media clients, every individual being surrounded by a network of media aiming at over-information and disregarding the limited memorizing capability of the consumer. So the newspapers publish what has been repeatedly broadcasted by three different TV-networks. Thus the people read about a sporting event they have already been informed of by the previous day's TV or radio programs, but despite excessive repetition the actual information vanishes immediately from the recipients' memories. Considering this phenomenon some critics rightly question the over-emphasis on 'result and record' reporting and wonder why some journalists exclusively nurture this kind of coverage. Would not fewer but different aspects be more entertaining and more informative? Hence, the most important demand towards sport journalists focuses on the imbalance of their reports, requesting a more comprehensive coverage of that sport that is popular with a large number of people in terms of their own sporting activities and their interests as listeners or spectators. At present sport journalism seems to be limping behind the actual development of sport. Carate events, for example, often attract larger crowds than boxing, and it might well be that sport which still has a somewhat sectarian image is, in fact, progressing rapidly. On the other hand the sport media also have to pay more attention to new concepts and notions of physical activities developing outside of and as alternatives to traditional concepts of sport and attracting increasing numbers of people. These are, for instance, non-competitive forms of movement and dancing, body control and body experience as well as the sub-cultural spheres of surfers, rock climbers or hanggliders. Our demand to decrease the imbalance of sport coverage also aims at a better integration of 'outsiders'.

Of great significance in this respect is the integration of school, leisure and recreational sport, also comprising the work of voluntary organizers, children's sporting events with all their participants, people doing recreational sport, those with disabilities, senior citizens, foreigners, other minorities and their spheres of sport and physical activities.

In view of the present imbalance we finally have to regard as a grave deficiency that we are continuously exposed to the excessive presentation of Olympic champions' private banalities, whereas discussions of superior quality about sport are hardly ever even mentioned in the media. Especially sport policies and sport science are reduced to an almost unsurpassable shadowy existence despite their extremely important functions for the further development of sport in our society. However, being pushed to the fringes and into special publications with a low circulation which are read only by a small number of people, society can hardly profit from their achievements.

The inclusion of these essential contents is certainly not contrary to the entertaining function of the media, as journalists often maintain when confronted with the criticism of imbalanced reporting. Only notorious pessimists can reject the notion of sport as entertainment. In my view TV-audiences and readers indeed have a right to be entertained on a high intellectual and aesthetic level which, as a matter of fact, is the only basis to justify the presentation of outstanding supreme performances in sport.

However, when criticizing the entertainment value of TV-sport programs we should not ignore that they contrary to other genres of TV-entertainment like western movies or thrillers, do not feature murders and their victims. Often, they rather convey the ideals of fair and non-violent sport and competitions.

3rd expectation:
Sport journalists should present athletes as those individuals in our society they really are.

The image of top-athletes, as presented in the madia, is inadequate. The fact that the public largely associates the word 'athlete' with characteristics like 'egocentric', 'intellectually underdeveloped', 'packed with muscles', and 'ascetic' is after all a result of their presentation in the media. For many years the media have presented the supposedly 'typical' top-performance athlete. Those, however, who know athletes and are familiar with sport are aware that these generalizing characterizations could only evolve from dealing exclusively with competitive sport and in this respect solely with the final decisive competition, but not with the process of performance.

Table 22: Standards for the evaluation of sport coverage

1. The principle of truth

2. The principle of intelligibility

3. The principle of information

4. The principle of relevance

5. The principle of topicality

6. The principle of entertainment

This results in merely measuring performances and comparing them with previous achievements without taking into account the athlete's personality and background. Thus he/she is being degraded to a communication object, has become a fixed sterotype and deteriorated to a produced image.

Consequently, the athletes' criticism of the sport media is certainly justified, but what needs to be changed?

In the future athletes are to be presented as personalities - which they can be as well as any other people - journalists will have to change their attitudes towards them, focusing not entirely on their performance, but also on the persons, the individual human beings generating these performance. This will be a time-consuming and difficult process, requiring competent investigation as well as overcoming prejudice. The athletes themselves, male or female, will have to be willing to face open and honest discussion. In this respect it also has to be criticized that the image of the female athletes, as it is depicted by almost exclusively male sport journalists, is by and large unacceptable, reflected in the media traditional role expectations of a society dominated by privileged men. In sport women are also objects of mass media manipulation, and they are discriminated against in terms of the quantitiy of sport coverage, as empirical studies show. This is not only true as far as soccer is concerned, the dominance of male athletes in sport coverage becomes also apparent during the Olympic Games. Investigating the contents of coverage reveals - besides some positive aspects - a large number of chauvinistic and sexist modes of presentation. Women are, for instance, usually evaluated in terms of their outward appearance, their looks are continuously judged. Women are required to meet as beauty ideal and are not permitted to reject the female ideal our society has developed. They must always look nice and attractive and are often presented as sex objects for male curiosity. The aspect of sexuality degrades women to merchandise, thus allowing their commercialization and exploitation for advertising.

There are more than enough examples of such treatment. It has to be recognized that traditional role stereotypes and sexism are still common features of sport coverage. Critical sport journalists, however, should consider as a primary function and responsibility to make their clients aware of hitherto unquestioned female myths in order to assist our society in reflecting upon them and abandoning the notion that they are lower of nature. This kind of coverage, however, is only rarely to be seen.

4th expectation
Sport journalists should know and reflect in their work that their professional field increasingly has socio-political amplications and social functions.

Only due to the media sport has acquired characteristics of merchandise and has - like movies, cabarets, circuses and variety shows - become a fact of modern entertainment industry. Sport has its market, athletes have their market value, and both are dependent on consumers and audiences.

The media are also responsible for the national pathos regularly to be experienced in connection with sporting performances, for the dominance of commercial interests in sport, often reducing the athletes to puppets, and for the fact that the performance is separated from the athlete, that it becomes a part of national prestige, that the athlete is being caught and used in a cobweb of bureaucratic and economic system, and that the audience's sense of identity is abused for the sake of political and economic interests. That all this is closely related to and caused by sport journalism, that sport journalists play a major part in the development of sport is, however, recognized by a few journalists only and hardly ever accepted.

The problematic interdependence between the coverage of an event and its results on the one hand and the subsequent socio-political references and functions on the other hand is still not being reflected as a synthesis in sport coverage. To some extent this is caused by the division into departments, which usually results in the sport journalists' political incapacity by the politics journalists. Considering the existing and latent political manipulation of sport, this separation is to be regarded as dangerous and thus should be changed. Another reason, however, is the sport journalists' own understanding of sport, placing sport somewhere in a socially and politically free space, which is bound to make them blind for the effects these events have outside this supposedly free space.

If we demand adequate reference to society we have to recognize that ignoring relevant news is the most severe form of political manipulation, which we frequently realize, whenever political events become important in the context of sporting events, a striking example being the Western boycott of the 1980 Olympics in Moscow, where the majority of sport journalists was in favour of the boycott, even though they had almost unanimously been the mouthpiece of supposedly unpolitical sport a few months before.

Their unpolitical attitude is actually plain conservatism. That such an attitude is bound to cause embarrassment always became apparent during East and West-German sporting competitions. In the past, the word 'German' exclusively referred to West-Germany athletes when used by West-German reporters, thus actively supporting the West-German politicians' claim of sole representation of all Germans, East and West. The same applies to the treatment of human rights problems or the media presentation of so-called 'socialist athletes'.

Sport journalists have to realize that all their actions are determined by fundamental references to society including even the bare results, because they also may affect society. The sporting actitivies of every single individual have some kind of effect on the athlete as a citizen. What does this mean?

If a reporter only presents the course of a sporting event, like, for instance, talking only about the twice 45 minutes of a soccer match without considering the conditions under which the match has become reality, without taking into account aspects of health, ethics, economics or politics he does his duty only half. Our demands rather have to be that sport journalists look beyond the stadium walls and that their thinking does not stopp where the stadium ends. Economic, medical, psychological and political aspects are inherent in sport, but usually they are ignored by sport journalism.

Another form of mass media manipulation is the personalization of facts in sport. Successful athletes are presented in an illusory world which obscures the fact that sport is not determined by individual personalities, but rather by a large number of coaches, officials and successful managers as well as by unsuccessful athletes, who are essential for the success of the extraordinary and outstanding athlete.

Successful athletes are characterized by qualities and capabilities absolutely out of distance the readers' reach. But the subsequently caused unbridgeable distance between the athlete's and the recipient's positions is relativized by the fact that they are given an aura of "people like you and me" by the reporters.

This is achieved by presenting successful athletes in their roles as fathers or mothers, by repeatedly characterizing them as fellow country-men, as children of their mother country, and hence, as brethren of the recipients who identify themselves with the same country. Thus the top-athletes may be considered an idol by the recipient, and, despite the large social distance between him-/herself and the consumer, becomes one of 'us'. The usual features distinguishing the audience from the sport stars like, for example, their economic and social position, their position in the process of production, their potentialities in terms of social rise, income and consumption are thus negated. All this is done under the premisses of entertaining readers and audiences.

I agree with some critics who rightly suspect that the supposedly harmless journalistic means of entertainment in sport might have functions other than mere amusement and relaxation, because it is apparent not only in sport, that entertainment can also take on the functions of disguised instruction and manipulation. Often, entertaining programs have a stronger influence on the recipients than sober reports which aim at providing information.

5th expectation:
Sport journalists should become aware of their educational responsibility.

Most sport journalists are obviously unaware of the significant influence their products exercise on their recipients' motivational attitudes towards sport and in sport. Not only do they manipulate the people's active and passive interests in certain sport disciplines, they also direct public opinion about sport as well as their social significance. Moreover, they provide identification opportunities for students and other young people, which serve as points of orientation in terms of the students' attitudes towards physical education and sport clubs. Usually, sport journalists merely select, interpret, emphasize, dramatize and omit, but this is precisely how they give a particular meaning to sport. Consequently, all presentations of sport have effects influencing the recipients' consciousness, which is an inevitable result of journalistic work and need not be dangerous. However, dangers emerge, when journalists are not aware of these effects; unfortunately this still applies to a large number of sport journalists. Hardly any of them considers it a necessity to justify and give reasons for possible or desired effects. Today, the negative impact on physical education is already apparent. The students' interests in sport are generated in close relation to mass media presentation, imbalanced as it is and problematical from an educational point of view, thus preventing physical education and other school sport fully achieving their educational objectives. Rigid expectations towards sport, as defined by the norm concepts of competitive sport (soccer in particular), severely impede alternative concepts of physical activities convey the passive concepts of high-performance sport and thus place the active participation of ordinary people in sport into a world out of their reach. Sport coverage, however, not only influences our knowledge of sport and our imagination of what our participation in sport could look like, it also affects the reception, attitude, and consequently the actual behaviour of people involved in sport.

In connection with the problems of aggression, which recently has become increasingly significant in many sport disciplines, scientists have pointed out that sport coverage may directly affect the behaviour of athletes as well as audience, resulting in their increased aggressiveness, and that it generates conditions for aggressive behaviour within the sphere of sport as well as in other sectors. Furthermore it might provide spectators with excuses for their own inappropriate actions.

In this respect particularly the sport journalists' aggressive language usage is to be criticized, because it removes taboos in respect of the spectators' aggressive desire, reduces restraints, depicts aggressiveness as socially admirable behaviour, and thus perverts sport.

These effects are supported by the fact that athletes are raised to heroes, and competitions are given the aura of highly important social events, thus promoting the audiences' willingness for identification, which is also a condition for experiencing defeat as a major frustration, for provoking aggressive reaction, and for sensing opponents in a game as actual enimies.

On a national level such coverage may cause generalizations which result in the notion of hostile groups, nationalistic arrogance and chauvinism, and this influences national stereotypes also outside sport. For these reasons sport coverage is largely to be blamed for the fact that aggressive behaviour in sport has become legitimate or at least excusable, the consequence being the moral and ethical devaluation of the opponent.

If sport journalists want to take on their educational functions they can only meet the demands of public curiosity to a limited extent, a public supposedly wishing that defeat and spectacular failure enforces attention.

We are often confronted with the opinion that privately owned media have hardly any possibilities of educationally responsible coverage. This view seems erroneous to me, since it is becoming more and more obvious that the journalistic principles are violated in the same way by public radio and TV-networks as by private ones. The public networks are, in fact, primarily responsible for the degeneration of sport to 1:0 reports and for its development towards mere entertainment journalism which crawls along the surface of sport.

So far, all efforts to integrate lower social classes into an active movement culture have failed, which is hardly surprising in the face of a media-induced immobility. Passivity can only be reduced or prevented by those who have caused it; these are to a large extent sport journalists and their media, and in this respect primarily TV. Therefore the question is legitimate whether the print media and TV by apparently limiting themselves to entertainment and eloquent but rather uniformative reporting about sport meet their own standards. At least the public institutions have greater obligations in this respect.

What seems to be needed are a little more enlightenment, a good deal, more distance to sport itself and more critical identification. We may rightly expect sport journalists to foresee developments, to draw out attention to 'dead-end roads', and not to degenerate to uncritical conveyors of information, applying all their means of technical perfection solely for this purposes. Already today, they could be advocates for the public's rejection of that kind of high-performance sport which overstrains the human organism, and sport journalists could also make themselves advocates of athletes complaining about the fact that the human personality is in danger of deteriorating in modern sport.

6th expectation:
Sport journalists should proceed with due caution when dealing with sport organizations, officials and athletes; this is necessary to enable them to fulfill their function of being detached instructors and critics at the same time.

The relationship between sport journalists and athletes, coaches or officials is often characterized by too little distance, dubious companionship or even corruption. Interviews frequently resemble superficial 'Royal Court' coverage or degenerate to conformist parroting, and - not only during live-broadcasts - biased siding with the 'own' athlete or team has become the rule. Evidence for the frequent lack of distance between journalist and athlete is the fact that athletes are usually addressed by their first names.

Sometimes this lack of distance leads so far that journalists become official writers for sport organizations while still working as journalists. This double function currently held by many sport journalists is, however, unacceptable considering the principles of independent journalism.

Unfortunately there are countless examples of journalists devising the public relations of an organization, writing a club's publication or organizing sporting events. In some cases they have even been in charge of the public relations for a major sporting event while at the same time reporting and commenting on its competitions. Sport journalists who devote their potentialities to a sport organization are in danger of abusing their readers- und listeners' confidence, because they trust the commentator and rely on his neutrality and unbiased judgement, which should be based on critical distance and not on any ties that are in sharp contrast to their function as guardians. Wanting sport policy in the media to be more than mere shadow-boxing requires reconstructing as a fundamental condition that journalists must not become dependent on those carrying responsibility in sport policy. However, the relationship between journalist and sport official is not the only problematical one, the same applies to that between journalist and coach, and a recent Swiss study revealed that 87,5 % of the journalists and 97,2 % of the coaches also consider this a problem.

In the first respect coaches often see the causes of conflicts on the journalists' side, blaming them for being non-factual, biased, incompetent, not sufficiently informed, for publishing wrong or only half-true information, for magnifying and exaggerating insignificant side aspects, and for violating many athletes' as well as coaches' private spheres in this process. 19 % of the coaches interviewed have at least once demanded a counter-representation or correction because of alleged unjustified criticism, and one in four admits having felt insulted; one in three believes that individual sport journalists have accepted bribery. The journalists' image among the coaches is certainly not positive and needs instant improvement. The degree of dissatisfaction in terms of the relationship between coaches and journalists also becomes apparent when considering that 30,6 % of the coaches interviewed state that they have taken some kind of revenge on sport journalists for repeated criticism and that over 40 % of the journalists admit having given coaches a taste of their anger in one way or another.

These results - but also those of German and American studies - indicate that the problem or journalistic distance and neutrality is also very closely related to questionable attitudes of coaches and especially club officials towards the freedom and independence of the press. On an increasing number of occasions critical sport journalists have been denied admission to press rooms and even stadiums, and often journalists are selected on the basis of 'loyalty', or, what is even worse, their loyalty has been bought by bribery.

It has to be emphasized again and again that, in the face of such tendencies, more courage for enlightened criticism is urgently requested, in order to put sport into a position where it can be judged and evaluated by its own standards.

7th expectation:
Sport journalists should report competently on the basis of well-founded knowledge.

In my view investigative reporting in sport requires an orientation towards sport science. In the same way as a business journalist lacks competence without having studied economics and possibly is a very doubtful source of information in the sector of business and trade, a sport journalist is also incompetent if he does not or cannot make use of the results of sport science. For this reason a sport journalist should have sufficient knowledge of the analysis of movement, he should be familiar with the fundamental aspects of training, he should know about the development of tactics and skills at least in sport and should have some personal practical experience in sport. Moreover, he should be aware of the political, social and scientific implications which always affect sport, but what is required above all, is more precision in reporting. I am not talking about precision in terms of time or scoring statistics, but often important details remain obscure and the interpretations of sporting actions speculative for the reader of a newspaper; hence, we request more precise pictures and more precise investigation, background information and references to possible consequences.

However, nobody can seriously demand that sport journalists should have a university degree in sport science in order to be qualified to report on sport; no medical degree is needed to write an article about doping. Effort and goodwill granted, everybody can acquire sufficient knowledge essential for competent reporting and judgement. Experts waiting to be asked and ready to share their knowledge are to be found all over the place, and journalists are paid for obtaining relevant information.

This applies to innovative features in sport as well as to traditional ones. It seems to be the case that the media presentation of traditional sport like, for instance, soccer, team handball or athletics is particularly inadequate or superficial. Especially those journalists who maintain that soccer is just a game and that they therefore only talk or write about what they see, should at least report factually and competently on what can be seen, which is, in fact, what they obviously do not in most cases. In the studio so-called experts are invited to state what the reporters have said before, and if the TV-anchorman repeats for the fourth time what the commentator, the expert in the stadium and the expert in the studio have said before, this cannot even be justified on the grounds of entertaining journalism. Critical remarks about players, coaches, etc. are hardly ever heard; "they all do their best, they are all really good!" There obviously exists a "blood-brotherhood" between those concerned. What the political implications are may be left to the critic. There are, however, some journalists who have to be excluded from this criticism.

8th expectation:
Sport journalists should use the whole array of available journalistic tools, and they
should insist on the improvement of their present working conditions.

The analysis of daily newspapers, radio and TV-programs show that most journalists
do their work according to set patterns of behaviour and communication, which leads to
the widely known stereotypes of sport journalism. Interviews are particularly
problematical; in sport-talkshows, for example, we often get the impression that the host
does not want to know anything, what he rather wants, seems to be the star as a show
object. The hosts' quantitative share in interviews is usually very big, varying between 37
% and 72 %, with an average of about 50 %, whereas in interviews with politicians their
average share is about 26 %. What is also very surprising is the large number of
redundant and leading questions; over 50 % of all questions asked belong to this category.

Sport journalism is suffering from a lack of initiative to present, for the public
benefit and by means of new forms of journalism, that other side of sport referring to the
individual citizen. What we need is, for example, the development of a new type of social
report covering leisure and recreational sport, sport for minorities, sport for people with
disabilities, etc. Those devoting themselves to this facet of sport journalism perform a
necessary social task and will be rewarded with appreciation and sympathy.

Working in this sector could be challenging as well as attractive for sport journalists.

Similar criticism applies to the print media. The still increasing tendency towards a
monopolization of the press structure is indeed annoying; it causes the extensive use of
news agency material, which means we get to read exactly the same article in several
different newspapers. Avoiding redundancy requires journalists who are sufficiently
competent to edit this material, introducing or adding specific perspectives of individual
participants or observers of sporting events.

Another request concerns the frequently demanded, yet rarely printed comment.
Critical comments in sport sections unfortunately are still not more than a reduction to
school grades, in many cases they are too personalized, putting too much emphasis on
individuals. Consequently the criticism is justified maintaining that the press is largely
responsible for merciless audiences cheering the winner but ignoring those who finish in
fourth or fifth place in a major competition.

However, the possibilities of multifariously using journalistic tools to a large extent
depend on the sport journalists' working conditions. Severe economic pressure as well as
the dependence on publishers jeopardize journalistic freedom. Thus, in the interest of
objective and critical journalism our efforts have to concentrate on the reduction of these
pressures.

9th expectation:
Sport journalists should use language that is appropriate for the coverage of sporting
events and understandable for the recipients.

Whereas, for a long time, the metaphorical and chauvinistic use of language used to
be in the focus of the critics' attention, it must be noted now, after a period of
disillusionment, that the language of sport journalists does not succeed in creating good
entertainment, which the recipients rightly expect. The monotony of language usage
certainly need not be replaced by justly criticized military metaphors. Nevertheless seems

linguistic ingenuity and creativity still to be limited to a small number of journalists, while their majority still sticks to so-called 1:0 journalism, which is characterized by the fact that the journalists' main function of providing information solely consists of the presentation of results, figures and records. Rather would it be desirable that sport journalists to some extent comprehend themselves again as 'narrators of myths' telling travel stories and trivial tales.

Today, they are much too often underprivileged and use their tool, language, quite amateurishly. While neither daring to use the great forms nor knowing any alternatives, they escape into good behaviour, superficial descriptions of events, cold analyses and statistics, and into the mystification of individual athletes.

Altogether, however, we ought to recognize that the criticism of sport language is by no means as well-founded as the critics pretend. It often derives from questionable objectives, is based on doubtful research and uses inappropriate generalizations. Most critics are representatives of an outdated school of linguistics, and, above all, their criticism is much too seldomly orientated towards the most important criterion, that is, whether the examined expressions and phrases are intelligible or not. Thus, any demands concerning a different use of language in sport coverage are only acceptable if they do not jeopardize the intelligibility of statements. As a matter of fact, such criticism often fails to recognize the primarily entertaining character of sport journalism.

Despite this relativization of language criticism there still remains a number of aspects that require our attention. Considering language usage of white sport journalists in terms of writing or talking about ethnic groups of minorities, such as blacks in particular, there is clear indication of at least some remains of colonialism. This is apparently tied to the fact that sport journalists suffer from having to process and refine one and the same subject again and again, which, however, does only marginally distinguish them from political journalists. Regardless of our sympathy for the use of metaphors', it must therefore be pointed out that a 'stew of metaphors', as it is still to be found in numerous comments and reports, can certainly not be an appropriate means to overcome this monotony.

10th expectation:
Sport journalists should make more efforts to receive better basic as well as advanced training, which must be expected due to their extraordinary position in our society.

The training of sport journalists represents the most difficult problems in this field. A number of studies indicate that entering sport journalism is much easier than getting into any other journalistic sector, and the percentage of university graduates is much lower, too. Political awareness does not seem to be exactly highly developed among sport journalists either. Nor is the interdependence between their political awareness and the general political leading of the media usually recognized by them. They see their major function and objective in their audiences' entertainment.

Basically, sport journalists are not integrated into the group of their colleagues working in other departments, and thus drawing conclusions from their popularity to the reputation of their profession would be a grave error. The sport journalists' self-image is, in fact, too negative. However, they equal entertainment journalists in terms of their incapability to improve the quality of their work. The improvement of their reputation as well as the promotion of their self-esteem can apparently only be achieved by better basic training and better opportunities for advanced training as well as a stricter selection. Better education and training would not only support their ego but also give them greater flexibility, enabling them also to find employment in other departments; thus their fixation on the sport departments could be eased and a better integration into the staff of their paper or network achieved. The prospects, however, are doubtful since the majority of journalists themselves impede the professionalization of their job, and it is interesting in this respect that on the one hand particularly those journalists working with electronic equipment have got the lowest education and receive the least training, but, on the other hand, most ardently object to the improvement of these conditions.

Another problem that has strong effects and therefore should not be ignored concerns mainly TV. It is the internal journalistic star-cult which prevents proper and distinguished journalistic work, seducing freshmen in the field into trying to gain success not by means of effort but through gags or showy acts which have their effects on the audience. For the sake of the scoop which they believe to have up their sleeves, they investigate biasedly in order to achieve the desired effects. They manipulate their audiences, and should they fall on their noses in this process, vehemently lament about the vanishing of the freedom of the press.

The recruitment of ex-athletes as sport journalists is another problematical development. Supposing that this might help to make programs more informative or be supportive in the fans' and spectators' education has turned out to be erroneous; it has actually generated the opposite effect. Because ex-athletes neither receive any kind of journalistic training nor can possibly report on the technical know-how of sport, their contributions remain generally superficial if not altogether poor, and are, in most cases, not even entertaining. Usually they introduce a redundant jargon into the coverage of a competition, and at a closer look there is not more than superficial bla bla. Demanding better basic and advanced training of sport journalists requires talking about their economic situation. If their training is to be efficient and of a high standard we will still need independent professional sport journalists in the future. However, independent sport journalism has become almost impossible under the present conditions. Those who want to start a family and secure their retirement pensions depend on secure employment. The royalties presently paid are by no means sufficient to meet these demands particularly when considering the time-consuming work required for responsible journalism.

In the end this results in a growing number of part-time and hobby journalists, as they can be increasingly found in the field of sport coverage. It should also be recognized that this problem is to some extent responsible for or at least supports dubious companionship. To counter this development should actually be one of the fundamental duties of every sport journalist. They ought to recognize the importance of qualified training for the future existence of their profession. Their technical competence should only be considered a necessary basis, what is more important is the conscious reflection of their personal commitment. There should be no room for idolizing, petty jealousies and power struggles among radio and RV sport journalists. Instantly necessary, however, are intensive internal topical discussions, the exchange of experience, close cooperation with sport scientists and reading special literature. Those aspects which have been neglected in the past concerning junior training and qualification will have to be confronted speedily in a concentrated effort.

Final remarks

These ten expectations towards sport journalism are primarily based on observations presently to be made by external observers about sport journalists and their work. From the journalists' point of view they may be too far-reaching, premature, inadequate or even wrong. They will question their feasibility and refer to their specific working conditions. They will also point towards the pressures of topicality constantly forcing them to produce and deliver their work hastily, thus making ostensible pragmatism a major characteristic of sport journalism. They will also mention the hierarchical structure and organization of journalism, which disallows individual decisions, assigns pre-decided work to them and limits their choices as well as their freedom. Finally they will refer to the merchandise-character of journalistic production, which means that the criterion of saleability is the success criterion and that success is measured according to sales figures.

These arguments will have to be taken into consideration in future evaluations of journalistic performance, they can, however, serve as an alibi only to a limited extent in an attempt to escape critical, reflective as well as information- and education-oriented work in sport journalism. Our expectations towards sport journalism may be relativized by these arguments, but they will certainly not lose their justification.

With due scepticism I think that we can hardly expect sport journalism itself to initiate systematic change. The criticism of sport journalism has a long tradition, and another repetition of all the arguments is unlikely to bring about major changes. There are certainly some journalists who have undertaken a number of positive attempts, but all in all, those carrying responsibility in the editor's offices and studios are still repeating their stereotypic statements maintaining that the majority of recipients does not want to be confronted with the problems of sport, that they, however, seek entertainment and information, that soccer, and tennis are the most attractive kinds of sport to be presented, and that the audience wants results and absolutely topical information.

These statements will probably be maintained elsewhere, too, but nevertheless they have no solid foundation and should not be accepted uncritically. The impulse for change has to come from outside. It could be initiated by the recipients as well as sport organizations, by the churches, political parties or even by the government. Impulses could come from people not directly involved in the system of sport journalism, who have connection to insiders. But what is necessary is an impulse from outside, because social systems seek balance and harmony, they do not consciously initiate change. The sport journalists suffer from a lack of incentive for change, seeing no reason for it as the system works so smoothly with almost everybody making profit - and that is the point after all.

A *summary* of the criticism of sport journalism should contain the following key words:
Concerning the linguistic acts of commentators and TV-presenter: loud-mouthed, excessive use of superlatives, nationalistic tendencies, bombastic speech, political tactlessness, flowery expressions, not commenting on the actual pictures, low information and entertainment value of interviews, no inquiries and no problematization, no disagreement, frequent rhetorical questions, frequent self-answering of questions asked, informal addressing of athletes, not accepting athletes as equal partners, presenting themselves as the stars.

Table 23: Ten expectations about sport journalism

1. Sport journalists should take the recipients' wishes and interests seriously; sport coverage should be based on democratic principles.

2. In their reports sport journalists should give sufficient attention and the space it deserves to that world of physical activity and sport which they actually come across outside their offices and studios.

3. Sport journalists should present athletes as those individuals in our society they really are.

4. Sport journalists should know and reflect in their work that their professional field increasingly has socio-political implications and social functions.

5. Sport journalists should become aware of their educational responsibility.

6. Sport journalists should proceed with due caution when dealing with sport organizations, officials and athletes; this is necessary to enable them to fulfill their function of being detached instructors and critics at the same time.

7. Sport journalists should report competently on the basis of well-founded knowledge.

8. Sport journalists should use the whole array of available journalistic tools, and they should insist on the improvement of their present working conditions.

9. Sport journalists should use language that is appropriate for the coverage of sporting events and understandable for the recipients.

10. Sport journalists should make more efforts to receive better basic as well as advanced training, which must be expected due to their extraordinary position in our society.

Largely ignored are: technical explanation, precise descriptions of rules and actions in the various sport disciplines.

In the foreground are: tables, 1:0 journalism, figures and records.

Furthermore: TV-presenter seems to be a job for men only, women are discriminated against, the selection of presented material is imbalanced, it distorts reality, and the interests of the majority of recipients are disregarded, there is no real communication, the presented material lacks democratic justification, sport is not presented as a social reality but is reduced to show business, goals, gags; sport is being commercialized, and last but not least, sport is only statistics presented as pictures.

Chapter III:
Cooperation in Sport
with Developing Countries

Sport as a Means of Modernization in Developing Countries

1. The process of modernization - is there an alternative?

Since Gorbachev's Perestroika aimed at the transformation of Soviet society everybody has realized that the concept of modernization and the related theoretical arguments, which have been criticized for decades, are more attractive today than ever. There is no doubt that the transformation of the former Soviet societies will be based on the concept of modernization. In all of Eastern Europe modern western institutions are presently being adopted or reinvented. The same is happening in the southern hemisphere. Many developing countries quite understandably express the desire to learn from western societies what conditions are necessary for self-supporting economic growth and democratic structures, and how these conditions can be transformed to the societies of developing countries by means of developmental policies. In this process we realize that modernization theory, an American invention of the 1950s, is still valid today, its significance reaching far beyond the processes of industrial development. In the face of the failure of numerous development projects devised in accordance with a theoretical concept of modernization, the relevance of this theory must certainly be seen to be reduced. Many a project in Africa or South-East-Asia had unexpected negative side effects, some technological interventions were not accepted by the partners, measures designed in the First World failed due to an insufficient infra-structure in developing countries. The criticism indicating that the western model of modernization means the Americanization of the world's society (criticism of 'westernization') also seems to be justified. Some critical remarks of several schools of western marxism are also certainly worthwhile being discussed. The criticism rooted in the theory of imperialism and the resulting 'dependency theory' had strong effects everywhere in the Third World and doubtlessly contributed to the realization of key errors and mistakes in the concept of modernization, like, for example, the problematic role of the reactionary upper classes in developing countries. With due respect for the criticism of ideas concerning theoretical modernization, one thing, however, seems certain: the theoretical foundation, as presented, for example, by *Parsons* for American sociology or by *Zapf* in Germany, could not be shaken by it. The empirically apparent facts form a solid foundation for this basis. What are the characteristic features of this basis? In my view there are, primarily, six characteristics requiring our particular attention:

Firstly, essential features of a modern society are competitive democracy, a market economy, mass consumption and the idea of a welfare state.

Secondly, determinants of the modernity of a society are rationalism, activism, individualism and universalism (cf. *Münch* 1989). A non-modern society on the contrary, is characterized by social immobility, where education is not considered a civil right, and where conflicts are not actively resolved.

Thirdly, modern societies are defined by an efficient enforcement of civil and equal rights, by the recognition and resolution of social conflicts, by a diversity of social interests, and by the fact that elites are possible as well as desirable under certain circumstances.

Fourthly, it is especially important that modern societies are primarily characterized by allowing a rise in status and social mobility through growth of material affluence and wealth as well as fostering an increase of social competence for as many citizens as possible beyond the basic political and social rights.

Fifthly, it is worthwhile considering that in modern societies innovations by people acting individually and collectively and struggling against established interests must be permitted.

Finally modern society shows a tendency towards humanistic and ecological self-criticism (cf. *Luhmann* 1991, 92).

Thus modernization basically means rationalization and concentration on facts. A modern society consists of mobile individuals. Their mobility leads to an extension of their participation rights within the community or collective. My thesis, to be discussed on the basis of these characteristics, is the following:

Societies featuring the foregoing characteristics are more successful and more adaptable. That is: They are more modern than those which do not. The model of a modern capitalist society can be a suitable focusing point for the policies of developing countries, capable of guiding processes of reinvention as well as stimulating initiatives of 'self-invention'. Modern sport are a part of this model. Sport can take on an important catalyst function in processes of reinvention and self-initiation in developing countries.

Before explaining this thesis in greater detail, I would like to concentrate, as a second step, on some critical aspects characterizing the model of a modern society, which are important if developing countries choose to pursue this concept.

First, we have to consider that successful processes of modernization develop slowly and require many sacrifices. Particularly the success of some South-East Asian nations gives a clear picture of how time-consuming modernization processes are and what social, cultural and political conflicts accompany them. It also shows, however, that reinvention and self-invention are indispensable for the positive development of underdeveloped countries (cf. *Zapf* 1990a; *Menzel/Senghaas* 1986).

One of the fundamental questions concerns the sacrifices of modernization. A political concept aimed at the objective of modernization will continue to have problems. Criticizing the further modernization of our societies is justified. The frequently mentioned concern that 'we can't go on like this' points towards the social limitations of growth, the marginalization of population groupings, both in western societies and elsewhere, the meritable loss of our political capability to direct social systems, and to the global risks and dangers of world hunger and starvation, global pollution, climatic disaster, etc. Doubtlessly 'future' has a negative connotation for many people today. Now, at the turn of the century, we can observe the helplessness of scientists as well as politicians in the face of the structural impoverishment of the developing countries, unemployment, increasing inequality and the ecological crisis. In this respect the working population seems to be in a specific crisis. It seems that the social welfare state has spent its capital, because more and more workers are made redundant in the system of modern production.

We now have highlighted the central problems of modernization. The nature and dimension of these problems, however, can hardly be used as a principle objection against further modernization, especially because there is not a more efficient alternative to be seen. In the future we will rather have to put our hopes on the innovative capabilities of the basic institutions in modern societies, which means above all that these basic institutions will have to be preserved in the future. Modernization theory's answer to the various problems, probably has to be the same as the one it has given to those problems it has managed to solve in the past: the problems have to be distinguished and divided in terms of facts, time and social impact to strip them of their overwhelming dimensions. This means we need technical and social innovations for further differentiation and a rise in status or social mobility for the underprivileged groups (cf. *Zapf* 1990a, 21).

What sacrifices are justified if policies considered to be binding to the modernization process are to be pursued? This is one of the unanswered fundamental questions of the 20th century. The fear today that man's desire to rule over nature will lead to the inevitable destruction of the earth is justified more than ever. The fact that the successful management of problems of human life increasingly leads to destructive processes can be observed by almost everybody. The macabre side of enlightenment and modernity, the flip side of the modernity coin is becoming more and more obvious (cf. *Jaeggi* 1986, 26). Therefore we may justly ask why we don't abandon the individual, the human being, if their cognitive abilities and their moral competence are not sufficient for the solution of the most difficult problems. Why don't we at least give up the concept of rationalism and modernism in development policies? Why don't we pursue the concept that calls itself 'postmodernism' and pretends to solve at least some of the problems generated by 'modernity'? There is a lot of unnecessary argument in the philosophical and sociological dispute between representatives of post-modernity and those defending modernity. However, the fundamental aspects of this dispute clearly point out that modern society has become irreversible, having to rely entirely on itself with no way out to be seen. Functional differentiation and fully developed communication media have - after a modest beginning - acquired a dimension that can hardly be reduced again in the future. A concept of post-modernity therefore does not seem to be an adequate solution, neither in the sense of a backward turn, nor in the sense of hyper-modernity. *Luhmann* quite rightly points out that at a structural level there is absolutely nothing that deserves being called a solution for the problems caused by modernization (cf. *Luhmann* 1991, 101). Nor can the straight-forward, dogmatic defence of reason and progress, the uncritical clinging to ideas of evolution theory be a prospect for the further development of modernity. Socialist reality did, in fact, fail precisely because of this concept. The project of modernity rather has to follow Habermas' recommendations that the self-reassurance of modernity still needs to be stimulated by a consciousness in which historical as well as future-oriented thinking are fused together. In this respect enlightenment has to be understood as the courage to act with cool sobriety. This includes a farewell to matters of principle, man's liberation from controversies about absolutes as well as from ideological overburdening and its illusions. What we need is not resignation but moderation. However, pleasure, joy and creativity are also required (cf. *Jaeggi* 1986, 33). For this very reason it seems to be adequate that suitable modernization theories to a certain degree ought to be free of history and utopian ideas. They develop patterns neutral in terms of space and time for social development processes; the term modernization is no longer burdened with the notion of the completion of modernity (cf. *Jaeggi* 1986, 22). Modern society does not permit "ultimate ideas", it cannot bear authority and does not tolerate points of view from which other people's societies could conclusively be judged (cf. *Luhmann* 1991, 101).

2.   Sport - a phenomenon of modernity

You have probably been asking for quite some time how all this is related to sport and foreign aid in sport. Well, the answer is quite simple. The foregoing thesis has to be related to sport, and then could be phrased as follows:

Sport is a phenomenon of modernity. Promoting sport consequently means promoting the modernization of society.

Indeed, I maintain that sport can be an ideal means for the development of underdeveloped societies if these societies have the objective of transforming themselves into modern societies. This thesis must be well-founded, what I am going to try in my following analysis. I want to outline the modernity of modern sport and at the same time characterize them as an appropriate medium for a modern sport policy.

What characterizes the modernity of sport, what are their most significant modern features? In this respect we have to consider eight aspects:

1.   In modern sport we recognize a *specific rationality* based on the eco-system and thus representing the world picture of natural sciences. Modern sport is also determined by '*time*' largely similar to the use of the term 'time' in modern technology or modern administration. 'Time' in sport is defined by precision, quantifiability, universal applicability and an orientation towards the future.

2.   Modern sport is determined by *componentiality* and complexity. This can be experienced through clearly distinguishable components and structures which can be put together or assembled, like, for example, through talent-searching, training and competition. It tends towards bureaucratic organization, towards the division of labour, and thus towards the differentiation of their functions. In many of its apparent forms sport is to be characterized by its *complex structure of functions*, that is, practicing sport is an activity in which many different things happen simultaneously. This applies to the sporting activity itself as well as to the social processes related to it. Keeping pace with this complexity for the individual requires a specific adaptability of his or her consciousness. A special *way of thinking* is necessary.

3.   In modern sport *feasibility* can be experienced, a problem-solving attitude towards reality is dominant. Almost inexorably new techniques and skills are invented; the rules of sport are continuously changed and adapted in order to meet the needs of feasibility.

4.   Modern sport is characterized by *progressiveness*, recognizable in the fact that participation in sport is dominated by the principle of maximization. Thus sport reflects the engineering mentality of technical production, which makes sport unstable, never capable of remaining the same it is at a given point in time. Everything has to be improved continuously. The maxim being "higher - faster - longer".

5.   *Planning* is another characterizing feature of participation in modern sport. The desire to be successful in sport requires the long-term planning of activities. Weekly, monthly, yearly training schedules, diet and nutritional plans as well as competition calendars thus characterize modern high performance sport. Acting according to plans and schedules requires the ability to postpone immediate satisfaction in favor

of (a desired) long-term satisfaction, whose achievement requires accepting frustrations. Thus high performance sport has become a model of the principle of performance and achievement.

6. The modern system of sport is characterized by *sets of rules* which tend towards classification. For this reason we try to classify all new behavior patterns. The rules of sport are based on conventions and traditions, they require communication as a pre-condition and allow adaptation and change at the same time. It is essential that through rules in modern sport we enhance the expectation of *general justice*; therefore we assume that all athletes are basically equal. Thus the system of sport is tied to a moral standard. To keep up this moral structure of rules we need impersonal and official neutrality. Consequently every participant in sport may rightly expect that everybody is treated justly.

7. In modern sport the *control of emotions* is particularly significant. The refinement of this is a characteristic of the development of modern sport. This feature is also reflected in the further differentiation of rules in sport. Expressing emotions may be permitted, but only within a system of control.

8. A further characteristic of modern sport is the fact that *individuality* is desirable, which means the individual has a central position in sport, and individual values rank high in the hierarchy of values, comprising creative individual performances as well as aesthetic forms of prescribed behavior patterns. Individual freedom, individual autonomy and individual rights are taken for granted in sport as moral imperatives.

In my view these features of modern sport characterize the specific quality of modern sport in their reciprocal interrelation with modern society. They highlight the socializing potential inherent in sport. In this respect it is particularly important that these modern features primarily refer to those sport orientated towards the notion of competition. I maintain that these features contain the developmental potentialities which are supposed to bear fruit with projects of developmental cooperation in the field of sport.

3.   Modernization theory as a basis of sport-political intervention

The assumption which maintains that sport in its modern form contains developmental potentialities requires empirical proof. This proof has not yet been tried in any reliable and representative way, although quite a lot of evaluations of projects in Asia, Africa and Latin America may rightly indicate that there is, in fact, empirical evidence for this assumption (cf. *Digel* 1989). Its theoretical foundation and justification, however, are no less important. In this respect "The Homeless Mind. Modernization and Consciousness" by *Berger/Berger/Kellner* seems to be particularly valuable. According to their analysis, the development of a society to a modern one is primarily triggered by so-called "primary carriers", which are to be understood as 'technological production' and the 'bureaucratically organized state'. They are the carriers of modern consciousness and the cause of modernization. No less important for the progress of modernization are so-called "secondary carriers". These are 'social and cultural processes', their historical foundation being the primary carriers, but they are now capable of having their own independent impact. In *Berger/Berger/Kellner*'s view they comprise mass education, mass media, the private sphere of individual life, science as an institution but also urbanization and a mobilizing system of social stratification (cf. *Berger/Berger/Kellner* 1975). I tend to see sport as another independent secondary carrier of today's modern consciousness. The features of modern sport previously dealt with indicate that sport can be a very suitable carrier for developmental intervention. I am going to outline this by using three examples.

Example 1:
     It is very significant that even the most modern variants of sport feature traditional, as well as modern elements (cf. *Rittner* 1977). On the one hand there are superstition and scientific know-how and on the other hand irrational rituals and chance may appear along with calculation. These features highlight that sport may be suitable for mediating between polarized groups in a society on their way from tradition to modernity. In this respect one of the characteristics of sport is its potential for integration in terms of different ethnicities, social classes, age and gender groups. Thus sport obtains a mediating function between tradition and modernity. Whereas pre-modern manstems from an agonal culture, modern man is determined by the dominance of cognition. In sport especially physical action is important and considered equal to intellectual activity. Pre-modern man's first encounter with modern industrial production makes him realize that hard physical labour ranks beneath work of an intellectual nature. A miner, for example, has to accept that people working in offices, which requires neither physical strength nor is accompanied by unusual risks, earn higher wages. In the context of this learning process, teaching people that human performance is not only evaluated according to the physical strains required, sport as an agonal behaviour pattern can be an important assistance as a means of compensation.

Example 2:
     Sport can possibly also help to solve another typical problem of modernization policies. The division of human life into a private and public domain is characteristic for people pursuing their own paths to modernity. Today, this division is painfully forced upon people in many developing countries. Societies discerning a sensible and prudent path for themselves in the development towards greater modernity have to realize that they will need special assisting institutions in the field of social relations, because modern technological production generates anonymity with respect to the individual, and relationships are suddenly treated in the same manner as material objects in modern technology. This results in the permanent threat of anomy. For this very reason the social sector demands particular attention in any policy of modernization. It should be directed in a way which supports the individual against the unintentional effects of technological production. This requires structures of solidarity, and sport can be appropriate to this process, bridging the gap between private and public life, on the one hand by reflecting the intentional public structures through their ideal of justice and equality, and, on the other hand by providing the private feature of solidarity in their practice patterns. In this respect competition and association are the constituting factors of the sport system. Here, the function and role of sport as a mediating force, in the form of voluntary associations, becomes apparent. To a certain degree sport clubs are anti-modern, because they limit the mobility of their members. Consequently they are contradictory to the enlightened idea of a society consisting of an aggregate of freely acting members. However, this is the very basis of their integrating potential as a step towards modernity.

Example 3:
Furthermore, sport can be integrated into a modernization strategy not only because of their inherent combination of traditional and modern features but also because they distinctively contain and reflect the decisive values of the western world. As a system of symbols they are an appropriate means of demonstrating economic growth, free enterprise and a competitively based system of production to one's partners in developing countries. In the field of educational policies they can be an instrument of individual and social education, and in the sector of leisure-orientated consumer policies they can develop a future investment market with great potential. Thus sport can become a symbol of consumer and leisure orientation in developing countries in the same way as in western industrialized societies. Sport is an expression of modernity; modernity is a consequence or the result of social differentiation. Following this logic indicates that sport can contribute to development in the sense of modernization. Consequently, a developed society is characterized by a differentiated sport system featuring gyms, sport grounds, race tracks, professional and leisure sport as well as sport for people with disabilities.

My advocation of the modernization of underdeveloped societies through sport is based on the principle assumption that sub-systems within a society and their transfer effects on the consciousness of the individual are interdependent. I am therefore assuming that those elements of consciousness which are related to sport on the grounds of their close similarity can be transferred to other social areas, which are not directly related to sport. I am presuming sport can have effects similar to those of technological production. The assumption that these transfer effects exist is plausible in so far as they can be observed very frequently in the First World. Everyday life is, in fact, in all areas continuously confronted with material objects and processes resulting from technological production. In this respect sport seems to represent the behaviour model that is - more than anything else - very closely related to technological production on account of similar characteristics. The everyday consciousness as required in sport is congruent with scientific ideology and the technological mentality characterizing modern society in general. So, modern sport has become an independent secondary carrier, having their own ideology with an inherent dynamic capable of influencing or even generating processes of modernization.

4. On the necessity of a relative perspective

The potential of sport as an element of modernization, however, should not be overestimated. This becomes obvious when observing those three areas of development usually to be distinguished in modernization processes: industrial-economic development, social and political development.

Industrial and economic development has to aim at a fair distribution of resources and income, hence, at an economic system with an effective social structure. A just distribution of land and the smallest possible concentration of income appear to be particularly important and useful conditions in this respect (cf. *Menzel/Senghaas* 1986, 27 - 38).

The process of the political development of a society should aim at the progressive rationalization of the political system of government. The objective ought to be, above all, the enforcement of the rights of political participation for all citizens, that is, the outdated unequal distribution of political power and economic opportunities has to be overcome.

In the field of social development we have to initiate a process of change or transition, liberating the people from outdated traditional ties. Thus new forms of communication can be established, extending the sphere of direct experiences of primary groups such as relations within the family, at the workplace and among friends. The main indicators of this process are urbanization, the expansion of primary or elementary education as well as the degree of people's exposure to the influence of mass communication (cf. *Brandt* 1972, 62).

In each of these areas of development sport can, at the most, play a secondary role, even though sport seems to be an appropriate means for the third area due to their particular adaptability.

But the overestimation of sport is dangerous for another reason. The advocation of sport as presented here is generalized in the same way as the arguments of modernization theory. Theories of modernization tend towards outlining the conditions which have to be fulfilled to make industrialization a success. By and large they describe stages of development that have to be passed through on the way to industrialization and which are similar or equal to those passed through by industrialized societies. Thus development is a non-linear process (cf. *Lerner* 1970). In 1968, *Bendix* pointed out that these ideas are based on the unacceptable generalization of a limited historical experience (cf. *Bendix* 1968, 212). Today this criticism is more valid than ever. Many comparative studies show that it is irrelevant to comprehend industrial development as a uni-linear process. Rather there is a whole variety of alternative ways of developing, delineated by specific historical reference points. A generalizing model, however, obscures the insight into the independence and singularity of historical development processes. Even the inflexible distinction between tradition and modernity seems to be rooted in a problematical philosophical tradition that fails to hold its ground when evaluated on the basis of historical facts (cf. *Bendix* 1968). Here, too, *Luhmann* is right in observing that "today's features of modernity are neither yesterday's nor tomorrow's, and this is exactly what makes them modern" (*Luhmann* 1991, 89). .

The general development potential outlined here thus requires relativization. The functions of sport in the process of development may vary significantly from one developing country to another. Just like the economic conditions of industrialization in a developing country are dependent on the corresponding non-economic institutional conditions, the development of sport in these countries is determined in a specific manner by these factors. What is more, all functionalization of sport is problematical. Its hypothetical character is apparent. However, this need not be a disadvantage for the decisions necessary in the field of developmental cooperation in sport. If sport science has not so far been able to provide a definite answer to the question, whether sport, rightly or not, can be attributed certain functions, then this primarily points to the deficiencies of sport science. The relevance of certain assumptions about the significance or importance of sport, however, can hardly be diminished by this fact.

Finally, I want to emphasize once more, that, as a consequence of modernization processes in developing countries, sport is also very likely to develop. In societies featuring partial systems like education, health care and mass media the development of sport as a consequential system is very likely. But sport is not only a necessary result in the modernization process of a society. They are also to be seen as a symbolic amplifier system corresponding with the concept of modernity to a large extent. Through their bi-polarity of competition and cooperation sport represents - in their systematically organized forms - the eminent and typical features of modernity, they represent it for "technological production" as well as "modern bureaucratic administration", and athletes show the same features of identity and characteristics as "modern personalities".

Cooperation in Sport with Developing Countries - Understanding Foreign Characteristics, Learning From Each Other

Sport is characterized by having various important functions in society; that applies to sport in developing countries just as much as to sport in industrial nations. The person doing sport in Indonesia can justify his action as well as any member of a sport club, who has newly joined the senior group. Many of these functions of sport and the explanations given for the meaning of sport are debatable. Especially when it has to be proved empirically that sport really meets the meaning or the functions assigned to them. The biological functions are questioned as well as the social functions of integration which are assigned to the sportsman. Sportsmen are little concerned by such doubts. They do not need a justification for doing sport; they "believe" that sport is a fun thing to do, that it is healthy and gives them the opportunity to meet interesting people and, not least, they think it is sensible compensation for the strains caused by their work. Competitive sport - from its very first moment of existence - sought legitimation in the explanation that competition offers the chance to get to know other people, cultures, political systems and societies; and that this is reason enough to promote such sport events like the Olympic Games, World Championships and (international) contests between national teams. The belief that sport gives the opportunity for meeting and communicating with foreign people and that sport helps to understand each other holds justification enough for those people performing or having performed in one of the sport events mentioned. Despite all the criticism that has been voiced this belief is still prevalent. It is based on various experiences and is therefore plausible and reliable. Thus it is not surprising that these positive functions of sport are listed in connection with sport as a measure for development aid. Thus developmental cooperation in sport can be suitable - or perhaps is especially appropriate for mutual communication and learning between different cultures, for enjoyable contacts and the exchange of experiences between people from different worlds. These opportunities in sport shall be the subject of the following discourse, taking into account that the meeting of the so-called developed world and the developing countries in sport still is far too often moulded by protective treatment, a know-all manner and a tendency of imperial or even neo-colonial boasting behaviour. To change this negative image for the better shall be the scope of the following reflections.

1. Handball is not always equal to handball

More than 10 years ago I had for the first time the chance to travel to Africa as a representative of the National Olympic Committee (NOC) of West Germany. There my task was to instruct physical education teachers, coaches and coaches-to-be in modern team-handball. Before I started my journey I had accepted two fundamental assumptions. The NOC, as well as I, believed that playing team-handball at school and in leisure time could be a sensible activity for Africans. What is more, I believed that teaching handball in Africa must be similar to the methods used in Europe and that therefore I, as a European person could act as handball instructor with a clear conscience. During my first action as a so-called sport expert on a further training course for African physical education teachers in Togo and on a training course for representative coaches in Ghana I soon had to experience that both assumptions are valid to a very limited extent only.

Team-handball in Africa is - so I thought - handball under less desirable conditions. There would be a lack of suitable facilities and balls. Seeing the handball stadium in Lome (Togo) I soon was taught otherwise. Under virtually ideal conditions there was a stadium at my disposal for the training course, with a regular field, which was made of well contrasting colored asphalt and which was equipped with proper goals. There was a large covered stand, which also provided the silence required for my theoretical course. These were the facilities and conditions for team-handball I found in Togo, one of the smallest countries of Africa.

In Ghana, only 100 km away from Togo, as well as in some native countries of the course members (Benin, Niger or Mali) there are neither handball stadiums nor regular handball fields. Empty fields and parking lots are reserved for handball. There is a shortage of balls, and schools only have improvised equipment; proper footwear is far too expensive for students and athletes. Goals are two simple posts, if existing at all. We have to point out that such features cannot be interpreted as an indication for underdevelopment or even as an example for an alleged inability of the people living in those countries; for if we take the situation in West Germany after the Second World War, only 40 years ago, we see that the conditions for team-handball were very similar.

These exterior conditions of handball already show that there is no such thing as one African kind of handball: handball in Bourkina Faso and Benin - countries in which more than half the population suffers from malnutrition - is bound to be different from handball along the Ivory Coast or in Togo. And in Tunesia or Egypt handball is incomparably more developed than in any other country in Black Africa. Not least the different colonial backgrounds of the various African countries have influenced the development of handball. There are countries with British influence where until now handball is nearly unknown. Whereas in countries with French influence handball is played on a technically high standard. Technically some teams have reached the standard of any European top team. Such progress can be attributed to the fact, at least to some extent, that European coaches have given them intensive training. What is more, this progress is limited to a few teams, often only to the international team. Industrial countries of the First World describe this kind of support with the rather dubious term "foreign aid in sport". Not least politicians, but also sport officials, praise this supposedly very inexpensive but therefore very effective interference of successful eastern and western sport nations with developing countries.

Thus again and again the attempt is made to adapt people of the developing countries to conform to sport patterns as they have proved to be worthwhile in Europe. You can call it either good or bad luck that such an adaptation has yet failed to succeed. There are different reasons for that.

2. Features of distinction

The reason for practising sport being a different matter in Africa, Asia or Latin America than in England, Austria or Germany can be found first and foremost in the difficult general conditions for sport in developing countries. My first day of training in Togo led to such dehydration in my body, which in Europe can only be observed in wrestling, when athletes lose weight quickly in order to be allowed to a lower weight category. Training was possible only in the time between 6 and 9 a.m. and between 5 and 7 p.m. For the planning of the course I had to take into account the heat on the one hand and the dusk, which quickly led to pitchdark night - only to be illuminated by candlelight or a campfire - on the other hand. Training and playing team-handball under tropical conditions with 38 degree Celsius in the shade and 85 % humidity can be compared to heavy construction work in a city in Northern Europe in mid-summer. The length and the intensity of training have to be subordinated to these conditions, and this is one reason why the competitiveness and the standard of athletes and teams in the tropics can be developed and increased to a limited extent only compared with the standard of competitiveness in Europe. The health and the nutritional situation of the population have also an impact on the development of handball. Players lacking basic foods over a length of time cannot maintain regular intensive training. Here, it is a question if it is at all sensible to support the establishment of a system of sport, considering the fact that athletes at the same time endanger their health through taking part in sport. A risk whose consequences cannot yet be estimated.

Regardless of whether an answer to this question will be found; with climate and nutrition we have two factors at hand which challenge European sport experts to develop a certain sensibility if they really want to become partners of athletes in developing countries. These two factors lead us to look for assumptions that can explain why sport in this world differs crucially from sport in our industrial culture. Sport in developing countries grows in a very distinct way, due to the fact that the people belong to a different culture, live in a different environment and a different society. Ethnic distinctions are just as important in this respect as religious ones. Basketball in Nigeria therefore is bound to be different from basketball in Malaysia. The affiliation to a certain tribe or race also mould the mental abilities and the physical shape of the body.

The Islam influences the attitude towards the human body and thus towards sport in different ways than Buddhism or Hinduism. With social experiences, obtained in extended families in a rural environment - based on subsistence economy - the introduction to sport is another one than when living in a big city's ghetto without receiving formal education, without having family ties and without any perspectives. Something else affecting the formation of sport in developing countries is the fact that people in other societies and cultures do not necessarily strive for the same goals as for example people in Sweden. In this respect the materialistic attitude can be as strange to developing countries as the entire system of values of modern and postmodern life, to which people of the post-industrial society correspond.

In sport such discrepancies can be found in all possible variations. Why is it that in Malaysia, a country with a population consisting of 55 % Malaysians, 34 % Chinese and 10 % Indians, Indians tend to play hockey and here often produce especially successful athletes, whereas Chinese mostly gather to play basketball, table tennis and badminton and the Malaysians in this multi-national state are likely to play football, cycle or prefer unarmed combat disciplines? Why do school classes and the staff of banks and firms march publically on the streets in Indonesia, wearing colorful uniforms, and hold competitions during those marches? And why are Sepak Takraw championships held in the event of the Asian Games? Why is it that in some Saudi-Arabian countries the use of sport facilities is organized in a way that men and women do not use them at the same time? Is sport developing differently in Islamic countries according to the prevalent beliefs? Is sporting activity equally acceptable for Sunnites and Schiites? Those and other questions occur when observing closely the variety of sport in developing countries as they are established today, and when comparing it to our industrial, e.g. developed, country. It is essential not to expect that everything works in the same way as we are used to in Europe. When obeying this rule we cannot only help our partners in developing countries more efficiently, but - first and foremost - we ourselves can learn from it. Thus the connection between sport of the developed and the developing world can become a special type of intercultural communication. This will not always yield positive results. Anyway, the degree of experiences which possibly can be obtained by German coaches, physical education teachers, sport scientists and sport journalists during their work as experts in developing countries proves that we can get good results.

3.   The principle of "winning" is relative

During the team-handball class mentioned, which I taught in Togo, the participants had many of problems learning the skills and tactics of handball. It was especially difficult for my African colleagues to attack their opponents cleverly such as European players usually do. Furthermore, it was difficult for them to apply a systematical manner of playing so that the aim, to win the game, remained the crucial scope of the game; something which for European players appears to be self-evident. Often they were clumsy in using their body in the game, fouls were too obvious, not very cunning; when fouling, it happened in an extraordinarily hard and clumsy manner, not aiming at the actual purpose. Over and over again during the game I was able to observe unnecessary artistic "interludes". The players reacted with laughter and delight when someone messed up a throw. Both teams laughed when the keeper made funny movements during the attempt to catch the ball. In class with German sport students - people who often are even less talented and motivated than their African colleagues - it has proved to be worthwhile to confront the students with a special problem. I ask them to play handball in mime. This method I have chosen in order to examine if the students understand the concept of the game. Apart from not having a ball the game proceeds as usual, all the normal rules are valid. Compared with a handball game with a ball I observed that, above all, teams which normally are apt in playing are virtually incapable of playing handball in mime. For example before one minute has elapsed the students do not know who is in possession of the ball. Suddenly two or three balls are in the game; no one knows exactly what to do. During the handball training course in Togo mentioned above I set the same problem for the African colleagues. However, the result turned out to be different. Handball in mime played by African players differs distinctly from the manner in which Germans handle the problem. The game was characterized by liveliness and lots of laughter. It lasted for ten minutes. Two teams were opposing each other, there were two goals, a regular field, and the players never lost the ball. When an attacking player was feinting, a defender cleared the situation using the appropriate movements. When a player tried to score a goal the keeper tried to save the ball. I experienced the handball pantomime of the African players as a perfect non-lingual system of communication. Is it that Africans have a special ability for pantomime? Is it that the game concept of both, Africans and Europeans, is different? Is it that Europeans want to win; does every European player want to score whereas Africans mainly want to enjoy playing? Is their playing less competitive, more cooperative and focussing on solidarity? What is the scope of Africans playing? Why is it that they are able to apply tactics without the ball while they tend to do solo runs, play more individually and less cooperative by the ball? *Nitschke*, a socio-historical scientist, made some important observations on this issue: In most European sport disciplines the athlete's attention is directed to a target which lies outside his body, e.g. in high jump. One has to jump as high as possible over a bar. As opposed to that in most sport cultures outside Europe the athlete's attention is aimed at his own body. He makes experiences with his body, e.g. in all variations of the traditional judo as well as in many African dances. It is not the principle of beating which constitutes the partner's scope of all efforts in judo. Instead, experiences with giving way to or diverting movements are main features of Asian unarmed combat disciplines. With non-European movement patterns people obviously can make different experiences from those made in European sport (cf. *Nitschke* 1985). Are such experiences useful for Europeans? Indian yoga exercises, Asian unarmed combat disciplines and African dances seem to clearly prove this fact. But do Europeans make the same experiences as Chinese, black and Indian people? There are many of questions to be answered. In my view, they are worthwhile being discussed.

4.   Our values do not have to match with those of our partners

The next example also deals with team-handball. In the event of a training course in Padang, Sumatra, an island more than 10.000 km away from Togo, handball was on schedule. After an exhausting course of lectures the Indonesian participants played handball together with three German colleagues. The Indonesian teachers had become interested in the game to which they had been introduced by two German sport experts. They were prepared to establish regular training in their leisure time from then on - as the first Indonesian handball team, as it was. Their play was moulded by the well known movement patterns of basketball. Similar to the play of their African colleagues a certain talent for artistic throws was apparent. The Europeans present experienced the game as problematic in many respects due to the fact that - being educators - they always combined sport with educational scopes. Among the Indonesians a typical reaction to a mishap commited by one of the players during the game was gloating. Once in possession of the ball the players tried to score by doing solo runs. Even in positions without any chance to score they made an attempt. Such a play, from a Euro-educational point of view, is regarded as unfair and anti-social. Thus, we would think that social learning is what those players required.

But both, this analysis as well as the conclusion, are nothing but rash; and from the Indonesians' point of view it would be even wrong. When I pointed out my observations after the game the Indonesians were amazed by the worries I had expressed. Neither those who had laughed nor those who had to "tolerate" the laughter regarded their actions as a problem. They did not perceive the solo runs, the supposedly unfair throws just above the keeper's head as negative actions as Europeans would do.

What is the conclusion we must draw from this experience? Surely it would be erroneous to deduce that everything is relative, and that in the final analysis no universal statements can be made. However, it seems worthwhile to say that other cultures have different values, and that therefore in sport not necessarily the same values and norms that we regard as right have to be valid.

Similar observations could be made on the training of Nigerian athletes, on physical education classes in Madagascar, on handball and football matches in Egypt and on competitions in Venezuela, Malaysia or Indonesia. In all these countries and many more we can observe that only at first glance sport appears to be always the same. With the help of internationally accepted rules Indians can compete with Columbians in any sport discipline they like, likewise French or German sportsmen can compete with athletes from Morocco or Madagascar. Yet, if we take a closer look at the performance in the various disciplines we always have to question who is doing sport and which discipline is performed by what kind of person. We have to ask ourselves what are the disciplines in which women are allowed to participate, or from which they are excluded? Who are the people supporting sport and what is their incentive to do so? Asking those questions we soon realize that sport in developing countries offers a wide variety. We ought to take advantage of this fact and respect it highly. For Europeans this appears to be not quite as simple as it seems. Here are two further examples.

5.   Not everything can be inferred rationally

The first example shows the experience of a colleague who has been working as a football instructor in Togo. The fact that sport experts, when successful, enjoy a privileged status in societies of underdeveloped countries may well be considered unfortunate. The fact that success in a Junior World Championship or in an Africa Cup is no evidence for an actual development is most obvious, when looking back on 40 years of German sport aid. However, it is also worth to be mentioned that we as well can learn from the other cultures, the players and our partners. This is the reason to quote passages out of a letter of a German colleague: "Togo will be in the 1987 Junior World Championship in Chile! I can hardly believe it, but it is true. Playing against Morocco, the No 1 in African soccer, we have qualified for the final in South America. All Togo is out of control. For the first and maybe for the last time a team of Togo will participate in a World Championship, playing against the best in the world. Never before have I had to shake so many hands. Strangers congratulated the team and me in the streets; from everywhere we heard: 'Entraineur merci, maintenant on va chercher la Coup du Monde'. Well, this we will never achieve but just to participate is great ...".

My colleague describes how this sensational success in the qualifying round against Morocco took place under difficult circumstances. Since he can explain the success of his team only partly, such observations that people often smile at, hardly ever believe and normally even despise have been important to him. "However, football in Africa is a different thing, much more emotional on the field as well as among the spectators. For the first time in many years the stadium of Lomé was nearly sold out and from many corners we could hear the noises of the drums, which were meant to support us. But maybe it was an entirely different kind of support which influenced the result much more decisively. I mean the witch-doctors who had bewitched the rival team and the goals and who had exactly predicted the match's course and result. I don't believe in such things (not yet). However, it was imposing to see the measures taken by the witch-doctors and the team. My team started to impress the Moroccan rivals from the first moment on, when they loudly sang a battle song. Their skipping and jumping around during the official presentation and in the time between the two national anthems gave the opponent an idea of our determination. Psychologists will rate all this old hat. Though in connection with the following actions many of those details become more important and intensify the impression. A special liquid was spilled on the surprised Moroccan players by two witch-doctors, when they left the changing-room. Simultaneously the witch-doctors spelled them with magic formula. They took care that no drop of the magic liquid was spilled on us. Similarly they bewitched the teams' benches and goal - a rite which the whole audience enjoyed. The Moroccans noticed it with great dismay. A piglet and a goat were driven through the goal and many other things were done ...".

As a conclusion of these observations he writes in his letter: "Our German-European way of thinking and rating things cannot serve as a model for African behaviour patterns. Altogether we must say: The more we live here the more important African issues and problems become for us. Europe, so strong in terms of technology and economy, loses more and more of its significance. Europe is only a small part of the world compared with Africa; but it tends to take itself too seriously - it is too egoistically interested in its own progress, likely to forget the Third World." Cultural openness seems to be the maxim this German soccer coach recommends to us concerning sport in developing countries.

If we are prepared to such open-mindedness we can spare us some disappointments in our cooperation in the sector of sport. Often European sport experts as well as North-American experts tend to expect their partners in developing countries to be grateful in order to achieve appreciation for their work. Thus a German sport scientist, who fell ill during a stay as an expert in a developing country, wrote: "Four days now I have been lying down with fever, headaches, diarrhea and a lack of appetite. Now I can see how I receive all the gratitude I deserve for all the years here. As long as I am healthy, as long as I commit myself to the work, as long as I function well, I'm welcome and I'm interesting for my colleagues. Now that I am ill my colleagues visit me only scarcely. As soon as I have regained my strength they will start again to get on my nerves, to fleece me, to beg for help for their work from me, to invite me to events and ask me for presents and souvenirs. In such situations as now I consider my colleagues' mentalitiy to be unbearable, but there is nothing I can do. On the treadmill of everyday's life when I feel fit again, when I work together with them all day long such things are pushed into the background. I ignore such things or I often don't allow them to affect me." This German colleague's consternation is understandable. However, it might help him if he learned from this example that he was judging his colleagues by European moral standards. Those standards must not necessarily apply to other cultures. Forms of gratitude need not be universal and helpfulness need not apply to the same circle of persons as it is customary in Europe. To be aware of this, of course, does not mean that this colleague's discontent is overcome automatically. But it probably helps to cope with the situation if he stops blaming others.

6.   Standards for successful cooperation

Fifteen years have passed since my first employment in Togo. Nearly every year I have had the opportunity to present my knowledge in sport science and practice to partners in developing countries, thanks to sport aid programs of the Federal Government of Germany organized by the National Olympic Committee, by the agency of technical cooperation (GTZ), by institutes of sport science at German universities and by many other sponsors. It seems reasonable to ask if it is sensible at all to send sport experts to developing countries with the aim of helping those partners in establishing appropriate structures in sport. In the past this question has been answered in various ways. Taking into account the German government's scopes, stated in their sport commentary on this issue, it appears to be reasonable to send German experts e.g. to Kenia, Madagascar, Burundi or Malawi, Ruanda or Ecuador every year. Their task is to smooth the way for a cultural cooperation with countries with which up to now no close links have existed in terms of cultural and scientific relations. The expert working on this field of sport is expected to provide an impetus for progression in development, in such way that by transferring the learned behavior of individuals or groups, other sectors in society can benefit, so we assume. Communication between different ethnic and social groups is what is to be encouraged. Social barriers are to be gradually eliminated by practising sport. Thus the establishment of homogenous communities will be brought about. Physical education it is hoped will help organizing structures in developing countries in a more dynamic way, structures which so far are often static and are hindering further development.

The question if these scopes really can be met, if they will be met and if, in a final analysis, it is desirable for the progress of underdeveloped countries to meet them has so far not been answered adequately. Taking stock we must say that successes in German policy of sport development have been rather modest. This result has to be admitted especially if we regard as scope the establishment of a sport system equal to the one in Germany. Comparing the present situation with the one fifteen years ago, in Togo as much as in many other countries, it seems that - from Germany's point of view - sport development has stagnated. Progress with which scope whatever does apparently not take place.

However, we must ask if this is an appropriate judgement of taking stock and of defining values. It is not only in the field of sport that we have long since realized that many a development aid project has failed to succeed because the socio-cultural conditions have not sufficiently been taken into consideration. Often the reasons lie in the attitude of governments in developing countries themselves. They have a rather ambivalent attitude towards their own tradition and history and therefore towards wide sections of the population. At the same time the reasons can be found in the concepts of aid programs of industrial nations. It is not unusual that these concepts are mainly designed to overcome ancient cultural values, traditions and ethnological findings. Animism and magic cults need not necessarily represent obstacles for progress, as in the world of sport still is believed, today. With this we do not want to support the "yearning for wilderness" in sport. We must not consider everything suspicious or dangerous that cannot be justified rationally. However, it is advisable to employ caution and discretion in intercultural judgments. Applying such an attitude it should be possible to find in other cultures what we miss in our own without being taken in for commercial exoticism. Such a boom of commercializing everything African or Indian as attractions is already taking place at present.

We must not accept everything offered by foreign cultures, and in reverse our culture cannot always be accepted by our partners. Abandoning newborn babies, stoning adulteresses and ritual sacrifices are elements of cultures which do not deserve to be regained or adapted by other cultures. Cultural identity should not become an end in itself. Cultural relativism ends at the point where slavery, apartheid or fascism start.

7.   There is no demand for ethno-centrism in sport

In the field of sport in intercultural contacts such extremes are hardly of any importance. Here it is much more significant that sport representatives of the First World realize that the assumption that sport constitutes a culturally homogenous sector is completely wrong, even in view of the original home countries of the Olympic Games. There are still some Olympic officials supporting this theory. Not only by chance do we distinguish between the playful manner of southern countries and the vigorous manner of playing soccer in England. Fist ball is a predominantly German game; whereas cricket and rugby are at home in anglo-saxon regions, and lacrosse is a typical feature of French and Spanish speaking countries. Such differences can be denied only if one estimates the world of sport in an ethno-centrical way, i.e. from one standardized, exclusively true point of view.

To give up such ethno-centrism also means accepting that sport, in order to be enjoyable, not always have to be performed just as perfectly, luxuriously and expensively as we are used to today. Balls made of banana leaves, skipping ropes made out of rubber from old tires, batons out of bamboo, self-meshed goal or volleyball nets, self-constructed sport facilities - there are enough examples which show clearly that sport culture is possible without three stripes, DIN norms, plastics, without luxury in sport and sport industry.

Sport comprises the extraordinary opportunity to be able to mediate between cultures which in their future process of development cannot remain detached. Mediation here means "giving and taking", we have to co-operate so that both sides contribute their abilities. The one-way street on which e.g. German sport promotion is proceeding must be equipped with new traffic signs. "Beware! Oncoming traffic!", should read the hint which draws our attentions to experts of foreign cultures who have joined us to broaden our own sport and exercise culture. Not basketball, tennis nor any further disciplines in swimming, athletics or gymnastics should be admitted as Olympic disciplines. Rather is it about time to allow that sport patterns of other cultures such as Capoeira or Sepak Takraw are introduced to the Olympic Games.

This is especially important because for some time now we have observed a change in mind on the cultural sector in developing countries. The sole concentration on achievements of industrial societies as orientation for their policies has confronted developing countries, especially on the cultural sector, with a threat to their original traditions. Therefore we can detect in nearly all these countries a recollection of almost forgotten games and dances (nevertheless, energy and expenditure spent on modern sport are obviously higher, and the recollection of original tradition is often linked with and motivated by tourism and folklore). However, in such a manner a situation has risen in the developing world in which a meeting of modern sport and a culture of games and other motions is taking place; and the latter is claiming its own rights. If modern sport does not take this as a threat but rather as a challenge then an interesting mutual learning on the sector of sport could be achieved in the near future.

8. Mutual learning does not mean domination

We should not misunderstand the meaning when talking of mutual learning as a maxim for meetings with athletes from the developing world. Far too often for "learning" we imply as an equivalent "knowing everything, down to the smallest detail". Our world outlook is scientifically oriented, and thus we hold an insatiable curiosity. Even those people who in public demonstrate an aversion against everything scientific, which nowadays has become popular and attractive, are moulded by this view. We want nothing to remain mysterious. Especially in meeting with foreign cultures campaigns for comprehension take place which often have no other scope than the domination of what is comprehended. Marianne Gronemeyer, a German theologian, precisely discribed this phenomenon: "Comprehension often is acquired by mowing down everything". What is it sport experts in developing countries can learn from this? When cooperating with partners of developing countries we should try to put ourselves in our partner's position, we should look at our sport disciplines from their point of view and give their sport disciplines the same weight as ours. We should take up what is useful for us of their experiences and pass on those experiences we believe to be of use for our partners. However, we should also accept the limits of comprehension, that is to say, we must learn to respect differences and contrasts. Differences, not uniformity is what constitutes the variety of a culture. Especially in sport, in view of a dangerous but welcome tendency to unification this realization is worthwhile being considered. Far too quickly and often untimely embraces take place between sportsmen or sport officials at meetings of developed and developing nations. The saying "We are one big family" in sport often generates a feeling of "We agree with each other" where such understanding is not asked for.

This does not only apply to inter-cultural meetings in sport. What is desirable in sport should be required in political meetings with representatives of developing countries as well. In conclusion, this realization shall be further clarified by remarks made by the German President Richard von Weizsäcker:

"If we offer just money and technical aid to people in underdeveloped countries they will accept it just as passively as they accept misery and dependency, today. If we intend to convert them in their religious beliefs they will not understand us. However, if we learn that for example their Coran contains all the advice and ethical incentives necessary - up to the point of family planning - then we can support them better to help themselves actively by taking advantage of our aid. Here, cooperation in development programs starts to become mutual giving and taking. In the course of centuries our own culture has become a certain scientific-technological civilization. Gradually such an intellectual way of thinking has eliminated alien elements and is consistently heading towards computerization. This is the perspective which determines most of our needs and scopes. Within this development we feel superior to other cultures. However, those other cultures have different standards. They do not rate the law of cause and effect to be important. They do not construct right angles. They have a different understanding of time and space as well as of the nature of death. Their relation to living and dead ancestors is a different one. They believe in energies and powers which cannot be proved by a right-or-wrong test. Powers that, even though we unfortunately cannot see them, offer this to nature, to the position and value of a human being and to ethics of truly human social life! And every system of values that allows human dignity is justified, it is "life-fostering".

Sport Development in Young Nations - Some Recommendations

1. Sport in the process of development

What is to be understood by the definition of an underdeveloped country? This is a question which can be answered with reference to the background of the conception of a developed society. In common theoretical discussions about questions concerning foreign aid it has meanwhile become customary to document conditions of underdevelopment with statistical data. Most significant are the demographic situation and the per capita income, the health conditions of the populations, the quality of public communication, the achieved technological standard, the life expectancy of the population, the nutritional situation of the people and the distribution of wealth. These indicators for development are fixed by the western industrial nations as well as the quality border data which tolerate a decision about the question concerning underdevelopment and development.

If one looks closer at the economic discussions on development and underdevelopment it has to be noticed that sport in this type of debate is not an issue. Whether sport is practised in a country or not, seems at first glance not to be an indicator for development or underdevelopment. Sport neither seems to have caused underdevelopment, nor has it promoted the process of it. The situation of sport looks totally different, if we try to answer the question which features an ideal model could have for the development of a less developed country. Depending upon the different developmental political strategies and different conceptions of objectives, sport can have different functions. If we want to present these facts, above all, we can distinguish between three different concepts (cf. Table 24).

First of all, there is the ideal of a developed society which is characterized by the features of democratic industrial and consumers society. The ideal for this are western industrial nations, because a free social trade and market system is looked upon as the suitable instrument for the distribution of earned wealth.

In this concept of development sport can play an important role. As a symbolic system it is suitable for demonstrating economic growth, free enterprise and competitively orientated production in a metaphorical way to our partners in developing countries. In the field of educational policy sport can be an instrument of individual and social education, and in the area of recreationally orientated consumer policy sport can develop a profitable investment market for the future. Just as sport have become a symbol of a consumer and recreationally orientated society in the western industrial nations, this should also match with developing countries. Sport is an expression of modernity, modernity an impression of development. If one follows this line of thought the assumption suggests itself that sport can make a contribution to development. A developed society distinguishes itself accordingly among other things by gyms, sport fields, race tracks, professional sport, recreational sport, sport for people with disabilities etc.

Table 24: The role of sport in developing countries

Condition of underdevelopment	Process of development	Condition of development
■ low income per person	modernization à la capitalism	democratic industry society
■ high mortality rate		
■ low life expectancy		
■ bad health conditions		
■ low savings investment quote	modernization à la socialism	socialistic industry society
■ low public communication		
■ low technological standard		
■ inadequate nutrition situation	strategy of dissociation	dissociated society
■ unjust division of wealth		
■ unfavorable demographic situation		
■ inadequate educational and cultural org.	basic needs strategy	autonomous society with relative economic dependency
■ (...)		
s p o r t ?	s p o r t ?	s p o r t ?

At a first glance the role of sport in a developmental process of a young nation looks totally different, if one looks at the second model for development. Contrary to the foregoing philosophy of development this condition of development presents itself differently for socialist countries, and therefore for all those developing countries which have socialist-orientated politics. The idea of an ideal socialist society is the point of orientation for development. Private property is of minor importance only. The central point of this policy is the human relation between socialistic personalities and sport. Therefore it seems to suggest itself that a strategy of modernization is limited first of all to a developmental aid policy of the western industrial nations. Looking closer this proves to be superfluous, because the means of directing the process from underdevelopment to development by socialist countries are also definitely to be understood as methods of modernization. According to this, sport has an important position in the model of a socialist society. Sport and physical culture are indicators for the standard of development of the so-called socialist personality. Therefore it is not a surprise that socialist countries look upon the development of sport as an important vehicle to transport their idea of a socialist society as a model of development for developing countries. By the way, we have to state today, that it does not work.

Besides the named models of development a third model has been tried to be realized for some time. A few developing countries neither saw a socialist nor a democratic consumer society as their developmental objective. It is more desirable to develop conditions in which developing countries develop their own cultural identity independent of other societies, that social justice and the satisfaction of basic needs are a matter of fact, and that growth takes place within the system of society, which is in harmony with nature as well as in harmony with the needs of the people. Participation in political decisions, work for all and the chance of political, social and economic equality are in this respect further aims characterizing the desired conditions of development. The differences between societies, nations and cultures are accepted as something desirable, particularly in relation to this model or ideal. This must not be obscured by the point of reference "Socialism", nor by the point of reference "Capitalism". The process from underdevelopment to development will not be pushed ahead through an exclusively externally directed programme of modernization, or through one-sided industrialization of society. It is rather suggested that the development in the country itself be undertaken if possible without external help. This means a strategy of dissociation is suggested, and an inwardly focused development is to be striven for. At most, a selective cooperation with developed countries is the only possible consideration. Or else the principle of self-governing is in the focus of attention. In this strategy modern sport plays scarcely a role as a product of western industrial society. External sport aid has to be rejected in favour of an inwardly focused body and movement culture.

None of these development models which I have described, has turned out to be successful in the course of developmental policy practice. It is therefore hardly surprising that science as well as politics have designed and tried new ways of development. Meanwhile, in the discussion about modernization strategy on the one hand and dissociation strategy on the other hand a concept of development has crystallized, which, with regard to its objectives, can be defined as the basic-needs model. This strategy is a result of the knowledge that the dissociation strategy is not realistic and modernization strategy has only seldom proved itself as being fully successful. In this respect it is the basic-needs strategy which primarily wants to initiate the process of development via a basic satisfaction of external needs. Especially food, housing, clothes and education have to be secured for all in this respect, and an elementary of basic system of public services must be established on this basis (cf. Table 25). The objective is in respect a social system guaranteeing the possibility of an appropriate participation of all in the important political, economic and cultural decisions. Here, too, the solution is secured by an inwardly focused auto-central development in a similar way as in the dissociation strategy, and it is also a matter of the development of an independent commonwealth. Education plays an important role in this basic-needs strategy in so far, as it is assumed that the basic needs strategy can be transformed via appropriate education policies into a general development strategy, which helps the Third World to progress from a state of underdevelopment to a state of development. Support from outside is regarded as sensible as long as the national identity of the developing country is respected, and as long as interferences are orientated towards the model of basic needs. Therefore sport can only become important

Table 25: Ten fundamental human needs

- A clean and beautiful environment
- A clean and adequate water supply
- A minimal requisite of clothing
- A well-balanced diet
- A simple house, which one can live in
- Fundamental health care
- Simple communication facilities
- A minimal requisite of energy
- Complete education
- Cultural and intellectual needs

in this kind of developmental political dimension in so far, as sport is defined as a basic need only under certain conditions, and in so far, as sport can make contributions to development policies if they are integrated in educational measures in the formal as well as in the informal sector of education.

This limitation suggests that modern sport as a whole with their large variety of manifestations probably can hardly be supported in terms of developmental policies by means of arguments of the basic-needs theory. Furthermore this limitation suggests that the usual attempts to justify sport-related developmental policy in young nations must be made the subject of a critical analysis.

2.   Attempts to justify the promotion of sport

Fundamental to all attempts of justification is the assumption that sport development policy provides impetus for the developmental process in general. This impetus-function is considered ensured particularily if sport in the Third World appears as "a means of social engineering". If this is the case further desirable functions of sport become valid, and through the effects of this "sport therapy" we finally get the desired social structures, and thus the desired new type of man in the Third World as a result of the following functions:

o   the idea of competition is immanent in sport, it stimulates an incentive for the performance of the individual, the group and the nation

o   sport is based on the acceptance of rules, it teaches fair-play, cooperation and respect for the laws and rules of the community

o   sport requires training, it teaches determination and discipline

o   sport of women and girls supports the process of emancipation

o   sport can have a possible influence on the process of nation building

o   sport has integrating and supporting effects with regard to linguistic, ethnic, social and religious differentiations

o   development aid in sport furthermore can contribute to equality in international top-performance sport between the First and the Third World.

These functions related to sport can point out, how we have to imagine the "New Man" in the Third World. Obviously he is the enlightened sport-citizen of the 20th century.

In this or similar ways sport scientists, politicians and advisers in the First World and in developing countries as well have assigned functions of development policy to sport. All these assignments of functions have in common that they are - above all - expressed on a background of positive experiences with sport in the First World. In so far they actually have some kind of empirical basis. Not considering negative experiences with sport (e.g. hooliganism, doping, injuries), however, makes them also become ideological utterances. This tendency is strengthened if you consider the state of science, so far achieved with regard to the functions assigned to sport. Taking into account the negative functions of sport and the present situation of science, we must have quite serious doubts with regard to the mechanism and effects of sport in the First World. Considering these doubts, it seems to be downright dangerous if sport in the Third World are assigned the same insecure function, if sport is presented as a kind of universal therapy, and if, in this respect, a transfer-assumption is made, which has not even proved to be good on the level of much more similar systems than that of different social systems. But this assignment of functions is also debatable for the reason that with regard to empirical aspects it has proved to be wrong already today in some Third World countries. This shall be exemplified by means of pointing out six of the above described developmental functions of sport.

▪   *Sport development aid as an instrument for personality development*

The assumption that sport can provide basic qualifications for a capacity to act, which is to be achieved by the people in the Third World, - examples of this would be the orientation towards achievement, individualism, openness towards the future, empathy, and the capability to abstract persons, things and situations -, this assumption is plausible, but in empirical respects it is not sufficiently secured. In particular it is debatable, whether these basic qualifications, exemplarily described in sport, get into conflict with existing basic qualifications in those societies in which sport is supposed to contribute to development. This especially applies to the performance orientation, and thus to the idea of performance incentive; it applies to the desired individualism and, not least, also to the problem of promoting intelligence. Therefore it must be warned of the psychological overestimation of sport, and its export to developing countries, connected with the assumption that the personality structures of the partners in developing countries could be changed by the intervention of sport.

- ### Sport development aid as an instrument for integration

The argument that sport can make contributions to the process of nation-building in all those countries whose borders were only defined by the colonial powers, where tribes and cultures with the most diverse traditions are confronted with each other, turns out to be ideological after some close consideration, at least it is only rarely supported by empirical findings. The contrary rather seems to be true. This is shown firstly by analyses results in respect of the First World, referring to the accomplishments of integration of sport clubs, or those which have the problem of violence in sport as a subject. But it can also be shown in respect of observations made in developing countries. So is, for example, commitment in sport in many developing countries differential according to religion, race and tribe-membership. This point of view, differentiating according to branches of sport, shows that certain branches are only practiced by certain races, and that between the sport-branches there are hierarchical variations in respect of religion and race. In Malaysia - for example - we can observe a differentiated commitment to sport of Indians, Malayans and Chinese in different branches of sport.

In the First World sport can only fulfill integrating functions when organizational conditions exist, such as the structure of sport clubs. The integrating function of sport in the Third World is only seldom debatable, because the necessary conditions for a realisation of this function are scarcely existing here.

Nation-building furthermore can, however, also be interpreted as a negative effect of sport, especially, if success is chauvinistically raised. Sport are supposed to demonstrate the supposed quality of a political system; in reality, however, social inequality and violations of human rights are frequently covered or hidden. The question, to what extent sport might get into conflict with the religious system of developing countries, is also in contrast with the function of nation-building. There is much indication that particularly in those countries where the fundamental variant of Islam plays an important role sport meets difficulties as to its display. This applies in particular to the participation of women in sport in countries whose religion is shiite-islamic; there the commitment of women in sport is decreasing. Obviously the integrating effects of sport are also limited in this respect.

- ### Sport development aid as an instrument for identification

It is also questionable, to what extent sport is a suitable instrument for idenfication, that means, to what extent sport can be a positive possibility of identification in places, where urbanization, high social and regional mobility, and the loss of importance of over-lapping social groups take place. So, if we consider the results of sport science research, too, we see that sport as an opportunity of identification is primarily discussed via the successful top-performance athlete. It is assumed that sport idols have a positive socializing function during some periods in our lives, especially for adolescents. Whether this should however be regarded as positive, and whether idols have the same kind of effect in the Third World as in the First World, seems to be debatable. On the one hand such processes of idol-building are linked to a differentiated system of mass communication, and just this does not exist in almost all underdeveloped countries. On the other hand the successful top-performance athlete can actually have a negative model function. At least the unattainability of his sporting performance can also cause a distance to an individual's own active practicing of sport.

Table 26: Olympic ranking list (1896 - 1992)

		Participation since	Gold	Silver	Bronce
1.	USA	1896	784	604	527
2.	USSR	1900	453	413	701
3.	Germany	1896	342	356	365
4.	Great Britain	1896	173	221	215
5.	Italy	1900	152	127	131
6.	France	1896	151	169	182
7.	Sweden	1896	135	145	167
8.	Hungary	1896	134	140	142
9.	Finland	1908	100	78	112
10.	Japan	1912	90	84	95
11.	Australia	1896	80	76	95
12.	Romania	1924	59	70	90
13.	Czechoslovakia	1900	49	50	51
16.	Canada	1900	46	67	84
15.	Poland	1924	46	54	108
14.	Netherlands	1900	46	52	71
20.	Bulgaria	1896	40	69	58
19.	Norway	1900	40	39	35
17.	Switzerland	1896	39	63	57
18.	Belgium	1900	38	49	49
25.	Cuba	1900	38	27	24
21.	Denmark	1896	32	62	59
23.	New Zealand	1908	27	10	8
22.	Yugoslavia	1912	26	31	34
24.	Turkey	1908	26	15	12

■   *Sport development aid as an instrument of equality*

We must also warn of the legitimation of sport-promoting interventions by means of the reference to equality between First and Third World in international sport, which certainly does not exist. Those believing that by means of sport-promoting measures the partners in developing countries would be offered an equal starting position, from which they could compete in international top-performance sport misjudge the actual indicators for top-performance in sport. In so far it is also inadequate to justify sport promoting measures in developing countries by means of the argument that on the basis of a comprehensive concept of school- and recreational sport they can catch up with the world's absolute top-performance sport (cf. Table 26).

- *Sport development aid as an instrument for compensation and regeneration*

It seems to be certain that sport has the function of compensation for the unusual strains of industrial labour. Without any doubts sport can fulfill this function in the Third World, too. But sport is practiced as a means of compensation by those groups who can refer to scheduled working hours in urban areas. This reference points out that sport obviously has a chance to develop if they meet conditions of production which show a separation between leisure and labour, and which provide sufficient spare time for regeneration and recreation. Such conditions, however, only exist in the metropolitan areas of the Third World, and considering the financial circumstances and the distribution of wealth in most developing countries, at present only a privileged class is able to practice sport in their leisure.

- *Sports development aid as an instrument for the satisfaction of basic needs*

Regarding sport as a value in itself helps us to escape the question, why we "export" sport to underdeveloped societies of the Third World. This opinion can be recognized at least partly in respect of those arguments relating the status of a basic need to sport. The reference of an Indian journalist who said, he had never seen a child getting enough food by sticking a ball into his mouth, may be polemic, but it defines precisely the problem we are confronted with here. If it is already difficult to find reasons for defining education as a basic need, - considering the at least partly failed investments in education in the Third World - sport can at best be justified in the form of physical education with reference to the necessity of a comprehensive education. It seems t be the case that sport - in the sense of such comprehensive education - can have a positive influence on the process of development as one aspect of public health only if they intervene in the form of those variants, which cause positive effects in respect of health and fulfill useful functions in respect of education. Large parts of the differentiated system of sport, as we know it today, are, however, beyond question. On the background of the real living conditions in some developing countries, it seems to be cynical to grant sport the status of a basic need. Many developing countries can - today and in the near future - do without sport, not without rice and water.

Let us sum up again the attempts of legitimation and justification: It is a feature common to the outlined supporting arguments that sport is regarded as a positive system of values, which by means of the feature of fair-play is somehow removed from the world, and thus symbolizes a better world. The fact that sport is a glittering phenomenon, always in danger due to negative influences, when they want to put into practice their positive values, is hardly ever recognized in this discussion. In so far, the partner in the Third World is offered a product whose dark sides are not mentioned by the retailer, but which rise to the surface daily after the product has been bought.

3.   *To promote sport means: To build up structures*

According to what has been described so far, the question could arise, how it is nevertheless possible - bearing in mind such criticism - to believe in a concept of the promotion of sport as I do?

In view of the political, economic and social situation of developing countries the function and role of sport should be defined on the basis of the following question:

What can sport achieve for the advancement of their societies?

I think sport can take on five fundamental functions, which are:

First, a *socio-emotional function*. Sport addresses the needs of individuals providing for the management of tension and conflict; it also provides opportunities for the generating of a feeling of togetherness, a sense of belonging, friendship, and companionship. Sport as a ritual is a source of reassurance and the reinforcement of cultural beliefs.

Second, it can take on a *socialization function*. Sport is important agents inculcating cultural mores and ethical values into the individual and supporting the development of a personality; through sport people can learn and adopt desired behaviour patterns and beliefs.

Third, very significant is also the *integrative function* of sport; it is means assisting with the harmonious integration of disparate individuals into a collective and their identification with it; striking examples of this function are local and national sport teams.

Fourth, sport has a *political function* and is used as political tool. In a sense this could be seen as an extension of its integrative function to the national level of a collective or community. In another sense sport is used as a political means of sanctioning other nations. However, the greatest significance of the political function of sport lies in its potential impact on education, social welfare and health.

Finally, sport can take on a *social mobility function*; there is reason to believe that sport can effectively promote the social mobility of less fortunate members of society, the poor, or ethnic minorities. It can indeed enhance the increase of social prestige and subsequently also provide economic regards.

The foregoing arguments have shown that sport has not caused the state of underdevelopment, but that in the process of development it *can* play a certain role in the Third World similar to the First, and that sport if considered an important means can obviously be supportive in a society's way from underdevelopment to development. As to the question of timing and speed of this process, different developing countries are to be judged by different standards. On the one hand it still is, however, an unanswered question to what extent sport actually supports, neutralizes, or impedes the process of development of a Third World society.

On the other hand almost every developing country already boasts a large variety of sport structures: sport facilities like gyms and stadiums, sport associations and institutions, Olympic Committees, athletes, coaches, and physical education in schools. All these structures function more or less efficiently and successfully, and nobody advocates their abolition. But we can also sense the disappointment about the huge but fruitless investments made in the past. On this political basis we are to ask for a more realistic and practical policy of promoting sport in the future. In my view the dominant aspect of any policy will have to be the contribution of a measure for the solid establishment of sport structures.

But what are the criteria for structure-supporting sport promotion? Approaching this problem from the practical side brings to mind the following five control questions that have to be answered comprehensively before any sport development aid project is being realized:

(1)   Does the measure support the process of institutionalization?

The discussion of problems of sport development aid, but also experiences in the field, indicate that sport-promotion-measures can really contribute to the promotion of sport in Third World countries only, if they go along with processes of institutionalization. In so far it will be important for future sport promotion projects to observe the level of organization of the project, and to aim at those structural connections, sport is embedded in. (These could be clubs, federations, industries, communities, churches etc.)

It would be necessary that particularly in rural regions specific initiatives of the state provide fresh impetus to the foundation of voluntary associations. What is imaginable in this respect is - above all - a connection between social work and sport projects in order to establish such associations, for example, in suburban and rural areas.

(2)   Does the measure contribute to a differentiated structure of sport education and training?

Developing sport structures means taking further measures concerning additional infra-structure related to the development of voluntary associations. Fundamental to this are "elementary educational structures" in which physical education has an important function for the comprehensive development of physical, intellectual and emotional abilities.

Sport-related elementary educational measures should be embedded in projects of rural regional development but also in projects in areas of urban agglomeration. This has to be connected to traditional forms of dances, games and competitions and to the specific local conditions and facilities. Measures for a formal education must be related usefully to informal innovations of or in education. This also applies to the development of training facilities, for professional and spare time sport personnel. Finally it should not be forgotten that spare time commitment has to be encouraged.

(3)   Does the measure contribute to an improvement of guiding structures of sport?

Efforts with regard to structures of education and training are not very helpful if they do not go along with the development of those sport structures making the practicing of sport possible.

One part of this is the development of a differentiated system of sport facilities which can be justified economically and, with regard to our present knowledge, also ecologically. In particular, it must be considered that the rural and suburban residential areas of underdeveloped societies are provided for. Suitable are in this respect especially those sport facilities which can be built with simple materials on the basis of inexpensive and possibly self-produced resources, and which are integrated into the lives of the people.

(4) Does the measure support the development of a differentiated system of sporting competition?

The development and extension of a differentiated system of sporting competition must also be regarded as a structure-building measure. In this respect it will be particularly important in the future that Third World countries confine themselves - taking into account their specific economic, cultural and climatic conditions - to a selection of branches of sport, and that they create and establish their own highlights in sport independently of the First World.

(5) Does the measure contribute to the development and extension of an infra-structure of mass communication?

With reference to structural aspects the development of a sport communication system is also important. In this respect their own facets of sport coverage have to be provided. Not only top-athletes, records and high-performance-events ought to be covered. 'Sport for all' must be an important topic of mass media.

I believe that a sport policy committed to these five guideline-questions is to the advantage of the majority of the people of developing countries and will be successful in the future.

Table 27: Success of developing countries at the Olympic Games in Barcelona 1992

Developing Countries	Gold	Silver	Bronze	Total
China	16	22	16	54
Cuba	14	6	11	31
North-Corea	4	-	5	9
Kenya	2	4	2	8
Indonesia	2	2	1	5
Jamaica	-	3	1	4
Nigeria	-	3	1	4
Brazil	2	1	-	3
Morocco	1	1	1	3
Ethiopia	1	-	2	3
Iran	-	1	2	3
Namibia	-	2	-	2
Algeria	1	-	1	2
Mexico	-	1	-	1
Peru	-	1	-	1
Bahama Islands	-	-	1	1
Surinam	-	-	1	1
Ghana	-	-	1	1
Colombia	-	-	1	1
Pakistan	-	-	1	1
Phillipine Islands	-	-	1	1
Puerto-Rico	-	-	1	1
Thailand	-	-	1	1
Quatar	-	-	1	1

Table 28: Success of developing countries compared with the total number of attainable points at the Olympic Games in Barcelona 1992

(Gold = 3 points; Silver = 2 points; Bronze = 1 point)

	Total number	percentage
Number of possible points	1591	100%
Developing countries	**579**	**36,4%**
Industrial countries	1012	63,6%

Table 29: Success of developing countries referring to all successful countries at the Olympic Games in Barcelona 1992

	Total number	percentage
Number of countries	64	
Developing countries	**24**	**37,5%**
Industrial countries	40	62,5%

Table 30: Success of developing countries compared with the total number of attainable medals at the Olympic Games in Barcelona 1992

	Total number	percentage
Number of medals	815	100%
Developing countries	**142**	**17,4%**
Industrial countries	673	82,6%

Table 31: Distribution of medals in Athletics at the Olympic Games in Barcelona 1992

	Gold	Silver	Bronze
USA	12	8	10
GUS	7	11	3
Germany	4	1	5
Kenya	2	4	2
Cuba	2	1	4
Spain	2	1	1
Great Britain	2	-	4
Czechoslovakia	2	-	-
China	1	1	2
Canada	1	1	1
Morocco	1	1	-
Ethiopia	1	-	2
Algeria	1	-	-
Netherlands	1	-	-
France	1	-	-
Greece	1	-	-
Korea	1	-	-
Lithuania	1	-	-
Jamaica	-	3	1
Namibia	-	2	-
Japan	-	2	-
Bulgaria	-	1	1
Nigeria	-	1	1
Finland	-	1	-
Mexico	-	1	-
Romania	-	1	-
Sweden	-	1	-
South-Africa	-	1	-
Australia	-	-	2
Bahama Islands	-	-	1
Italy	-	-	1
Colombia	-	-	1
New Zealand	-	-	1
Poland	-	-	1
Quatar	-	-	1

Chapter IV:

The Future of Sport

158

The future development of sport

When talking about the future of sport, we first and foremost have to consider the problems sport is facing at present. In Germany, for example, not only high performance sport is affected by manifold problems. With regard to the environmental threats confronting our society, the legitimacy of our whole sport system is being questioned. 'Sport for all' - a democratically based and very successful policy - cannot be realized without getting into conflict with our natural environment. High performance sport is increasingly subject to financial pressures. We are shocked by the violence on the sport fields, and doping is still an unsolved problem in sport.

A more precise characterization of this legitimacy crisis is based on the answers to eight questions (cf. Table 32):

Table 32: Questions concerning the development of sport

1. What is the meaning and/or significance of sport?
2. What are the ethical standards and values of sport?
3. Who are the clients of sport?
4. What are the different forms of organization in sport?
5. What are the functions of sport?
6. To what extent is the system of sport autonomous?
7. In what respect is sport subject to economic pressures and commercial utilization?
8. Is the system of sport still orientated towards unity?

Why are both the internal and external structure of sport in danger of disintegration, and why are the traditional features of sport presently in a state of flux?

According to my studies the specific changes concerning the German system of sport is related to general social changes in our society. Most obvious is a change of ethical values, or more negatively expressed, we are facing an ethical crisis. The problems confronting sport are a reflection of a societal crisis, which, in fact, seems to be a crisis of accepting the technological revolution. In the language of system theory it is a consequence of a process of functional differentiation, at the end of which are a lot of partial systems, each having its own problems of governing and directing.

1. The change of values

In social science literature it has become customary to distinguish two value standpoints (cf. Table 33, 34). On the one hand there is the "industrial" and on the other hand the "post-industrial" value standpoint, the respective terminology originating from the American sociologist *Inglehart*.

Does a comparison of these two standpoints indicate progression, regression or normality? Is this conflict of values unique or does it appear regularly in the development of a society?

From my point of view the change of values is a relatively normal phenomenon in the process of a society's evolution; different values are indicators of the pluralism within advanced societies.

Values become visible and concrete in real individuals, and another look at table 34 may reveal that an individual - in terms of his or her values - may sometimes lean more to the left and in other respects more to the right column. In my view this is quite typical of our present situation. The change of values runs right through humanity, it varies depending on age, gender as well as social background, and it is continuously influenced by external factors. Consequently every individual has a set of values of his or her own.

Table 33: Changes in values of American adults, 1981 - 1989

Value	Percent Affirming	
	1981	1989
Having a good family life	82 %	89 %
Having a good self-image	79 %	85 %
Being in good physical health	81 %	84 %
Having a sense of accomplishment	63 %	69 %
Working to better America	51 %	67 %
Following a strict moral code	47 %	60 %
Having an exciting, stimulating life	46 %	48 %
Having a nice home, car and other things	39 %	41 %

Source: "Social Values", 1989, pp. 35 - 44

However, the change of values takes place in a social context, and it seems important to focus on the features of this change. Looking at table 34 shows that discipline, obedience, loyalty, and subordination have lost their dominant positions and are of secondary importance only, whereas emancipation, freedom, equality, creativity and political participation have become increasingly important, while the highest-ranking values are self-realization, cooperation, and - particularly for adolescents - questions concerning the meaning of life.

These are not consequences of our economic prosperity in the sixties, of an educational revolution and a revolution of the media, of the student revolt, of women's lib, peace, and environmental movements, or the continuously increasing number of pressure groups. Rather are they related to changing working conditions as a consequence of our society's economic development, of unemployment and an ecological crisis. But they also reflect our apparent disappointment with technological progress.

Table 34: Change of values

Materialism	Postmaterialism
■ traditional educational ideals (diligence, discipline, obedience)	■ democratic-egalitarian ideals
■ strict gender differentiation	■ partnership orientated ideal of man, decreasing willingness for role-specific integration and subordination
■ willingness to adapt, discipline, obedience, loyalty, submission	■ emancipation, freedom, equal treatment, creativity, self-realization, self-determination
■ standardization	■ tendency toward uniqueness
■ efficiency, rationalism, result-orientation	■ need-orientation, individuality, process-orientation
■ achievement, carreer, power, upward mobility, status seeking, striving for high income and consumption	■ quality of life
■ work orientation	■ leisure orientation, growing importance of private domain
■ striving for material and social security	■ readiness to take risks
■ abstinence	■ enjoying life to the full extent
■ ascetism	■ hedonism
■ secularism	■ new creeds
■ dominance of man over nature, belief in progress and technology	■ harmony between man and nature
■ belief in authority, obedience, tendency towards acceptance	■ participation, openness of political decisions
■ science - as a doctrine	■ scepticism towards scientific rationalism
■ "protestant" ethics	■ ethics of "voluntary simplicity"

What used to be propagated as being synonymous with a superior quality of life in the seventies, has become doubtful or even hazardous for many people today; this finds its expression in the fear of nuclear power plants and is manifested in a trend towards nostalgia, which has been lasting for decades now.

Summarizing at this point we can in general contend a rejection of the traditional values of industrialized societies; and we may justly maintain that the search for the meaning of life as well as the question about the meaning of life have gained greater importance than they used to have in the past. There is also strong indication that the values pertaining to work are undergoing a process of change; certain social groups have lost their religious values. Whereas competition-oriented values have lost much of their significance, individual development, self-realization and consumption have become more relevant, and we notice an increasing tendency towards hedonism.

2.   Values of sport in transition

Is sport affected by the change of values to the same degree and with the same speed as society? In terms of speed the system of sport, that is, for example the sport clubs, has succeeded in keeping to its traditional values for a long time and has also successfully managed to defend itself against untimely modernization in contrast to many other sectors of society. Hence, the development of sport and sport clubs took place relatively slowly in comparison with the general development of society, and consequently is much less strongly influenced by tendencies towards change. Sport rather is still subject to value-orientations that are to be defined as industrial and modern, thus following the trend towards technological progress and the path of modernization. This can best be shown in the field of high performance sport, and table 35 shows the effects of this trend.

The foregoing table indicates that at present sport is primarily dominated by industrial values; their consequential attitudes continuously play a significant role in the decisions of club officials and association functionaries. How can activities of sport clubs become more efficient by means of technological interventions? What new and better sport facilities can meet tomorrow's requirements? How can we fund top performance in sport in the future? Which scientists can assist in our athletes' optimal training, psychological and physical fitness in competitions?

Table 35: Social development and change of sport

Sport in the fifties	Sport today
■ every day knowledge and experience	■ scientific rationalism
■ honorary work	■ work on a full time basis
■ amateur	■ professional
■ direct participation as a spectator	■ indirect participation as a spectator
■ self financed competitions	■ subsidized competitions
■ competitions without supplementary interests	■ commercialization of competitions
■ simple rule system	■ differentiated rule system
■ simple organization	■ differentiated organization
■ accidental promotion of talents	■ scientific orientated promotion of talents
■ competition as a free space	■ political and economic utilization of competition
■ competition as comradeship, as a sociable happening	■ strict separation between competition and sociability

Table 36: Change of values in sport

Industrial sport vs.	Postindustrial sport
■ pressure for high-performance; objective standards of performance	■ no pressure for high-performance; subjective standards of performance
■ dominance of competitiveness	■ no dominance of competitiveness
■ dominance of skills	■ subordination of skills
■ dominance of rules	■ decreasing importance of rules flexibility
■ homogeneous groups	■ heterogeneous groups
■ object orientated action	■ communicative action
■ youthfulness	■ sociability
■ high-performance / achievement	■ happiness
■ records	■ quietude, tranquility
■ success	■ health, well-being, joy

These questions highlight the trend towards modernization followed by the majority of people responsible in sport, especially by officials in high performance sport.

However, there also appears to be a contrary movement; there are already some sport scientists today who believe that we are in a period of transition concerning our comprehension of sport, and that this movement is gathering momentum and gaining increasing support from people involved in sport. The large array of sub-cultural currents outside the sport clubs illustrates this quite clearly; we are witnessing the growth of a 'movement culture' beside the traditional patterns of sport in our society. Whereas the typical values of the traditional sport systems first and foremost comprised youthfulness, success, high performance and records, the new values centre on social contact, happiness, tranquility and health (cf. Table 36).

From a moral point of view sport appears to have reached a crucial state. There are more and more people involved in the system of sport who are becoming aware and warn of the growing self-delusion of sport officials and other people carrying responsibility in clubs and associations, however, many still refuse to admit that they are leaving their own ethical platform in the trend to modernization.

Table 37: Percent of adults participating in outdoor recreational activities, by age, 1965 and 1982

	Age					
	18 - 24		25 - 44		45 - 64	
Activity	1965	1982	1965	1982	1965	1982
Bicycling	26 %	43 %	15 %	35 %	3 %	35 %
Horseback riding	18 %	15 %	8 %	9 %	2 %	3 %
Golfing	15 %	14 %	10 %	11 %	6 %	9 %
Tennis	14 %	33 %	5 %	15 %	1 %	7 %
Canoeing	8 %	13 %	3 %	9 %	1 %	4 %
Sailing	6 %	9 %	3 %	7 %	2 %	4 %
Boating	38 %	29 %	28 %	26 %	20 %	15 %
Waterskiing	17 %	16 %	7 %	10 %	1 %	2 %
Swimming	75 %	67 %	56 %	55 %	27 %	33 %
Fishing	38 %	39 %	35 %	37 %	30 %	27 %
Hunting	20 %	14 %	15 %	13 %	9 %	11 %
Camping	16 %	34 %	15 %	27 %	6 %	15 %
Hiking	14 %	20 %	7 %	18 %	4 %	9 %
Walking	61 %	61 %	52 %	57 %	42 %	50 %
Birdwatching	4 %	9 %	6 %	11 %	7 %	11 %
Picknicking	71 %	52 %	71 %	58 %	47 %	40 %
Pleasure driving	76 %	57 %	66 %	56 %	53 %	45 %
Sightseeing	62 %	49 %	60 %	54 %	49 %	43 %
Attending outdoor sport	59 %	50 %	44 %	44 %	29 %	30 %
Attending outdoor concerts	18 %	37 %	14 %	28 %	10 %	19 %
Ice skating	18 %	9 %	7 %	6 %	2 %	1 %
Skiing	8 %	15 %	3 %	9 %	1 %	3 %
Sledding	20 %	16 %	13 %	11 %	2 %	2 %

Source: Based on *Robinson*, 1987, p. 36

All this is an expression of the ongoing process of differentiation in the sport system. The more people want to participate in sport, the more the system of sport becomes functionally differentiated. A lot of its functions are not at all related to high performance sport, but are articulated by means of separate models of sport. The simplistic figure of the pyramid, as shown in table 38, has outlived its usefulness.

What has acquired much greater significance recently are, for example, patterns of relaxed movement and the innovation of new sport disciplines partly taking on the character and the function of social movements.

They are accompanied by the vast expansion of informal activities, like for instance, many forms of recreational sport. On the whole sport has increasingly taken on the function of a general aid in life, and it is becoming a very important factor for integration. Its socio-political significance has also increased, it is more and more prescribed as a cure for the ills of our society and the problems of its members. Sport provides facilities for rehabilitation and resocialization, for the older generation, for ethnic minorities (i.e. the

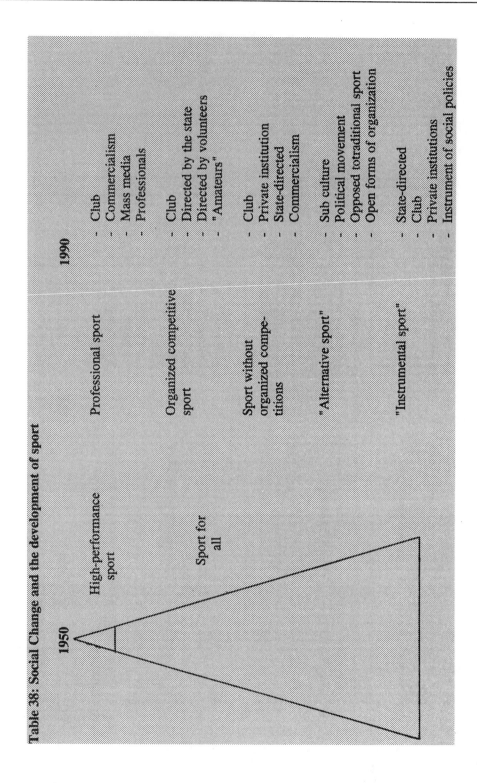

Table 38: Social Change and the development of sport

1950		1990	
High-performance sport	Professional sport	Club, Commercialism, Mass media, Professionals	
Sport for all	Organized competitive sport	Club, Directed by the state, Directed by volunteers, "Amateurs"	
	Sport without organized competitions	Club, Private institution, State-directed, Commercialism	
	"Alternative sport"	Sub culture, Political movement, Opposed to traditional sport, Open forms of organization	
	"Instrumental sport"	State-directed, Club, Private institutions, Instrument of social policies	

integration of Turkish workers into German mainstream society), and for fringe groups. These examples sufficiently indicate that there is a huge demand for sport subsequently to the problems of our complex society.

In the future therefore we should recognize that, within the internal structure of sport, different models have developed. In my estimation we can already distinguish five models in sport today, as reflected in table 38. *First*, there is the traditional model of performance-oriented sport, based primarily on the values of competition, performance, victory and defeat. This model is well-established in the clubs and meets the needs of a large number of people.

Besides this the model of commercial sport, comprising circus, show and media sport is growing rapidly, threatening the existence of the competition-oriented model of the sport clubs, or at least influencing it strongly. This *second* model comprehends sport as show business and thus enhances the professionalization of sport.

The *third* model could be named 'spontaneous sport'. Its moral standards and self-image derive from values such as fun, joy, happiness, and some further intrinsic values. It is mainly orientated towards recreation and leisure, elements of performance and competition being not fundamental to it. It is primarily practiced during holidays and spare time but has also become apparent in new forms of youth culture; originally practiced by and in unorganized groups only, it has meanwhile also gained entrance to the sport clubs, where it frequently competes with the more traditional competition-oriented model of sport. Its structures are purposely contrasting to those governing our actions in everyday life, and especially those determining industrial work.

Besides this so-called 'spontaneous sport' we can observe another (*fourth*) facet of body culture that has also grown and been established outside the clubs. It comprehends body culture as an expression of a particular way of life or even a political life style, its objectives being the generating of real alternatives in sport; it exists totally independent of institutionalized sport, is mainly to be found in sub-cultural groups, and there predominantly in the surroundings of universities.

Finally, there is a *fifth* model, the model of instrumental or functional sport. In its context sport is primarily seen as a social service; it is determined by its supposed positive functions, such as its socio-emotional, socio-integrative, political, biological, health-supporting, and its socialization functions. This model is generally considered very significant for education, and the instrumental effects concerning health are certainly very important, too.

In my view the sport movement, that is, the people carrying responsibility in the institutions of sport will have to make their political choices among these five models.

The prospects of modern competitive sport

1. Introduction

Is modern top-level competitive sport nearing the end of its days? This question immediately crops up when the current situation of top-level competitive sport is viewed in the light of a comparison drawn by Kaspar Wolf, a Swiss sport scientist. The Olympic Games of the ancients lasted a thousand years until they finally degenerated and vanished from history. The medieval tournaments stayed alive for 500 years until they too disappeared from the scene. Modern top-level competitive sport is no more than 100 years old, and nevertheless the question is already arising today: how long will it continue to survive? In view of all the many conflicts which can be observed today in competitive sport, and which are the source of problems and worry for athletes, coaches and officials, one could indeed easily come to the conclusion that the modern system of high level competitive sport has no future, that its end is near and that all efforts to prevent its demise will be in vain (cf. *Wolf*, quoted by *Babst* 1985, 185).

Political exploitation of sport, economic interests which encroach upon the autonomy of sport, the questionable interest taken by the media in sport, the insatiable demands on the part of the public for ever better levels of performance, the still-increasing threat to the health of athletes, the objective limits to achievement in sport, the enormous material expense involved in training and production of top sport performance, the enormous increase in measures to monitor and supervise training and competitive events, the participation of children in highly competitive sport as a necessary preparation for setting records, the ongoing institutionalization and bureaucratization of sport organizations, the ever greater dominance of science and technology in sport, all of these represent problems that today are confronting top-level competitive sport and for which no satisfactory solution has yet been found.

In spite of this worrying situation, I believe that top-level competitive sport still has good future prospects. To be sure, my belief is somewhat biased, since I fervently hope that top-level competitive sport will be able to look forward to a positive future. After all, it is mainly those whose professional training has been intimately tied up with sport who talk about the future of high level competitive sport. This results in subjectivity leaving very little room for a realistic assessment of the real problems facing top-level competitive sport. This also applies to me. Anyone who thinks it would be a shame if top-level sport was to completely disappear is biased. Consequently, in the following essay I have no choice but to present my biased point of view. The reader should take this into consideration when judging my argumentation.

Formally, I would like to divide my treatise into four parts. To begin with, I would like to characterize the current situation of top-level competitive sport. On the basis of this review, I will then present my arguments why high-level competitive sport is capable of playing a meaningful role as a provider of exemplary societal values, in spite of the dangers which are inherent in it. This will also allow me to sketch the prerequisites under which the continued existence of top-level competitive sport would be desirable. In the third part I would like to present a selection of those factors which, in my opinion, are of fundamental importance for the future development of top-level competitive sport.

Finally, I will close with a few recommendations on how to proceed in order to ensure positive prospects for the future of top-level competitive sport.

2.   Current problems of top-level competitive sport

In order to find out the meaning and purpose of top-level competitive sport today, it is important to consider its current situation first. When one speaks of top-level competitive sport, it is natural to first think of the athletes that perform so excellently in the stadiums. The names of Becker, Moses or Thompson are synonymous with the concept of top-level competitive sport. However, this is only half of the truth. Top-level competitive sport today is a modern institution in which athletes and what they do occupy only a fairly modest place among a great many others. The other places are occupied by a great diversity of people, groups and organizations. These include coaches, managers and sport officials. They also include the sporting goods industry, the manufacturers of sport equipment, sport scientists, the spectators in the stadiums and of course also business and the world of politics. Within this complex, top-level competitive sport has developed into a multifaceted institution which can be described today as a growth sector of the first degree. Actually, no one can truly be surprised about this any more. The reason is that the development of competitive sport has proceeded along the lines of common social patterns (cf. *Neidhardt* 1985, 71 - 75). Much of what we can observe today in top-level competitive sport, in other words, is by no means new. For that reason it is by no means as dangerous as it is generally assumed by critics. Top-level competitive sport is now undergoing structural changes of the kind which took place long ago in other areas, for example in science, religion, law and the arts. This development can be appropriately described by saying that it involves certain aspects of "differentiating out"; activities which previously played no central role and which could, at least to some extent, be engaged in an ad hoc or amateurish way, are now separated out and specialized. The result of this is that "virtuosos" emerge who turn their speciality into a profession, while behind them an "infrastructure" forms and grows with positions and organizations which are exclusively directed at backing and assisting the performance of these virtuosos. "Improvement of performance" is then the "real purpose" of this newly created institution (cf. *Neidhardt* 1985, 71). This process is now well under way in top-level competitive sport. It is being greatly accelerated by the fact that there is an extensive social demand for ever greater achievement in sport. This demand is being fueled primarily by the entertainment and consumer goods industry, which is responding to the entertainment and consumption needs of the public. This development is also favored by the fact that the population is enjoying increasing amounts of leisure time, as well as by climbing income levels of the majority of the population and by a growing interest in fitness, health and a physically active life style.

One consequence of this development is that today recreational sport and top-level competitive sport have almost completely separated from one another. Or at least, the distance between top-level competitive sport and leisure sport has grown significantly. These two variants of sport differ from one another with respect to their active participants and to the officials in charge of them, and especially as regards their funding. They also have quite different functions. Health and fitness, for instance, are no longer regarded as important functions of top-level competitive sport, whereas popular sport sees in them its primary legitimation. The same holds for the educational function of sport; this is rarely placed in doubt in popular sport, but is increasingly denied in the case of top-level competitive sport. As a result the top-level athletes of today have very little in common with those athletes who work in their clubs week after week, and then take part in matches at weekends in the hope of qualifying for the next-higher class. Top-level athletes have virtually nothing in common with those who get together on a recreational basis to play volleyball, do gymnastics or other physical activities, and afterwards meet in their clubhouses for a round of drinks (cf. *Digel* 1986a, 14 - 43).

Today's top-level athletes have much more in common with industrial producers, whereby they are, so to speak, both employers and employees at the same time. They are caught up in a tightly woven planning system. Long-term training plans, precisely calculated budgets and schedules, regular check-ups of their physical condition and equipment, calculation of finances for participation in major athletic events, observance of the rules and stipulations of the sport associations; these are what characterize the activities of top-level competitive athletes today.

3.   Performance as a symbol

Is all of this an indication that top-level competitive sport has no positive meaning? Or could top-level competitive sport even represent a threat? Several critics who deserve to be taken seriously are of the opinion that top-level competitive sport is nothing more than a counterpart to the working world (cf. Table 39). They serve as an escape value for letting off pent-up dissatisfaction, they distract from political injustice, it stabilizes our social order. Further, it is claimed, in top-level competitive sport the athletes are manipulated, unable to make decisions of their own, the victims of coaches, managers and officials; in a somewhat shortened form, this is the essence of their criticism. In my opinion, this criticism is neither deliberately malicious nor unjustified. Top-level competitive sport can indeed promote confirmity and have a compensatory function, acting as a substitute for failures. It is true that top-level performance in sport has long been "mechanized", and in a certain sense athletes are in danger of turning into machines themselves. Athletes can become part of an apparatus which is, in turn, part of a totalitarian culture (cf. *Rigauer* 1969, 76 - 84; *Rigauer* 1979, 70 - 86; *Maier* 1975, 82 - 83; *Vinnai* 1972; *Lenk* 1985, 12 - 13; *v.Krockow* 1974; *Lenk* 1972 among others).

Table 39: Criticism on top-level sport

- Top-level sport is manipulated, regimented work
- Top-level sport serves as an escape value for pent-up dissatisfaction among the population
- Top-level sport distracts from political injustice
- Top-level sport stabilizes the existing social order
- Athletes are immature and manipulated, unable to make their own decisions

Nevertheless, I believe that top-level competitive sport can still play a culturally meaningful role even today. In spite of all the danger signs which can today be observed in top-level competitive sport, there is no reason why it cannot continue to be a realm of experience in which individuals are granted the opportunity of attaining the maximum degree of humanly possible perfection in and through their own achievement. As such, top-level competitive sport can still serve as an ideal model for our competitive society. It embodies the most effective symbolic demonstration of the basic principles of an achievement-oriented society, the principle of competition and the principle of equality of opportunity (cf. *v.Krockow* 1974; *DSB* 1975; *Grupe* 1980; *Lenk* 1985 among others).

Moreover athletes can set an example of a disciplined way of life and of self-realization. If we ask ourselves which sectors of our society such attributes and principles are still being actively expressed in, then we must conclude that the principles of human achievement, incorruptible comparison of performance, competition and equality of opportunity can still be observed - more than anywhere else - in athletic competition. The principle of achievement as it exists in the realm of sport permits an almost utopistically pure representation of competitive achievement such as cannot be found in any other area of life, not even in the working world (cf. *Grupe* 1982, 176 - 182; *Lenk* 1985, 22 - 24).

Peter Arnold has described how he experiences this phenomenon as an athlete: "While running I realize that there is something symbolic about what I am doing. It has something to do with the actual experience of my own, living organism. While running I am more acutely aware than when doing anything else that I am the vessel and manipulator of my own vital energy. This realization makes running symbolic for me. The reality of my living body during this activity is symbolized by the pace, the effort, the breathlessness and the pain of running" (*Arnold*, quoted by *Lenk* 1985, 69). The fact is also of symbolic significance that an important aspect of top-level competitive sport is the learning and mastering of difficult types of movement. It often takes months until an athlete masters a given skill. In the genuine sense of the word, these motor skills in athletics must be "achieved", and such achieved movements become a means of expression of the human personality. Movements in sport are the result of goal-oriented self-discipline and a certain kind of learning process. Anyone who acts in sport must act as an entire person (cf. *Lenk* 1985, 65 - 67). On the basis of this kind of argumentation, Lenk and Grupe are proponents of the view that to surpass the realm of the average, to lead the human body to the limits of its possibilities, to develop a tactic or technique to achieve its ultimate perfection, that all of this has a symbolic character for a society which is necessarily dependent on cultural progress. It follows from their view that cultural progress must be the basis of all social progress (cf. *Lenk* 1985; Grupe 1980). These interpretations are worthy of attention, although it should be added that progress must not be understood as a value in its own right. Nevertheless, there is considerable evidence to support the view that societies which have raised mediocrity, and averageness to the status of ideals remain caught in just this mediocrity, and stagnate in a state of dissatisfaction. By contrast, those societies which cultivate individual achievement and attainment of the maximum possible level of performance appear to be capable of solving those problems which urgently require being dealt with to permit continued existence of society per se. In other words, the real purpose and role of achievement in sport could be to point the way to that kind of general social achievement which is needed to solve the problems confronting society.

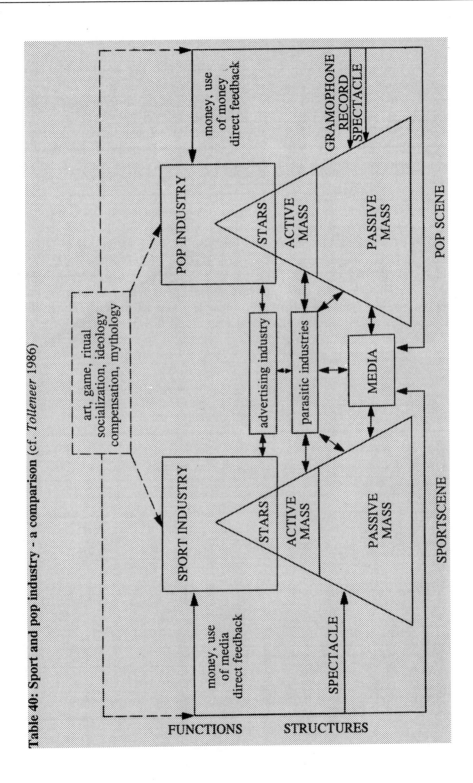

Table 40: Sport and pop industry - a comparison (cf. *Tolleneer* 1986)

Why then, it could be asked at this point, is it so important for the principle of achievement to be symbolically expressed in top-level competitive sport? This question can only be answered if we can first clearly define the role which the principle of achievement should play in our society in general. In my opinion, in our social order the principle of achievement should be the central criterion for distribution of individual opportunities and rewards. Neither the principle of success nor favoritism, seniority, birth and inherited privileges, coincidence, creed, race or skin colour, should determine the standing of individuals in our society. In an enlightened democratic society there can be no alternative to the principle of achievement, which of course needs to be socially anchored.

If my assessment of top-level competitive sport is correct, then it must be welcomed if human beings symbolically apply and express this principle in sport. It is my view that top-level competitive sport is worthy of being promoted and that they respond to important social interests. For this reason, it is also desirable for efforts to be made in order that top-level competitive sport may have good future prospects. Because of this, the problems and risks associated with top-level competitive sport cannot be simply ignored. The conditions under which top-level athletic performance is currently achieved frequently negate the symbolic role of sport, or at least detract from it. The violations of ethical principles which can be observed in many sport disciplines weaken the cultural value of top-level competitive sport, and it is impossible to disregard the fact that the principle of competition is increasingly generating dehumanized conditions in top-level sport.

- When the successes of a few top athletes can only be achieved at the expense of thousands of losers, when success in sport becomes more important than achievement, then the symbolic role of the entire system of top-level competitive sport is weakened or endangered.
- When the amount of time which athletes must invest in order to achieve first-rate performance becomes so great that the development of their personalities becomes one-sided, then athletes are no longer capable of embodying positive symbolic values.
- When the intervention of the state, business interests and the media, result in manipulation of athletes and irresponsible actions on their part, then top-level competitive sport has lost its meaning.

Table 41: Threats to modern top-level competitive sport

- Abuse of sport for political ends
- Business interests
- The questionable interests of the media
- Expectations by the public as regards ever greater levels of performance
- Growing threats to the health of athletes
- Material expense for training and competition
- Participation by children in high-pressure competitive sport as the necessary preparation for setting records
- Institutionalization and bureaucratization of sport organizations
- The growing influence of science and technology on sport

All of these dangers are evident; they must be countered in order to preserve the meaning of top-level competitive sport. In order to do so, it is necessary to confront the problems which are afflicting top-level competitive sport today.

4.   Factors likely to influence the future development of top-level competitive sport

A search for factors which will have a major influence on the future development of top-level competitive sport reveals that relatively dependable answers can only be given for those aspects which can today already be described with the aid of documented statistics. However, future developments will also be influenced by a number of other complex phenomena, and the extent of their relative influences can only be speculated upon (cf. Table 42). I would first like to briefly sketch those factors which can be assessed relatively exactly. If those trends are regarded which can be reliably discerned and foreseen at this time, then there is some justification in making the claim that top-level competitive sport continues to have positive prospects for the future. There will be enough athletes during the next decades who will be willing to commit themselves in top-level sport. In the future as well, sufficient numbers of coaches und full-time sport officials will be available who are willing to support the activities of athletes at the professional level. First-rate sport facilities will also be available in the future for top-level competitive sport. Presumably, the public will devote even more interest to the phenomenon of top-level competitive sport, which could in turn lead to increased involvement of the mass media in the field of top-level sport. One consequence of this interest could be greater activity by sponsors. Since the state cannot remain uninvolved in the phase of such a significant public development, state support for top-level sport can be expected in the future as well. Finally, there will also be a sufficiently large number of technologists and scientists willing to give top athletes and their coaches the support they need behind the scenes of the "sport theatre". All of this will happen in accordance with the basic rule which dictates that something will always continue to develop as long as everyone in it profits from everyone else.

In short this means: top-level competitive sport will continue to find powerful sponsors in the future. They will play such an important role that the state and the business sector will be more likely to increase than to lessen their interest in them. We live in a society in which the need for "grandiose identification" is widespread (cf. *Herms* 1985, 102 - 104). For the business sector, therefore, it is very lucrative if it can offer suitable identification objects to the people, and the state could see in them a possibility for implementing social policy; indeed, a political obligation could even be discerned. Top-level competitive sport, so it seems, is excellently suited for fulfillment of this obligation.

To be sure, such a positive picture of the future development of top-level competitive sport can only be obtained by restricting one's view to the surface of top-level competitive sport, in other words if one is not willing to regard all those intended and unintended effects and secondary effects which are already manifesting themselves today as top-level competitive sport rapidly are differentiating and proliferating.

Within this context, even relatively simple aspects become problematic, and some of the more complicated factors reveal themselves to be problems that will be quite difficult to solve.

Is it really true that there will be enough top athletes if the number of sport disciplines continues to grow? What kind of rivalry will develop among the sport associations as fewer and fewer children and young adults become available for more and more sport disciplines? How will they deal with this situation? Will the pyramidal structure of competition which is valid in the youth sport sector today break down?

Table 42: Indicators for the future development of top-level sport

Sport specific	In general
■ Recruitment of new athletes	■ Demography
■ Coaches	■ Labour market and conditions of employment
■ Full-time officials	■ Leisure time
■ Sport facilities	■ Public economic resources
■ Spectators	■ Income and distribution of income
■ Sport media	■ Cycles of life and the situation of families
■ Sport sponsors	■ Living and transport conditions Urban development
■ Patrons	■ Environment
■ State support	■ Public health
■ Sport science	■ Mass media
■ Sport technology	■ Education
■ Sport consumption	■ Impact of political participation
■ Athletes	■ Situation of the youth
■ Support by patrons	■ Trends in recreational activities
■ Assistance for sport facilities	■ Recreational consumption
■ Sport ethics	■ Entertainment needs
■ Sport rules and standards	■ Political developments
■ System of competition	■ Peace
■ Clubs and associations	■ Economic stability

Table 43: IOC Earnings by sponsoring

Topsponsors of the IOC	US-Dollar
1985 - 1988	100.000.000
1989 - 1992	170.000.000
1993 - 1996	200.000.000*

* estimated

How will the spectators be distributed if increasing numbers of competitive sport disciplines and competitive events are offered? Who will receive the money provided by sponsors and patrons? What will happen if the system of sponsorship and support enters into an economic crisis? What share of the financial support will be claimed by voluntary (unpaid) officials and others? Who will be willing at all to work on a voluntary basis within a system in which everything and everyone is paid for? Which sport association will be the first to abandon cooperation with the others and go its own way in pursuit of selfish interests? What will happen when the influence of technology and science becomes so intensive that it becomes possible to accurately predict the outcome of competitive events? Who will provide additional funds to sport facilities if the demands made upon them continue to grow as they have in the past? How will top-level competitive sport be organized in the future?

All of these questions have to do with complex phenomena which must be taken into account if we wish to guarantee a positive future for top-level competitive sport, and if individuals wish to contribute their share to this development as training supervisors, coaches or responsible club officials.

4.1 Top-level competitive sport as a paid activity

The first complex factor which I would like to deal with in this context can be given the heading of "top-level competitive sport as a paid activity". It is intimately connected with the issue of social security for athletes and the question of how to reintegrate athletes into society after they end their carreers in sport. To some extent, these aspects have been and continue to be discussed under the heading of "amateur sport", although the discussion surrounding this topic is still primarily characterized by hypocrisy and cowardliness. The discussion is hypocritical because it is conducted by sport officials who should and do know better; it can be described as cowardly because the courage to take the necessary decisive steps towards solving the problems cannot be observed anywhere, i.e. no solution is being offered to the real problems of the athletes. Arrangements such as those made in connection with admitting athletes like Boris Becker to take part in the Olympic Games in Seoul can no longer be discussed seriously by anyone except sport officials who are out of touch with reality. Objective observers can only smile at such discussions and rulings. It is high time for it to be recognized that the concept of the "amateur" is of no use for dealing with the problems facing athletes today. It is a left-over from a time in which it was still (wrongly) supposed that first-rate performance in sport represented a private kind of event. That is precisely what it was not, not even at the time when this was being put over as an ideology. It is true, that a certain number of wealthy persons, not infrequently members of the nobility, were able to practice top-level competitive sport as genuine amateurs at the expense of others, without realizing that their actions themselves "exploited" those at whose expense their elitist sport took place. It is particularly in the light of this background that it becomes apparent that the question of payment is by no means an ethical or moral problem, such as is claimed by the proponents of the amateur concept. The development towards the emergence of top-level competitive sport as a job is quite a normal one within the scope of the ongoing general professionalization of the sport system. It can therefore rightfully be assumed that the development towards professionalization of sport will continue (cf. *Neidhardt* 1985, 72 - 73). Increasing numbers of athletes will achieve ever-greater incomes in the field of sport.

In doing so they will be practising a "temporary profession". This development will contribute to more open recognition of professionalism in top-level competitive sport in the future, and will benefit top-level competitive sport itself. It will be endowed with a system of rules which is appropriate for a professionally practiced comparison of performance. Fears that this development could endanger the age-old, elegant moral inconsequence of top-level performance in sport appears to me to be unjustified in this context (cf. *Neidhardt* 1985, 74). The question as to whether sport will continue to be possible in the future if the outcome of sporting events ceases to be materially inconsequential can be answered with yes, simply on the basis of the fact that during recent years the existence of material rewards in sport has not endangered their existence. Remuneration for achievement in sport neither questions the principle of equality of opportunity, nor does it contradict any other of the ethical ideals of athletics. Moreover, it is in fundamental agreement with those standards and values which have proven themselves the world over in industrial societies and achieved recognition. "Good pay for good work" is a moral maxim which deserves to be defended. The question whether payment of athletes gives rise to a new set of moral values in sport is therefore of central importance. A much more important aspect is that the payment of athletes gives rise to a series of secondary problems which are more difficult to solve. One of them has to do with the fact that when victory in sport results in monetary gain, losing can mean financial ruin. In other words, if payment of athletes is accepted the question arises how to provide them with a measure to social security. The way professionalism in athletics is taking shape today, professional athletes take a much greater risk than that experienced by all of the other persons around them who also live in a professionalized sport environment. Consider the coach, the sport scientist, the managers and full-time sport officials, or the sport journalists. Their professions are relatively safe compared to that of the athletes. For the athlete, sport as a job can only be one of limited duration. It usually only lasts a few years, in soccer up to a maximum of 15, in other sport disciplines frequently just four to five years. This results in considerable social problems, for which scarcely anyone in the sport establishment feels responsible (cf. *Neidhardt* 1985, 72 - 73).

The business sector and the state only profit from athletes as long as they continue to perform. Once their professional carreers have come to an end, they become worthless for them from an economic point of view. The aging athlete as a social problem is thus by no means rare. On the contrary, we are dealing here with a conflict of a fundamental nature which could grow worse in the years ahead. It is not true that this conflict does not arise until the end of an athlete's carreer. Basically, it is present throughout each athlete's entire professional life. A survey of former olympic athletes revealed that 61 % of them regarded their withdrawal from active competition as having thrown up major problems in their lives. And almost unanimously they were of the opinion that, as one of them put drastically: "Somehow, our society-geared top-level competitive sport, as it is, must be changed in such a way that the value of each individual is based on more than one ability, and so that, when this ability no longer exists, the individual is not treated like something inferior. Athletes should direct some of their energies towards other things besides just training and competition. They must do this even before they retire from active sport, before the athletes' drop out or burn out. This process could start right at the beginning of their training." Orlick, who carried out this investigation, adds: "The challenge is not only to achieve outstanding performance in sport, but at the same time also to avoid destroying the rest of ones life in the process" (*Orlick*, quoted by *Lenk* 1985, 130 - 131).

This problem is not just the fault of the sport associations, the coaches, the officials, the states or the business sector. It is also the fault of the athletes themselves. Today's successful athletes rarely think about the fact that, in the final analysis, their success is always borne on the shoulders of others. In order for one athlete to become an Olympic champion in one sport discipline, thousands of losers are required. Where the future of top-level athletics is concerned, it will presumably be the case that individual athletes will become ethically more indiscriminate in this respect. The pressures placed upon them will cause them to concentrate even more on short-term, fast success. Such behavior is, however, harmful to the profession of top-level athletes. Like any other profession, top-level athletes also need collective representation of their interests. If athletes think not just of themselves, but also of the young athletes who will follow in their footsteps, and of those who have already finished their careers, perhaps having only made third place or having failed to achieve any fame, then individual athletes must be interested in joining up with other athletes to gain collective bargaining power. It will, therefore, be important for athletes to establish an organization to represent their own interests. If they join together

Table 44: The development of sport and finals in the history of modern Olympic Games

Olympic Games		Sport	Finals
1986	Athens	10	42
1900	Paris	14	97
1904	St. Louis	17	102
1906	Athens	11	77
1980	London	23	105
1912	Stockholm	13	106
1920	Antwerp	20	150
1924	Paris	18	131
1928	Amsterdam	15	122
1932	Los Angeles	15	126
1936	Berlin	20	144
1948	London	18	150
1952	Helsinki	17	149
1956	Melbourne/Stockholm	17	151
1960	Rome	17	150
1964	Tokyo	19	163
1968	Mexico City	18	172
1972	Munich	21	195
1976	Montreal	21	198
1980	Moscow	21	203
1984	Los Angeles	21	221
1988	Seoul	23	237
1992	Barcelona	25	257

(without winter sport competitions)

in a kind of union this could contribute to furthering and gaining acceptance for the collective interests of athletes. An "Athletes Union" would also be in the interests of survival of the sport system itself.

4.2   Just rewards for achievement in sport

The key question in connection with the problem of professionalization is that of just payment for performance in sport. Currently, the sport establishment tends to accept inflationary payment to a handful of athletes, while the majority are excluded from financial rewards of any kind. If this approach is maintained, then the system of top-level competitive sport has no chance of surviving. Instead of fulfilling an important cultural function by setting a positive example, top-level competitive sport would then only be symbolic of a success-oriented society. This would discredit achievement-oriented, democratic society. The sums, which are currently paid to top athletes such as Boris Becker for their athletic successes are in blatant contradiction of the ideal of just rewards for human achievement.

Table 45: International olympic movement leadership positions

	total	men N	%	women N	%
International Olympic Committee	91	85	93,4	6	6,6
Presidents, IOF	30	28	93,3	2	6,7
Secretaries General, IOF	30	27	90,0	3	10,0
Presidents, NOC	172	166	96,5	6	3,5
Secretaries General, NOC	166	162	97,6	4	2,4

cf. *Olympic Movement Directory* 92

To be sure, such contradictions also exist in other sectors of society, for instance in the entertainment industry, in connection with the production of some consumer goods and in some areas of science. However, these examples cannot let sport off the hook. In the interest of justice and fairness in sport, it must be asked whether it is acceptable for athletes to take enormous financial and physical risks to achieve top-level performance in those sport disciplines which are not favored by the media and the IOC, while in those kinds of sport favored by the media and the IOC the economic risks for the athletes are relatively minimal. The question must also be asked whether we can continue to tolerate the present situation, namely that top-level performance by athletes is prepared for and made possible as a team effort by their training supervisors, coaches and clubs, with successful athletes then privately marketing their athletic success with the support of managers and the private business sector. The problem of justice in sport also brings us to the question as to which criteria are applied in top-level sport today for determining the ranking lists. If rankings are set up according to criteria that have nothing to do with sport, instead of being based exclusively on the outcome of competitive events, then the solidarity of the community of athletes is placed in doubt (cf. *Heinemann* 1985, 83 - 95). Finally, the problem must be faced of female athletes in sport. Their participation rates are still increasing, but their rights and their influence on sport politics are still very low (cf. Table 45 and 47).

Table 46: Sport and professionalization in Germany

1. Acknowledged professional sport

Boxing	Tennis	Ping-Pong
Golf	Figure skating	Cycling
Motor sport	Riding	(USA/Japan)
Ice hockey	American football (USA)	Horse racing
Soccer	Dancing	

2. In the process of professionalization

Handball	Skiing (alpine)	Track and field
Basketball		Ocean sailing
Volleyball		Windsurfing

3. Professionalized to a lesser extent or not at all

Gymnastics	Sledding	Fencing
Canoeing/kayaking	Sailing	Rugby
Ski jumping	Shooting	Water polo
Polo	Rowing	Bobsledding
Weight lifting	Cross-country-skiing	Wrestling
Swimming	Badminton	Glider flying
Speed skating	Roller derby	Field hockey
Karate		Diving
Bowling (German skittles)		

(cf. *Fischer* 1984, 197)

Table 47: The modern summer Olympic Games athlete participation

Olympiad	total	males	% of males	females	% of females
Athens 1896	311	311	100,0	0	0,0
Paris 1900	1330	1319	99,2	11	0,8
St. Louis 1904	687	681	99,1	1	0,9
London 1908	2035	1999	98,2	36	1,8
Stockholm 1912	2547	2490	97,8	57	2,2
Berlin 1916		games cancelled			
Antwerp 1928	2607	2543	97,5	64	2,5
Paris 1924	3092	2956	95,6	136	4,4
Amsterdam 1928	3014	2724	90,4	290	9,6
Los Angeles 1932	1408	1281	91,0	290	9,0
Berlin 1936	4066	3738	91,9	328	8,1
Tokyo/Helsinki 1940		games cancelled			
London 1944		games cancelled			
London 1948	4099	3714	90,6	385	9,4
Helsinki 1952	4925	4097	89,7	518	10,3
Stockholm/Melbourne 1956	3342	2958	88,5	384	11,5
Rome 1960	5348	4738	88,6	610	11,4
Tokyo 1964	5140	4457	86,7	683	13,3
Mexico City 1968	5531	4750	85,9	781	14,1
Munich 1982	7830	6659	85,0	1171	15,0
Montreal 1976	6189	4915	79,4	1274	20,6
Moscow 1980	5512	4320	78,4	1192	21,6
Los Angeles 1984	7078	5458	77,1	1620	22,9
Seoul 1988	8527	6364	74,2	2163	25,8

(cf. D.A. *Kluka*, ICHPER Journal, 28 (1992) 3)

4.3 Survey of sport disciplines

From the inequality of rewards and opportunities available to athletes today it is only a short distance to the third factor which could influence the future prospects of top-level competitive sport. This factor has to do with the relative standing of the various sport disciplines. Although I have stated, in a fairly general manner, that the tendency towards professionalization in top-level competitive sport cannot be halted, it must nevertheless be recognized that not all sport disciplines are equally suited for professionalization; this, in turn, depends primarily on the degree to which they are capable of being commercialized.

In an analysis which was carried out of 52 sport disciplines, for instance, half of them were determined to be relatively unsuited for professionalization (cf. Table 46). Similar to the question of ranking of athletes, the question as to the ranking of sport disciplines also arises. The yardstick for determining the suitability of a sport discipline for professionalization is today no longer the quality and quantity of athletic performance, nor is the effort invested by athletes in training. Ultimately, it is the degree of attractiveness which a sport discipline is capable of exerting on the public which governs how suitable it is for professionalization and commercialization. The questions whether the balance among the various sport disciplines can be maintained and whether the injustices in the evaluation of sport disciplines which can already be observed today can be eliminated in the future cannot be answered at this time. Much seems to indicate that in the future solidarity in sport will decline as the importance of money grows (cf. *Heinemann* 1985, 95). This is already apparent in the discussion on distribution of television earnings, and in that on payment of athletes. The attempt which is being made to balance out these developments by providing state assistance to neglected sport disciplines does not have much chance of succeeding. Or at least in the past it has been shown that this approach is capable of only partially solving the problem of balance. It can be assumed that in the immediate future an increasing number of disadvantaged sport disciplines will be opposed by a shrinking number of preferred ones. In the final analysis, the matter of a balance among the various sport disciplines will therefore be governed by the existence of an arrangement between the wealthy minority and the poor majority in sport. Will it be possible to find redistributing mechanisms to ensure a financial transfer from the rich athletes, the rich associations and the rich clubs on the one hand, to the many have-nots on the other hand?

4.4   An arrangement between the sport establishment, the state and industry

The efforts to achieve a more just balance by means of appropriate sport policies have to do with the injustices which have been necessarily generated by increasing social demands being placed on sport, i.e. by the progressive differentiation of the sport establishment. These inequities have been primarily the result of intervention by the state and business interests in the system of sport. In view of this, the question as to an arrangement with the state and the business sector will have special significance for the future development of top-level competitive sport. In order to understand the problem, it is important to take another, closer look at the foundation on which top-level competitive sport is based. Even today, top athletes are still recruited primarily from the normal sport clubs. The goal of normal club athletics is to provide their members with the best possible opportunities and means to put their own interests into practice where games, athletics and physical activity are concerned. As a rule, decisions on how to achieve the club objectives are made democratically by all of the members. A sport program is agreed upon, of course within the limits imposed by the size of the club and the willingness of its members to bear the costs incurred. Heinemann has stressed several times that, beyond this, normal clubs only produce for themselves, and not for others (cf. *Heinemann* 1984, 17 - 51; 1985, 88). The situation is fundamentally different in the top-level competitive sport sector. The goal of top-level competitive sport is to produce for others, i.e. to take their orientation from the interests and wishes of third parties outside of the sport institutions. Top-level competitive sport must acquiesce to the conditions under which a competitive event becomes especially attractive to spectators, since only then can they sell their merchandise. The athletes themselves must accept this market orientation. They are forced to come to terms with the fact that this is the inevitable consequence of their professionalism. In this connection, the curious situation can occur that the spectators do not want to see the professional orientation of athletes, or even that they have an interest in it remaining hidden; and as a result, the athletes ritualize their activities, i.e. they disguise their professional orientation (cf. *Heinemann* 1985, 87 - 93).

So on the one hand we have the sport clubs with their inwardly directed interests, and on the other hand the institution of top-level competitive sport, the interests of which are outwardly directed. This conflict of interests could not be more drastic. Most of the 60.000 sport clubs in the Federal Republic of Germany are no longer directly involved in the presentation of "top-level competitive sport as merchandise". This is now primarily the affair of the athletes, who as a rule occupy positions in the regional and national associations. Because of this, top-level sport in the Federal Republik of Germany are dealt with for the most part at the highest level, without giving consideration to the fact that the real conflict of interests is situated at the bottom of the sport pyramid. As regards an arrangement among the sport establishment, the state and industry, it would be logical to first strive for an arrangement at the highest level. However, this carries the risk that the arrangement could be contrary to the interests of the base of the sport system itself, namely the clubs. After all, these continue to be the ultimate source of top-level competitive sport as a merchandise, even when it only benefits itself to a limited extent from the profits that are made. The key question demanding an answer today is: how will it be possible for sport, state and industry, to come to a mutual agreement that is in the interests of all concerned? One requirement for finding the answer to this question is that the sport sector be aware of what its interests really are. The question of an arrangement between sport on the one hand, and the state and industry on the other, is therefore also a question of interests and one of who is in charge. For sport the question as to who is in charge is intimately linked to the question of its autonomy. Will sport be able, within the context of an arrangement with the interests of the state and industry, to continue to determine and enforce its rules independently and appropriately? In my view, the question of the autonomy of sport is today rarely dealt with in a realistic manner. It by no means follows that sport is autonomous if it can set its own rules if the results which these yield are increasingly in the interests of the state and industry, while ignoring the interests of the athletes, the associations and clubs. This danger is present every time that external experts are fetched to act as supposedly independent sport officials and determine the rules in sport, without being familiar with the elementary interests of sport. This tendency can already be observed in several sport associations. In this way, the interests of sport are being undermined and/or corrupted (cf. *Digel* 1986b, 16 - 19; *Neidhardt* 1985, 76).

But what, one could interject at this point, are the real interests of sport? What is the point of solidarity in sport? If relations between sport, industry and the state are governed exclusively by economic criteria, then this can pose an acute threat to solidarity within the sport community, as Heinemann has repeatedly pointed out (1985). In the foreseeable future as well, there will be a large number of recreational athletes and voluntary officials standing opposite a minority of paid athletes, coaches and managers. This fact alone makes clear, that sport is unable to finance all of its interests on its own. It will continue to depend on voluntary work by a large number of persons, and at its grass-roots level it will continue to be confronted with the needs of normal club members, which are virtually incompatible with simultaneous intensive support of top-level sport within the clubs. And because of this it will be important for sport officials and the clubs and associations in this situation to be sensitive to the question of the standing of club members, to the question of the role played by voluntary work and to the question as to the functions which sport clubs should and want to fulfill. The same kind of sensitivity will also be required on the part of all those officials at the level of the national sport associations who are responsible for obtaining the new financial resources needed to maintain top-level competitive sport. The clubs will of course also have to make sensible decisions on economic matters. The financial structures of the clubs have undergone important changes during recent years. The proportion of the overall budgets of German sport clubs accounted for by contributions and fees from the members has fallen to 45 %, and in individual cases as low as 10 %. The rest is covered by externally provided funds. The solution to the funding problem will therefore be more just distribution of income and expenditure, and it will not be acceptable for recreational athletes to finance top-level athletes so that these can later turn to profit-marketing themselves on their own (cf. *Heinemann* 1985, 92).

The question of solidarity in the sport community is frequently discussed today in connection with the much-cited organizational unity of sport. The necessary balancing act between the sport associations and the clubs which I have already sketched, does not depend in my view on all of sport being monolithically organized, especially since the current situation in sport in the Federal Republic of Germany is characterized by the fact that sport is organized in a non-uniform way. In the same way that it is impossible for uniformity of the contents of sport to be achieved in the foreseeable future, it is also unrealistic to demand or expect organizational unity in sport. A differentiated type of organization in sport can indeed even result in increased efficiency, and this does not necessarily mean that top-level competitive sport must then play a morally weakened role. It will be important, however, for the dealings between the various organizational systems involved in sport to be regulated by fair contractual agreements that will create a situation of equilibrium. I believe that to achieve this will be the most important political task facing sport officials during the next few years.

4.5 The limits of athletic achievement

Economic analysis of the future of top-level competitive sport often ignore the fact that in the final analysis the development of top-level competitive sport primarily depends on the individuals involved, i.e. on the athletes and their physical and mental capabilities. It is a very lucky thing for top-level competitive sport that it is still not possible to exactly calculate the limits of athletic achievement. The real limits cannot be identified by experimental means. In spite of this, there are of course also biological limits to performance in top-level competitive sport, and in the course of further developments it will be necessary to take these into account. However, I think it is also important to recognize that they must also be culturally determined, i.e. ethically defined, limits. These are expressed in norms which we have established for ourselves and of which I assume that the future of top-level competitive sport will largely depend. These limits can also be violated, and it is possible to discuss whether ethically defined limits are meaningful at all, or whether other types of limits are called for. The question as to where sport stops and where it turns into something else is related to the question of ethical evaluation in the light of the ideas of humanity and morality (cf. *Digel* 1984, 199 - 213; *Lenk* 1985, 55 - 63, among others). In order to answer these questions, a serious brand of sport ethics is required which goes beyond superficial and noncommittal speculation. It is not enough to simply stress the principle of fair play. The kind of sport ethics which is needed must also be firmly rooted in the consciousness of the athletes, and no less in that of coaches, training supervisors and officials (cf. *Lenk* 1985, 62).

The question as to the limits of athletic achievement arises today at various different levels. For one, it is facing athletes in connection with the relationship between training and athletic achievement. The value of training for approaching the limits of what is humanely possible is becoming increasingly questionable. The demands and expectations as to performance, which are applied to athletes from the outside have led in some sport disciplines to such an enormous effort in terms of training, talent and scientific, technological, practical, physiological and psychological coaching and supervision that one must ask oneself whether the results achieved justify the effort invested. The reason is that usually only minimal additional gains are made; improvements in performance are advancing in ever-smaller steps. In view of the additional risks which this causes for the athletes, this development must be regarded as extremely dangerous. In order to achieve even small performance gains, athletes must put up with ever growing risks of excessive stress, accidents, permanent injury and other harm, all in order to advance a little bit more masterly in a specialized skill. If this is compounded by public pressure to perform, by the goal of competition being to win medals, or if sport is the only road open for athletes to advance socially, in other words if sport becomes and ends in itself, then it loses all its desirable attributes. This questionable development is encouraged by the existence of doctors who practice a kind of sport medicine in which they are willing to use medical tools to manipulate athletic performance, without stopping to consider that their task as physicians is actually quite a different one. The limits of top-level sport are - and this should be emphasized once more - not just of biological nature. They are also defined by the rules of sport, by the idea of sport and by the ethics of sport. Lenk rightfully points out that the principles of equality of opportunity and of giving everyone a fair chance would justify the existing prohibition of drug-use in athletics even if the use of anabolic steroids and other drugs were not dangerous from a medical point of view. The same applies to violence, cheating and manipulations of every kind (cf. *Lenk* 1985, 55).

The problem of locating the limits of top-level competitive sport also includes the quantitative aspect of competitive events. Here too, there is much to indicate that the ongoing proliferation of World Cups, European championships and similar competitions at the national level is doing its share to push top-level competitive sport too close to its limits. Even today, coaches complain that the endless succession of competitive events is preventing them from effectively applying their knowledge to the training of their athletes. This enhances even further the dangers to which athletes are exposed, thus lastingly endangering the "stuff of which competitive events are made". This example helps to make clear just how necessary it is for top-level competitive sport to be willing to voluntarily exert a certain amount of self-restraint.

The problem of the limits of athletic performance is, finally, also linked to the question of how to evaluate winning and victory in athletics in an ethically justified manner. When the reality of top-level sport is characterized by coaches' slogans such as: "Winning is not everything. It is the only thing", "Every time you win, you're reborn; when you lose, you die a little" or "Nice guys always finish last", then top-level competitive sport has lost its symbolic value; it has gone beyond the limits of what is acceptable. In the long run, it will be impossible to win over enough athletes for the ethical principles behind top-level competitive sport in the face of such cynicism. This

Table 48: The prospect of modern top-level sport

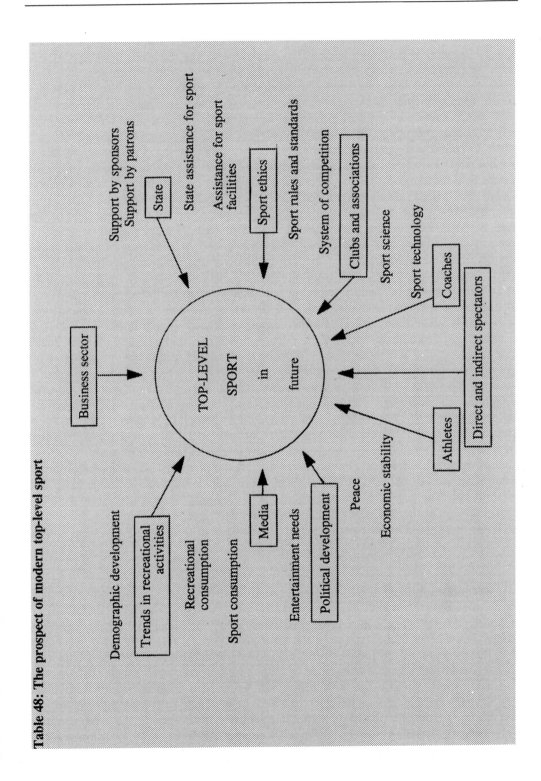

Demographic development

Trends in recreational activities

Recreational consumption

Sport consumption

Entertainment needs

Political development

Peace

Economic stability

Business sector

Support by sponsors
Support by patrons

State

State assistance for sport

Assistance for sport facilities

Sport ethics

Sport rules and standards

System of competition

Clubs and associations

Sport science

Sport technology

Coaches

Direct and indirect spectators

Athletes

Media

TOP-LEVEL SPORT in future

criticism should not be misunderstood. I'm not advocating an idealistic approach on the lines of "winning is not important; all that matters is playing the game and how well one plays" or comforting sayings like "participating is more important than winning" (cf. *Lenk* 1985, 45 - 46). Such slogans cannot be taken seriously by today's athletes. I would just like to make clear that, in the long run, emphasizing victory in athletics to the exclusion of all else is bound to raise doubts as to the validity of sport as a whole. This questioning will of course then also take place at the highest levels. If top-level competitive sport comes to reflect and symbolize the rivalry between different social systems, and this is without doubt already the case at some competitive events and within the scope of certain sports, then the symbolic role of sport that I consider to be so valuable is also placed in doubt; the bounds of meaningful athletic activity have been exceeded. Today it is unfortunately the case that, in international top-level competitive sport, this athlete or that team is most likely to win medals which is in a position to carry out major scientific research programmes in a wind tunnel, which has a staff of specialists in biomechanics serving as advisers, which applies modern methods of sport psychology and which, of course, can rely on a competent team of physicians who are also willing to exceed the usual limits imposed by medical ethics. It is in this way that the principle of equality of opportunity in sport has been distorted. This distortion places the developing countries at an especially great disadvantage. If technological superiority is a sufficient condition for success in a given athletic discipline, in other words if the training effort by individuals, their special talents and experience cease to be the deciding factors governing who wins and who loses in sport, then a boundary has been exceeded which sport has set itself in the form of its rules. It can be regarded as fortunate that in the majority of the Olympic disciplines the technological aspect alone does not yet carry enough weight to govern success and failure. The escalation of competition, however, is rapidly leading to a situation in which it is virtually impossible for any sport to completely do without technology (cf. *Lenk* 1985, 59 - 62). There is little chance of halting this trend.

However, this prognosis is only correct if organized sport fails to take appropriate action. By means of autonomous rulings, they could succeed in influencing this development. The capability for autonomous action by sport associations must therefore be regarded as having the potential for playing a major role in resolving the question of the limits of top-level athletic performance. On the basis of this insight, it is now possible to provide a few pieces of useful advice for the future.

5.   Recommendations

In future, the following eight recommendations should be taken to heart by officials, athletes and coaches in the sport clubs and associations:

1.   The associations must more openly acknowledge the professionalization of athletes. It should cease to be looked upon as something immoral when athletes earn money from sport. Sport must stop being part of a semi-criminal shadow economy. Conversely, this also implies that taxes must be paid on profits made from sport.
2.   The professionalization of athletes is the logical consequence of the comprehensive demands placed by society on top-level competitive sport. It is plain that athletes require a special kind of social insurance. This must be financed and organized by

the sport associations. The responsibility for doing so must not be turned over to the state or to the business sector.

3. In order for athletes to obtain the social insurance they need, it is essential for all athletes to join forces to collectively advance their interests. A union-like organization of athletes must be formed. Such an organization would be important, not only for the welfare of the individual athletes, but also for the survival of the entire sport system as such.

4. The associations must develop systems of payment for their athletes that are acceptable in terms of payment for work done and which ensure just distribution of earnings among young athletes, winners, losers and retired athletes.

5. The associations must, if they wish to attain a position of strength opposite the state and industry, practise solidarity in their dealings with one another. Strong associations must grant financial support to weaker associations. To this end, practicable arrangements and rules must be elaborated and contractually fixed.

6. The sport establishment must not lose sight of the fact that its strength lies in its ability to autonomously define its own rules. This applies both to the issue of the limits of athletic performance and to the question of commercialization.

7. The sport establishment must have the courage to impose definite sanctions. To do so, it requires a monitoring system and effective penalties, i.e. the world of sport must come to terms with the fact that it needs even more rules and regulations. The athletes must comprehend that their future depends on complying with the rules laid down by the association. In relations between athletes and their associations, it is therefore important for the athletes to understand that sanctions imposed, i.e. the power of the sport establishment, are employed in the common interest of all the athletes.

8. It must be accepted that clubs and associations search for new ways of financing their activities. Nonetheless, it must also be kept in mind that the search for new approaches to funding can also lead to new dependencies. It is therefore important for organized sport to monopolize access to the goods they have to market, namely to top-level competitive sport. The privilege of access to competitive sporting events must be reserved for the sport establishment itself. Once the sport establishment has gained control of this monopoly, the problem of outside manipulation will have been largely solved. The sport establishment will then have sufficient authority to impose and enforce sanctions against undesired interference. These could extend to the refusal to grant broadcasting rights and to prohibiting advertising using the medium of sport; athletes could be prevented from participating, and those physicians could be permanently banned who violate the ethical ideals of sport. Only in this way it is possible to ensure that top-level competitive sport will retain its symbolic function with an educational influence on other areas of life.

In other words, on the one hand the sport associations must not relinquish control over their dealings with the business sector by entrusting it to private agencies or even to the athletes themselves. On the other hand, neither should they ever forget that, ultimately, their foundations lie in the sport clubs. In order to protect their own interests, therefore, the associations must take care to select individuals to serve as their top-level officials who are familiar with the business world, i.e. who have learned to act in accordance with economic principles, while at the same time making their decisions in the interest of sport.

6. Concluding remarks

Our society depends on individual motivation and achievement. Great importance must be attached to promoting and encouraging both attributes. Top-level competitive sport is ideally suited for symbolic representation of both. By the same token, however, it can also discredit them. This already occurs frequently enough. Questions having to do with sport ethics are therefore destined to play a key role in determining the future prospects of top-level competitive sport. The greatest problems facing top-level competitive sport are those involved with application and enforcement of ethical and humanitarian ideals. These represent a major challenge not only for athletes, but also for coaches and officials. Because of this, I would like to conclude with the following statement:

For educational and ethical reasons, we are in need of top-level competitive sport which has learned to let its behavior be guided by sensible moderation instead of sacrificing its principles for the glamour of top-level athletic performance. This calls for training supervisors, coaches and athletes that make a genuine commitment to ethics in sport and who exert their influence on others to adopt the same convictions. The athletes must be coached and guided in a responsible manner to make those experiences possible in top-level competitive sport which could be so significant for the further evolution of our society.

References

ANDERS, G./G. SCHILLING (Hrsg.): Hat der Spitzensport (noch) eine Zukunft? Magglingen 1985.

ANDRESEN, R./H. RIEDER/G. TROSIEN (Hrsg.): Beiträge zur Zusammenarbeit im Sport mit der Dritten Welt. Schorndorf 1989.

ARBEITSGRUPPE SOZIALBERICHTERSTATTUNG: Wandel von Lebensformen. Entsolidarisierung durch Individualisierung? In: WZB-Mitteilungen 44 (1989), 15 - 19.

ARBEITSGRUPPE SOZIALBERICHTERSTATTUNG: Entwicklung der Wohlfahrt. Veränderte Lebensbedingungen und Einstellungen. In: WZB-Mitteilungen 47 (1990), 16 - 20.

BABST, C.: Die Gegenwart der Diskussion um die Zukunft des Spitzensports. In: ANDERS, G./G. SCHILLING (Hrsg.): Hat der Spitzensport (noch) eine Zukunft? Bericht des 23. Magglinger Symposiums 1985, 177 - 193.

BALL, D.W./D.W. LOY: Sport and Social Order: Contributions to the Sociology of Sport. Reading (Mass.) 1975.

BAT (Hrsg.): Freizeit-Daten. Zahlen zur Freizeit-Situation und Entwicklung in der Bundesrepublik Deutschland. Auswahl und Bearbeitung: H.W. OPASCHOWSKI. Hamburg 1982.

BECK, U.: Risikogesellschaft. Auf dem Weg in eine andere Moderne. Frankfurt 1986.

BECK, U.: Der Konflikt der zwei Modernen. In: ZAPF, W. (Hrsg.): Die Modernisierung moderner Gesellschaften. Frankfurt 1991, 40 - 54.

BECKER, P.: Sport in den Massenmedien - Zur Herstellung und Wirkung einer eigenen Welt. In: Sportwissenschaft 13 (1983) 1, 24 - 25.

BELL, D.: Die nachindustrielle Gesellschaft. Frankfurt/New York 1976.

BENDIX, R.: Nation-building and Citizenship. New York 1964.

BENDIX, R.: Modernisierung und soziale Ungleichheit. In: FISCHER, W. (Hrsg.): Wirtschafts- und sozialgeschichtliche Probleme der frühen Industrialisierung. Berlin 1968, 179 - 246.

BERELSON, B.: Content Analysis in Communication Research. Glencoe 1952.

BERGER, P.L./G. BERGER/H. KELLNER: Das Unbehagen in der Modernität. Frankfurt/New York 1975.

BERTRAM, H.: Einleitung. In: BERTRAM, H. (Hrsg.): Gesellschaftlicher Zwang und moralische Autonomie. Frankfurt 1986, 9 - 30.

BINNEWIES, H.: Sport und Sportberichterstattung. Ahrensburg 1975.

BÖHME, G.: Hat der Fortschritt eine Zukunft? In: Universitas. Zeitschrift für Wissenschaft, Kunst und Literatur 41/9, 1986, 929 - 938.

BRANDT, G.: Industrialisierung, Modernisierung, gesellschaftliche Entwicklung. In: Zeitschrift für Soziologie 1 (1972) 1, 5 - 14.

BREED, W.: Soziale Kontrolle in der Redaktion: eine funktionale Analyse. In: AUFERMANN, J. u.a.: Gesellschaftliche Kommunikation und Information. Frankfurt 1973, 356 - 378.

BÜHL, W.: Die "postindustrielle Gesellschaft": Eine verfrühte Utopie? In: KZfSS 35 (1983), 771 - 780.

CAPLOW, T./H.M. BAHR/J. MODELL/B.A. CHADWICK: Recent social trends in the United States 1960 - 1990. Frankfurt 1991.

DANKERT, H.: Sportsprache und Kommunikation. Tübingen 1969.

DARROW, M.: Sport im Rundfunk. Sehgewohnheiten während der Fußball-WM 1982 und Ergebnisse einer gemeinsamen ARD/ZDF Untersuchung. In: Media Perspektiven 1 (1983), 47 - 56.

DEUTSCH, K.W.: Soziale Mobilisierung und politische Entwicklung. In: ZAPF, W. (Hrsg.): Theorien des sozialen Wandels. Köln/Berlin 1970, 329 - 350.

DEUTSCHE FORSCHUNGSGEMEINSCHAFT (Hrsg.): Freizeit im Wandel. Düsseldorf 1984.

DEUTSCHER SPORTBUND (Hrsg.): Sport, Leistung, Gesellschaft. Eine zeitkritische Dokumentation des deutschen Spitzensports. München 1975.

DIGEL, H.: Sport und nationale Repräsentation. Spitzensport im Dienste der Politik. In: Der Bürger im Staat 25 (1975) 3, 195 - 202.

DIGEL, H.: Sprache und Sprechen im Sport. Schorndorf 1976.

DIGEL, H.: Mannschaftsbesprechung in Theorie und Praxis - Ein Versuch journalistischer Aufklärung. In: Leistungssport 9 (1979) 5, 372 - 383.

DIGEL, H.: Sportberichterstattung in der DDR - ein Modell? In: Leistungssport 10 (1980) 6, 510 - 521.

DIGEL, H.: Erwartungen an den Sportjournalismus. In: BINNEWIES, H.: Sport und Massenmedien. Ahrensburg 1981a, 37 - 61.

DIGEL, H.: Sozialistische Parteilichkeit als Merkmal der DDR-Sportberichterstattung. In: Publizistik 26 (1981b) 1, 86 - 103.

DIGEL, H.: Sport verstehen und gestalten. Reinbek 1982.

DIGEL, H./S. VOLKNANT: Der Sport in der DDR in der Presse der Bundesrepublik Deutschland. In: Publizistik 28 (1983), 3.

DIGEL, H.: Gesellschaftliche Entwicklung und der Auftrag des Sportvereins. In: KULTUSMINISTER DES LANDES NORDRHEIN-WESTFALEN (Hrsg.): Sportentwicklung - Einflüsse und Rahmenbedingungen - Eine Expertenbefragung. Köln 1984a, 52 - 67.

DIGEL, H.: Zur pädagogischen Bedeutung von Sportregeln. In: ADL (Hrsg.): Schüler im Sport - Sport für Schüler. Schorndorf 1984b, 199 - 213.

DIGEL, H.: Über den Wandel der Werte in Gesellschaft, Freizeit und Sport. In: DSB (Hrsg.): Die Zukunft des Sports. Materialien zum Kongreß "Menschen im Sport 2000". Schorndorf 1986a, 14 - 43.

DIGEL, H.: Jugend von heute - Führungskräfte von morgen? In: Olympische Jugend 31 (1986b) 10, 16 - 19.

DIGEL, H.: Sport in der Risikogesellschaft. In: KLEIN, M. (Hrsg.): Sport und soziale Probleme. Reinbek 1989a, 71 - 120.

DIGEL, H.: Sport in der Entwicklungszusammenarbeit. Köln 1989b.

DIGEL, H.: Wertewandel im Sport - Eine These und deren begriffliche, theoretische und methodische Schwierigkeiten. In: ANDERS, G. (Hrsg.): Vereinssport an der Wachstumsgrenze? Sport in der Krise der Industriegesellschaften. Witten 1990a, 59 - 85.

DIGEL, H.: Die Versportlichung unserer Kultur und deren Folgen für den Sport - ein Beitrag zur Uneigentlichkeit des Sports. In: GABLER, H./U. GÖHNER (Hrsg.): Für einen besseren Sport... Themen, Entwicklungen und Perspektiven aus Sport und Sportwissenschaft. Ommo Grupe zum 60. Geburtstag. Tübingen 1990b, 73 - 96.

DIGEL, H.: Sport in den 90er Jahren - Eine perspektivische Situationsskizze. In: Sportstättenbau + Bäderanlagen. Internationale Fachzeitschrift für Sport-, Bäder- und Freizeitanlagen 25 (1991) 1, 17 - 28.

DIGEL, H.: Zum Umgang Jugendlicher mit Sportsendungen im Fernsehen. In: Publizistik. Vierteljahresschrift der Kommunikationsforschung 37 (1992) 2, 183 - 196.

DÖBERT, R./G. NUNNER-WINKLER: Wertwandel und Moral. In: BERTRAM, H. (Hrsg.): Gesellschaftlicher Zwang und moralische Autonomie. Frankfurt 1986, 289 - 321.

DUNNING, E. (Ed.): The Sociology of Sport. A Selection of Readings. London 1976. 2nd Impression.

EDWARDS, H.: Sociology of sport. Homewood (Illi.) 1973.

EICHBERG, H.: Der Weg des Sports in die industrielle Zivilisation. Baden-Baden 1973.

EISENSTADT, S.M.: Modernization: Protest and Change. Englewood Cliffs 1966.

EISENSTADT, S.M.: Sozialer Wandel, Differenzierung und Evolution. In: ZAPF, W. (Hrsg.): Theorien des sozialen Wandels. Köln/Berlin 1970, 75 - 91.

EITZEN, D.S./G.H. SAGE: Sociology of North American Sport. 4th Ed. Dubuque (Iowa) 1978.

EMNID: Freizeitbedingungen und Freizeitentwicklungen. Bielefeld 1983.

ENGFER, U./K. HINRICHS/H. WIESENTHAL: Arbeitswerte im Wandel. Empirische Analyse zum Zusammenhang von unkonventionellen Werten und Arbeitsbedingungen. In: MATTHES, J. a.a.O., Frankfurt 1983, 434 - 454.

FEND, H./H.G. PRESTER: Jugend in den 70er und 80er Jahren: Wertewandel, Bewußtseinswandel und potentielle Arbeitslosigkeit. In: ZSE 5 (1985) 1, 43 - 70.

FEND, H./L.v. FRIEDEBURG: Zur Einführung: Jugend im sozialen Wandel. In: ZSE 5 (1985) 1, 1 - 3.

FISCHER, H.: Anmerkungen zur Erwerbschance im professionalistischen Sport. In: HEINEMANN, K. (Hrsg.): Texte zur Ökonomie des Sports. Schorndorf 1984, 196 - 214.

GEBAUER, G.: Wie regeln Spielregeln das Spiel? In: GRUPE, O./H. GABLER/U. GÖHNER (Hrsg.): Spiel - Spiele - Spielen. Schorndorf 1983, 154 - 161.

GERHARDS, J./F. NEIDHARDT: Strukturen und Funktionen moderner Öffentlichkeit. Fragestellungen und Ansätze. Berlin 1990.

GLUCHOWSKI, P.: Freizeit und Lebensstile. Plädoyer für eine integrierte Analyse von Freizeitverhalten. In: DGFF-Dokumente 2. Erkrath 1988.

GRUPE, O.: Vom Sinn (und Unsinn) des Hochleistungssports. In: Ethische, psychologische und sozialpsychologische Fragen an den Leistungssport. Symposium am 29. und 30. September 1980 in München. Eine Dokumentation. München 1980, 9 - 26.

GRUPE, O.: Bewegung, Spiel und Leistung im Sport. Schorndorf 1982.

GRUPE, O.: Hat der Spitzensport (noch) eine Zukunft? Versuch einer Standortbestimmung. In: ANDERS, G./G. SCHILLING (Hrsg.): Hat der Spitzensport (noch) eine Zukunft. Magglingen 1985, 13 - 42.

GRUPE, O.: Sport als Kultur. Zürich 1987.

GUTMANN, A.: Vom Ritual zum Rekord. Das Wesen des modernen Sports. Schorndorf 1979.

HABERMAS, J.: Technik und Wissenschaft als "Ideologie". Frankfurt 1968.

HABERMAS, J.: Theorie des kommunikativen Handelns. Frankfurt 1981.

HABERMAS, J.: Der philosophische Diskurs der Moderne. Frankfurt 1985.

HACKFORT, J.: Sport im Fernsehen. Münster 1975.

HACKFORT, J./S. WEISCHENBERG (Hrsg.): Sport und Massenmedien. Bad Homburg 1978.

HAMMELSBECK, O.: Die Bedeutung von Sport und Spiel für die moderne Gesellschaft. In: PLESSNER, H./H.E. BOCK/O. GRUPE (Hrsg.): Sport und Leibeserziehung. Sozialwissenschaftliche, pädagogische und medizinische Beiträge. München 1967, 66 - 83.

HEINEMANN, K.: Einführung in die Soziologie des Sportunterrichts. Schorndorf 1980.

HEINEMANN, K.: Einführung in die Soziologie des Sports. 2. überarbeitete Auflage. Schorndorf 1983.

HEINEMANN, K. (Hrsg.): Texte zur Ökonomie des Sports. Schorndorf 1984.

HEINEMANN, K.: Problem einer Ökonomie des Sports. In: HEINEMANN, K. (Hrsg.): Texte zur Ökonomie des Sports. Schorndorf 1984, 17 - 51.

HEINEMANN, K.: Voraussetzungen und Konsequenzen einer Kommerzialisierung des Leistungssports. In: ANDERS, G./G. SCHILLING (Hrsg.): Hat der Spitzensport (noch) eine Zukunft? Magglingen 1985, 83 - 96.

HERMS, E.: Die Bedeutung der Ideologisierung für die Zukunft des Spitzensports. In: ANDERS, G./G. SCHILLING (Hrsg.): Hat der Spitzensport (noch) eine Zukunft? Magglingen 1985, 97 - 113.

HILLMANN, K.-H.: Wertwandel. Zur Frage soziokultureller Voraussetzungen alternativer Lebensformen. 2. Auflage. Darmstadt 1989.

HINRICHS, K./H. WIESENTHAL: Arbeitswerte und Arbeitszeit. Zur Pluralisierung von Wertmustern und Zeitverwendungswünschen in der modernen Industriegesellschaft. In: OFFE, C./K. HINRICHS/H. WIESENTHAL (Hrsg.): Arbeitszeitpolitik. Formen und Folgen einer Neuverteilung der Arbeitszeit. 2. Auflage. Frankfurt/New York 1983.

HORTLEDER, G.: Die Faszination des Fußballspiels. Soziologische Anmerkungen zum Sport als Freizeit und Beruf. Frankfurt 1974.

HORTLEDER, G.: Sport in der nachindustriellen Gesellschaft. Eine Einführung in die Sportsoziologie. Frankfurt 1978.

HORTLEDER, G.: Die Sprachlosigkeit des Fernsehsports. In: HERMANN, I./A.-L. HEYGSTER: Fernsehkritik. Sprache im Fernsehen. Mainz 1981, 85 - 93.

HOVLAND, C.I./I.L. JANIS: An overview of personability research. In: SERENO, K.K./C.D. Mortensen (Eds.): Foundations of communication theory. New York 1970, 222 - 233.

INGLEHART, R.: The silent revolution: Changing values and political styles among Western publics. New York 1977.

INKELES, A./D.H. SMITH: Becoming Modern - Individual Changes in Six Developing Countries. Cambridge (Mass.) 1974.

INSTITUT FÜR FREIZEITWIRTSCHAFT: Der Freizeitsport der Bundesbürger bis 1990. München 1983.

JAEGGI, U.: Modernität und Aufklärung - oder was sonst? In: SCHÜTZ, W. (Red.): Politik und Kultur. Berlin 1986, 20 - 33.

JAGODZINSKI, W.: Gibt es einen intergenerationellen Wertewandel zum Postmaterialismus? In: ZSE 5 (1985) 1, 71 - 88.

JENS, W.: Fernsehen - Themen und Tabus. München 1973.

JONAS, H.: Das Prinzip Verantwortung. Versuch einer Ethik für die technische Zivilisation. Frankfurt 1984.

JONAS, H.: Wertfreie Wissenschaft und Freiheit der Forschung. In: Universitas. Zeitschrift für Wissenschaft, Kunst und Literatur 42/10, 1987a, 983 - 1002.

JONAS, H.: Ist erlaubt, was machbar ist? Bemerkungen zur neuen Schöpferrolle des Menschen. In: Universitas. Zeitschrift für Wissenschaft, Kunst und Literatur 42/2, 1987b, 103 - 115.

JUGENDWERK DER DEUTSCHEN SHELL (Hrsg.): Jugend 81. Lebensentwürfe, Alltagskulturen, Zukunftsbilder. Hamburg 1981.

KLAGES, H.: Überlasteter Staat - verdrossene Bürger? Zu den Dissonanzen der Wohlfahrtsgesellschaft. Frankfurt/New York 1981.

KLAGES, H.: Wertewandel und Gesellschaftskrise in der sozialstaatlichen Demokratie. In: MATTHES, J. (Hrsg.): Deutscher Soziologentag, Bamberg 1982. Frankfurt 1983, 341 - 352.

KLAGES, H.: Wertedynamik. Über die Wandelbarkeit des Selbstverständlichen. Zürich/Osnabrück 1988.

KLAGES, H./H.J. HIPPLER/W. HERBERT (Hrsg.): Werte und Wandel. Ergebnisse und Methoden einer Forschungstradition. Frankfurt 1992.

KLEIN, M. (Hrsg.): Sport und soziale Probleme. Reinbek 1989.

KLINGEMANN, H.D.: Neuere Analysen des Wertewandels in modernen Gesellschaften. In: Universitas, Zeitschrift für Wissenschaft, Kunst und Literatur 35 (1980) 4, 411 - 416.

KLIPSTEIN,M./B. STRÜMPEL (Hrsg.): Gewandelte Werte - Erstarrte Strukturen. Wie die Bürger Wirtschaft und Arbeit erleben. Bonn 1985.

KLUKA, D.A.: Women, sport and leadership: Paths through the olympic movement. In: ICHPER Journal 28 (1992) 3, 4 - 8.

KMIECIAK, P.: Wertstrukturen und Wertewandel in der Bundesrepublik Deutschland. Göttingen 1976.

KOMMISSION "ZUKUNFTSPERSPEKTIVEN GESELLSCHAFTLICHER ENTWICKLUNGEN" (Hrsg.): Zukunftsperspektiven gesellschaftlicher Entwicklungen. Stuttgart 1983.

KOSLOWSKI, P.: Evolution und Soziobiologie. Tübingen 1984.

KROCKOW, Chr. v.: Die Bedeutung des Sports für die moderne Gesellschaft. In: PLESSNER, H./H.E. BOCK/O. GRUPE (Hrsg.): Sport und Leibeserziehung. Sozialwissenschaftliche, pädagogische und medizinische Beiträge. München 1967, 83 - 95.

KROCKOW, Chr. v.: Sport und Industriegesellschaft. München 1972.

KROCKOW, Chr. v.: Eine Soziologie und Philosophie des Leistungsprinzips. Hamburg 1974.

KURZ, D.: Was suchen die Menschen im Sport? Erwartungen und Bedürfnisse der Zukunft. Referat. In: DEUTSCHER SPORTBUND (Hrsg.): Menschen im Sport 2000. Dokumentation des Kongresses Menschen im Sport 2000, Berlin 5.- 7. 11. 1987. Schorndorf 1988, 126 - 144.

LAASER, E.: Die Fußballweltmeisterschaft 1978 in der Tagespresse der Bundesrepublik Deutschland. Berlin 1980.

LASWELL, H.D.: The Structure and Function of Communication in Society. In: BRYSEN, L. (Hrsg.): The Communication of Ideas. New York 1948

LAZARSFELD, P.F./R.K. MERTON: Massenkommunikation, Publikumsgeschmack und organisiertes Sozialverhalten. In: AUFERMANN, J. u.a.: Gesellschaftliche Kommunikation und Information. Frankfurt 1973, 447 - 470.

LENK, H.: Leistungssport: Ideologie oder Mythos? Stuttgart 1972.

LENK, H.: Sozialphilosophie des Leistungsdenkens. Stuttgart 1976.

LENK, H.: Die achte Kunst. Leistungssport - Breitensport. Zürich 1985.

LERNER, D.: The Passing of Traditional Society - Modernizing the Middle East. Glencoe (Illi.) 1958.

LERNER, D.: Die Modernisierung des Lebensstils: Eine Theorie. In: ZAPF, W. (Hrsg.): Theorien des sozialen Wandels. Köln/Berlin 1970, 362 - 381.

LÜDTKE, H.: Kapital Freizeit. Kompetenz, Ästhetik und Prestige in der Freizeit. Erkrath 1989.

LUHMANN, N.: Öffentliche Meinung. In: LUHMANN, N.: Politische Meinung. Opladen 1971, 9 - 24.

LUHMANN, N.: Das Moderne der modernen Gesellschaft. In: ZAPF, W. (Hrsg.): Die Modernisierung moderner Gesellschaften. Frankfurt 1991, 87 - 108.

LUTHE, H.O./H. MEULEMANN (Hrsg.): Wertewandel - Faktum oder Fiktion? Bestandsaufnahmen und Diagnosen aus kultursoziologischer Sicht. Frankfurt/New York 1988.

MAIER, H.: Vergesellschaftung des Sports. Zum Problem der Reproduktion der Arbeitskraft. Gießen-Lollar 1975.

MAYER-TASCH, P.C.: Ökologie und Freiheit. In: Universitas. Zeitschrift für Wissenschaft, Kunst und Literatur 41/11, 1986, 1200 - 1205.

McCANN/ERICKSON: Der deutsche Mann. Lebensstile und Orientierungen. Frankfurt 1982.

McCLELLAND, D.C.: The Achieving Society. Princeton 1961.

McPHERSON, B.D./J.E. CURTIS/J.W. LOY: The Social Significance of Sport. An Introduction to the Sociology of Sport. Champaign (Illi.) 1989.

MENZEL, U./S. SENGHAAS: Europas Entwicklung und die Dritte Welt. Eine Bestandsaufnahme. Frankfurt 1986.

MERTES, H.: Der Sportjournalist. Ein Beitrag zur Kommunikationsforschung. Mainz 1974.

MOHR, H.-M.: Postmaterialismus in der Bundesrepublik? Frankfurt 1984 (Arbeitspapier Nr. 141, SFB 3, Frankfurt/Mannheim).

MOHR,H.-M./W. GLATZER: Werte, persönliche Konflikte und Unzufriedenheit. In: GLATZER, W./W. ZAPF (Hrsg.): Lebensqualität in der Bundesrepublik. Frankfurt/New York 1984, 277 - 233.

MÜNCH, R.: Die Kultur der Moderne. Frankfurt 1989.

NEIDHARDT, F.: Professionalisierung im Sport - Tendenzen, Probleme, Lösungsmuster. In: ANDERS, G./G. SCHILLING (Hrsg.): Hat der Spitzensport (noch) eine Zukunft? Magglingen 1985, 71 - 81.

NITSCHKE, A.: Nicht-europäische Bewegungsweisen im Sport. In: Sportwissenschaft 15 (1985) 3, 294 - 307.

NOELLE-NEUMANN, E./B. STRÜMPEL: Macht Arbeit krank? Macht Arbeit glücklich? Eine aktuelle Kontroverse. München 1984.

NUNNER-WINKLER, G.: Entwicklungslogik und Wertwandel: ein Erklärungsansatz und seine Grenzen. In: LUTHE, H.O./H. MEULEMANN (Hrsg.): Wertwandel - Faktum oder Fiktion? Bestandsaufnahmen und Diagnosten aus kultursoziologischer Sicht. Frankfurt/New York 1988.

OFFE: Arbeit als soziologische Schlüsselkategorie? In: MATTHES, J. (Hrsg.): Deutscher Soziologentag 21, Bildung 1982. Frankfurt 1983, 38 - 65.

OPASCHOWSKI, H.W./G. RADDATZ: Freizeit im Wertewandel. BAT-Schriftenreihe, Bd. 4. Hamburg 1982.

OPASCHOWSKI, H.W.: Arbeit, Freizeit, Lebenssinn. Opladen 1983.

PARSONS, T.: Evolutionäre Universalien der Gesellschaft. In: ZAPF, W. (Hrsg.): Theorien des sozialen Wandels. Köln/Berlin 1970, 55 - 74.

PFISTER, J./G. STEINMANN: Sozialer Wandel und makroökonomische Steuerung. In: STACHOWIAK, H. (Hrsg.): Bedürfnisse,Werte und Normen im Wandel. Bd. 1: Grundlagen, Modelle und Perspektiven. München 1982, 217 - 236.

PLESSNER, H.: Spiel und Sport. In: PLESSNER, H./H.E. BOCK/O. GRUPE (Hrsg.): Sport und Leibeserziehung. Sozialwissenschaftlaiche, pädagogische und medizinische Beiträge. München 1976, 17 - 27.

QUANZ, L.: Der Sportler als Idol. Gießen 1974.

RENSON, R./C. CAREEL: Sporticious consumption: An analysis of social status symbolism in sport ads. In: Int. Rev. for Soc. of Sport 21 (1986) 2 - 3, 153 - 171.

RIGAUER, B.: Sport und Arbeit. Soziologische Zusammenhänge und ideologische Implikationen. Frankfurt 1969.

RIGAUER, B.: Warenstrukturelle Bedingungen leistungssportlichen Handelns. Gießen-Lollar 1979.

RITSERT, J.: Inhaltsanalyse und Ideologiekritik. Ein Versuch über kritische Sozialforschung. Frankfurt 1972.

RITTNER, V.: Sport, Bedürfnisstruktur und sozialer Wandel. In: Stadion II, 2 (1975), 159 - 195.

RITTNER, V.: Sport als Kulturexport. In: Institut für Auslandsbeziehungen (Hrsg.): Zeitschrift für Kulturaustausch 27 (1977) 4, 34 - 41.

RITTNER, V.: Gesamtgesellschaftliche Entwicklungen und ihre Auswirkungen auf den Sport. In: KULTUSMINISTER DES LANDES NORDRHEIN-WESTFALEN, a.a.O. 1984, 44 - 51.

ROBINSON, G.J.: 25 Jahre "Gate-keeper"-Forderung. Eine kritische Rückschau und Bewertung. In: ANFERMANN, J. u.a. (Hrsg.): Gesellschaftliche Kommunikation und Information. Frankfurt 1973, 344 - 355.

RÖTHIG, P. (Red.): Sportwissenschaftliches Lexikon. Schorndorf 1983.

SCHAFF, A.: Wohin führt der Weg? - Die gesellschaftlichen Folgen der zweiten industriellen Revolution. Wien 1985.

SCHENK, M.: Publikums- und Wirkungsforschung. Theoretische Ansätze und empirische Befunde der Massenkommunikationsforschung. Tübingen 1978.

SCHEUCH, E.K.: Schwierigkeiten der Soziologie mit dem Prozeß der Modernität. In: ZAPF, W. (Hrsg.): Die Modernisierung moderner Gesellschaften. Frankfurt 1991, 109 - 139.

SCHNEIDER, P.: Die Sprache des Sports. Düsseldorf 1974.

SCHÖNHERR, H.-M.: Von der Herrschaft des Menschen zum Eigenrecht der Natur. In: Universitas. Zeitschrift für Wissenschaft, Kunst und Literatur 41/7, 1986, 687 - 698.

SEIFART, H.: Die Darstellung der Hochleistung in den Massenmedien. In: LENK, H. (Hrsg.): Handlungsmuster Leistungssport. Schorndorf 1977, 149 - 157.

SEYFARTH, C.: Wertwandel und gesellschaftliche Rationalisierung: Eine theoretische Diskussion aktueller Trendaussagen. In: LUTHE, H.O./H. MEULEMANN (Hrsg.): Wertwandel - Faktum oder Fiktion? Bestandsaufnahmen und Diagnosen aus kultursoziologischer Sicht. Frankfurt/New York 1988, 163 - 192.

SHANNON, C.E./W. WEAVER: The mathematical theory of communication. Urbana 1949.

SINUS (Hrsg.): Die verunsicherte Generation: Jugend und Wertewandel. Opladen 1983.

SPIEGEL (Hrsg.): Märkte im Wandel. Hamburg 1983.

STRÜMPEL, B.: Die Krise des Wohlstands. Stuttgart u.a. 1977.

STURM, H.: Methoden der Wirkungsforschung. München 1976.

STURM, H./J.R. BROWN (Hrsg.): Wie Kinder mit dem Fernsehen umgehen. Stuttgart 1979.

TOLLENEER, J.: The sports scene and the pop scene: A comparative structural functional analysis. In: Int. Rev. for Soc. of Sport 21 (1986) 2 - 3, 229 - 238.

TREML, A.K.: Ethik des Überlebens. In: CACHAY, K./H. DIGEL/G. DREXEL (Red.): Sport und Ethik. DVS-Protokolle Nr. 16. Clausthal-Zellerfeld 1985, 43 - 73.

VINNAI, G. (Hrsg.): Sport in der Klassengesellschaft. Frankfurt 1972.

VOLKAMER, M.: Der Einfluß der Massenmedien auf das Zuschauerverhalten. In: BINNEWIES, H. (Hrsg.): Sport und Massenmedien. Ahrensburg 1981, 17 - 29.

VOLKAMER, M.: Der Einfluß der Sportberichterstattung auf Sportler und Zuschauer. In: PILZ, G.A. (Hrsg.): Sport und körperliche Gewalt. Reinbek bei Hamburg 1982, 93 - 99.

WEISCHENBERG, S.: Der Außenseiter der Redaktion. Struktur, Funktion und Bedingungen des Sportjournalismus. Bochum 1976.

WINTER, J.: Natur und Pädagogik. In: Zeitschrift für Entwicklungspädagogik 9/4, 1986, 3 - 4.

ZAPF, W. (Hrsg.): Theorien des sozialen Wandels. Köln/Berlin 1970.

ZAPF, W. (Hrsg.): Die Modernisierung moderner Gesellschaften. Verhandlungen des 25. Deutschen Soziologentages in Frankfurt am Main 1990. Frankfurt 1990a.

ZAPF, W.: Modernisierung und Modernisierungstheorien. In: ZAPF, W. (Hrsg.): Die Modernisierung moderner Gesellschaften. Frankfurt 1990b, 23 - 39.

SPORT SCIENCE STUDIES

Series of the International Council of Sport Science and Physical Education (ICSSPE)

Volume 6   Herbert Haag

Theoretical Foundation of Sport Science as a Scientific Discipline

Contribution to a Philosophy (Meta-Theory) of Sport Science

1994. Size 6,5 × 9,4 in, 159 pages
ISBN 3-7780-6461-4 (order number 6461)
Price by surface postage US $ 20,—,
by airmail US $ 25.50

„Within this analysis four basic questions are answered in regard to a Philosophy (Meta-Theory) of Sport Science":

1. Aims and Objectives of Sport Science. Or: What is the function of Sport Science?

2. The Body of Knowledge of Sport Science. Or: What is the Content of Sport Science?

3. Research Methodology in Sport Science. Or: What is the Process of Gaining Scientific Knowledge in Sport Science?

4. Knowledge Transfer in Sport Science. Or: What is the Practice-Theory and Theory-Practice Paradigm?

With these four dimensions it is tired to develop theoretical foundations of Sport Science as a Scientific Discipline. This is especially important for a relatively young science like „Sportwissenschaft" (sport science). The discussion of these aspects should be lead on the national but also on the international level by help of the umbrella organisation for sport science, namely ICSSPE, which is providing an excellent platform for this. It is hoped that the presented analysis can contribute to a fruitful discussion within the scientific community of sport science.

Please send your order with a check directly to

Verlag Karl Hofmann · D-73603 Schorndorf
P.O. Box 1360 · Phone (0 7181) 402-0 · Fax (0 7181) 402-111

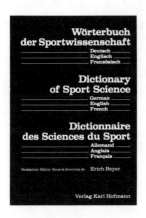

Dictionary of Sport Science

German, English, French
2nd edition 1992

Editor Professor Dr. Erich Beyer

The expansion of scholarly research and the progressive specialization into scholarly sub-fields of the relatively young sport science has, as it is the case in other fields of scholarly research, too contributed to the developmental tendency to an intensified differentiation of the technical terminology. The newer a field of scholarly research is, the less set its terminology. This is especially true of sport science, and this is the reason why it is difficult to communicate not only within one's own linguistic boundaries, but also in international cooperative efforts. To diminish such difficulties, to make the foreign scholarly literature accessible, and thus to further international cooperative work, an international team of about 140 scholars from Germany, USA, Great Britain, France, and Luxemburg have prepared this trilingual "Dictionary of Sport Science. German — English — French". 915 trilingual definitions of technical terms are classified synoptically and arranged in alphabetic order. International experts provided relevant annotations to indicate differing usages in the different linguistic domains. Clearly arranged indices help to find the terms.

The dictionary tries to provide greater clarity in dealing with sport science terminology and to stimulate a comparative scholarly consideration of the field. It is certainly a valuable source of information for scholars, teachers, and students.

Size 6,7 × 9,4 inch, 772 pages, ISBN 3-7780-3502-9
The dictionary costs US $ 47.— including surface postage, if you wish delivery by airmail it costs US $ 69.—.

Please send your order with a check directly to

Verlag Karl Hofmann · D-73603 Schorndorf
P.O. Box 1360 · Phone (0 71 81) 402-0 · Fax (0 71 81) 402-111